The Birds of
TOGO

An annotated Check-list

by

Robert A. Cheke & J. Frank Walsh

B.O.U. Check-list No. 14

British Ornithologists' Union, 1996
c/o The Natural History Museum, Tring, Herts, HP23 6AP, UK

First Edition 1996

ISBN 0-907446-18-3

Printed in Great Britain by The Nature Conservation Bureau, 36 Kingfisher Court, Hambridge Road,
Newbury, Berkshire, RG14 5SJ.

CONTENTS

EDITOR'S FOREWORD

This is the 4th. Check-list in the BOU series to cover part of West Africa. It is an important addition as it covers a major part of the Dahomey Gap (now known as the Togo-Benin Gap) in the Guinea forests, which separates Ghana (Check-list No 9) from Nigeria (Check-list No 4, 2nd edition). Togo has a wide variety of habitats, impressive rivers and beautiful mountain ranges, and these have been highlighted through a fine series of colour plates, which will be an important archive for future generations. Although 4 times smaller than Ghana, its avifauna (over 600 species) is comparable and mainly has a western origin.

Both authors have spent much time in the field and have had the use of helicopters to visit remote areas of the country, not visited by earlier workers. They have, particularly Robert Cheke, thoroughly reviewed the literature and the important skin collections made at the end of the 1890s by German ornithologists. This revealed several misunderstandings arising out of Togo's colonial history, during which its borders shifted several times, and these have been clarified. Many factors threaten the wildlife of Togo and the need for conservation is emphasised. One hindrance to conservation is a lack of precise knowledge of its fauna, but this is no longer true for Togo's avifauna. This check-list (No 14 in the BOU series) is comprehensive and will be a reliable, up-to-date base line for future studies.

Llewellyn G. Grimes

PREFACE

Soon after our first visits to Togo in the 1970s, we realised that many of the bird species which we were recording had not previously been collected or seen in the country. Until the mid 1980s our visits occurred mainly during the wet season and this limitation prevented us from preparing a comprehensive review of Togolese birds suitable for inclusion in the Check-list series of the B.O.U. This became a more realistic proposition after 1985. JFW was resident in Togo from February 1986 until June 1990, and RAC paid many visits during the dry months from 1985 until 1990.

In addition, we have used the field data of earlier travellers and other data provided from their collections. Of special importance are the collections of German ornithologists (described by A. Reichenow) and those of Belgian ornithologists (described by A. De Roo). However, our literature survey has not been an easy path because of complications arising out of Togo's colonial history. Its borders were shifted many times, and localities, listed in Togoland in early German literature, have had to be checked to establish whether they are indeed Togolese or Ghanaian sites. For some localities, it has not been possible to determine their precise position, for others our decision has relied on indirect evidence. For instance, Agomé Tongwe, the locality where Willcocks's Honeyguide *Indicator willcocksi* and Violet-backed Sunbird *Anthreptes longuemarei haussarum* were collected in the last century, is known to be the modern Agbome, in Ghana, solely on the basis of a statement in the gazetteer of Chapin (1954). Such specimens, discussed by Reichenow and still housed in the Berlin Museum, have been overlooked in the ornithological literature of Ghana (see Grimes 1987), often through the mistaken belief that they originated from present day Togo. Surprisingly, and to add to the confusion, Reichenow himself travelled to Ghana (then known as the Gold Coast) and collected there in August and September 1872 but appears not to have visited Togo!

A poster publicising the tourist potential of Togo refers to the country as "Africa in miniature". This reflects the varied nature of its terrain and habitats and the friendliness of its people. Within Togo are very dry and moist savannas, beautiful mountainous areas, forests, impressive rivers, varieties of coastal terrain and more besides. A total avifauna of 624 species is, therefore, not so surprising, and there is no doubt that more will be added in the future, especially when the avifauna of the forested zones is studied in more detail.

March 1996

Dr Robert A. Cheke   Dr J. Frank Walsh
c/o The Natural Resources Institute   80 Arundel Road
University of Greenwich   Ansdell
Central Avenue   Lytham St. Annes
Chatham Maritime   Lancashire
Kent   FY8 1BN
ME4 4TB   UK
UK

ACKNOWLEDGEMENTS

For invaluable assistance with specimens at museums we are very grateful to the following: P. Colston (Natural History Museum, Tring); J. Dean (Smithsonian Institution, National Museum of Natural History, Washington DC, USA); K. L. Garrett (Los Angeles County Museum of Natural History); Dr K. C. Parkes (Carnegie Museum of Natural History, Pittsburg); Dr M. Louette (Musée Royale de l'Afrique Centrale, Tervuren); Dr G. F. Mees (Nationaal Natuurhistorisch Museum, Leiden); Dr G. Mauersberger (Museum für Naturkunde der Humboldt-Universität zu Berlin); Dr R. P. Prys-Jones (Natural History Museum, Tring); P. Sweet (American Museum of Natural History); Dr B. Treca (IFAN Museum, Dakar); Dr J.-F. Voisin and Dr C. Erard (Muséum National d'Histoire Naturelles, Paris); Dr R. van den Elzen (Museum Koenig, Bonn); D. Willard (Field Museum of Natural History, Chicago, USA).

We are grateful to Mr. C. R. Vardy (Natural History Museum, London) for confirming the identity of the Polistine wasp *Ropalidia cincta*.

The late Dudley J. Cheke kindly translated German texts, particularly the whole of R. Büttner's account of Bismarckburg.

During many field trips made during our visits to Togo, we had the pleasure of the company of Samuel A. Sowah and in the latter years that of Mrs Joanna B. Taylor. Mrs Taylor also provided a substantial amount of information from the coastal and Misahöhe areas. Others who gave us their unpublished records included R. Alvarado, G. Bouman, T. Crisler, P. M. Claffey, J. R. Davidson, Dr J. Grunewald, Dr D. T. Holyoak, U. Kaiser, Dr M. Karam, H. Lege, Dr J. M. Lock (Minster Agricultural Group), P. Michelsen, D. Partridge, C. Perennou (International Waterfowl and Wetlands Research Bureau, now incorporated in Wetlands International), Dr A. Rougemont, M. B. Seddon, R. W. Taylor, C. Warneker, R. T. Wilson and Dr Y. Yamagata.

We particularly benefited from the skill of the pilots of Viking and Evergreen Helicopters especially A. Arne, C. Charles, D. Chinn, the late L. Cotter, G. Campbell, the late T. Johnson, P. Jutras, D. McLaughlin and L. Treadway.

For information on bird ringing and recoveries we thank Dr S. Baillie (BTO, UK), R. J. Dowsett (Tauraco Data Bank), J. Haapala (Finland), G. Jarry (Paris), J. Kazubiernis (Latvia), I. Kharitonova (Russia), C. J. Mead (BTO, UK), Dr T. B. Oatley (South Africa), R. Patapavicius (Lithuania), R. E. Sharland (Nigeria), Dr B.-O. Stolt (Sweden) and R. Wassenaar (EURING).

We are very grateful to the following who supplied special information: Dr W. R. P. Bourne (sea-birds); Professor R. Garms (German historical figures); R. Mai Jones (East European ringing schemes); Dr P. J. Jones (Quelea records); Mrs. Amberley Moore (Togolese history); Dr. A. Richford (species lists as of May 1991 from unpublished volumes of *The Birds of Africa*).

We are also grateful for the assistance in Togo of J. E. E. Henderickx, Mamman Nambiema and A. K. Opoku, and (while compiling the list) for the help of Mrs F. E. Warr (NHM library, Tring), Dr L. Birch (EGI library, Oxford), the librarians of the Natural Resources Institute and the librarian of the David Lubin Memorial Library (FAO, Rome) in supplying us with photocopies of articles. Our thanks also to Dr R. Luxmoore (World Conservation Monitoring Centre), who kindly supplied maps of Togo from which some of ours were adapted, and to Dr M. Packer (Oxford University), in particular, for allowing us permission to use the coloured vegetation map which he produced from satellite data.

Last, but by no means least, we are very much indebted to Dr. L. G. Grimes for his painstaking and thorough editing of our manuscripts.

LIST OF TABLES

LIST OF FIGURES

LIST OF COLOUR PLATES

Cover: Yellow-billed Stork *Mycteria ibis*, Mango, 16 October 1988. (J. F. Walsh)

1. Sudan savanna on rocky pavement near Namoundjoga, 8 April 1990. (R. A. Cheke)

2. Sudan savanna near Mandouri, 9 April 1988. (R. A. Cheke)

3. Aerial view of the Gambaga escarpment and cultivated land near Nano, 8 August 1989. (R. A. Cheke)

4. The Gambaga escarpment at Fosse aux Lions, 7 April 1990. (R. A. Cheke)

5. Cultivated land at Sawaga, 9 April 1988. (R. A. Cheke)

6. The Oti valley in flood, September 1988. (J. F. Walsh)

7. Northern Guinea Savanna in the Keran Park at the height of the wet season, 30 August 1984. (R. A. Cheke)

8. An elephant *Loxodonta africana* in Northern Guinea Savanna near Naboulgou, Keran Park, at the height of the dry season, 15 February 1987. (R. A. Cheke)

9. The Sirka forest reserve near Kara, 26 May 1979; yam plantations are in the foreground. (R. A. Cheke)

10. Flooded iron pan near Ketao, 18 August 1989; nesting ground of African Wattled Lapwing *Vanellus senegallus*. (R. A. Cheke)

11. Aerial view of the Kara R. valley and cultivated areas east of Kara, 27 June 1979. (R. A. Cheke)

12. Aerial view of intensively cultivated land with scattered trees and *Borassus* palms near Kara, 10 May 1979. (R. A. Cheke)

13. The Bafilo ridge viewed from the south, 30 October 1981. (R. A. Cheke)

14. A crag at Péwa, 25 March 1988; the habitat of Freckled Nightjar *Caprimulgus tristigma* and Mocking Cliff-Chat *Myrmecocichla cinnamomeiventris*. (R. A. Cheke)

15. Woodland near Péwa with *Euphorbia* spp. in the foreground, 8 February 1987. (R. A. Cheke)

16. Aerial view of the Aledjo forest, 14 July 1989. (R. A. Cheke)

17. Guinea savanna woodland and storm near Alehéridé, 31 May 1980. (R. A. Cheke)

18. Aerial view of the Anié forest reserve near Fazao, 26 April 1989. (J. F. Walsh)

19. Aerial view of the Kpaza R. valley with the Fazao mountains in the background, 27 June 1989. (R. A. Cheke)

20. Aerial view of mountain ridges near Fazao with their characteristic grassland and low density tree cover, and the thick gallery forest in the valleys, 13 July 1979. (R. A. Cheke)

21. Gallery forest and Koué R. in the Fazao-Malfakassa faunal reserve, 13 June 1980. (R. A. Cheke)

22. Guinea savanna woodland in the Fazao-Malfakassa faunal reserve, 13 July 1980. (R. A. Cheke)

23. The Boulo waterfall on the western escarpment of the Fazao mountains, northwest of Fazao, 24 September 1981. (R. A. Cheke)

24. The overgrown site of Bismarckburg, near Katchanké, 20 March 1990. (J. F. Walsh)

25. Forest at Misahöhe, May 1989. (J. F. Walsh)

26. Forest beside the Asawkawkaw R. along the border of Togo and Ghana, 26 May 1980. (R. A. Cheke)

27. Deforestation in progress near Déguingué, 20 March 1990. (R. A. Cheke)

28. Deforestation and burning near Amou-Oblo, 22 March 1990. (R. A. Cheke)

29. The forest on Mt. Tamania with the Amoutchou R. near Idifiou in the foreground, October 1985. (R. A. Cheke)

30. The Plateau de Danyi, 13 March 1985. (R. A. Cheke)

31. Hills along the border with Ghana near Yikpa-Dikpé, and close to known sites of Long-billed Pipit *Anthus similis* in Ghana. (J. F. Walsh)

32. Deforested hillsides near Badou, 26 April 1989. (J. F. Walsh)

33. Cultivations on deforested slopes near Badou, 26 July 1989. (R. A. Cheke)

34. Partially degraded forest near Badou, 26 July 1989. (R. A. Cheke)

35. Aerial view of gallery forest near Kpéssi on the Mono R. in the wet season, 12 July 1979. (R. A. Cheke)

36. Aerial view of gallery forest near Tététou along the Mono R. in the dry season, 1 December 1981. (R. A. Cheke)

37. The foreshore at Lomé with coconut palms and mixed flock of waders, 24 March 1985. (R. A. Cheke)

38. The harbour at Lomé with flock of waders, 31 March 1985. (R. A. Cheke)

39. L. Togo, Anécho, 8 March 1985. (R. A. Cheke)

40. Nestling Yellow-billed Storks *Mycteria ibis*, Mango, January 1988. (J. F. Walsh)

41. Smaller Banded Snake Eagle *Circaetus cinerascens*, Domaine Gravillou, 4 March 1990. (R. A. Cheke)

42. Male Plain Nightjar *Caprimulgus inornatus* near Tinkiro, 20 March 1990. (R. A. Cheke)

43. Long-tailed Nightjar *Caprimulgus climacurus* near Landa-Pozanda, 22 July 1989. (R. A. Cheke)

44. Male Standard-winged Nightjar *Macrodipteryx longipennis* near Landa-Pozanda, 10 March 1990. (R. A. Cheke)

45. Female Standard-winged Nightjar *Macrodipteryx longipennis* near Landa-Pozanda, 8 March 1990. (R. A. Cheke)

46. Jacana *Actophilornis africana*, Domaine Gravillou, 2 July 1989. (R. A. Cheke)

47. Crowned Cranes *Balearica pavonina* in the Oti R. valley, near Mango, 2 February 1987. (J. F. Walsh)

48. Great Snipe *Gallinago media*, Domaine Gravillou, 7 April 1990. (R. A. Cheke)

POLITICAL HISTORY OF TOGO

The ancient capital of the Ewé people was at Notsé, and remains of the ancient city's wall, dating from about 1500, may still be seen today (Allsworth-Jones 1990). The Portuguese, who had established a number of forts in coastal Ghana in the 1480s, probably explored thc Togolese coast (Fig. 1) in the same century. Nationals of other western European countries (Danish, Dutch, British and French) followed in later centuries as the West African slave trade flourished. In 1767, the French developed Anécho and Agbodrafo for the sole purpose of exporting slaves, but by 1865 they were trading posts of the French firm *Régis et Fabre*. A pioneering French group of missionaries from Lyon travelled to Atakpamé in 1866.

German missionaries arrived in 1847 and, subsequently, the people of Anécho wrote to the German Emperor asking for his protection. As a result, King Mlapa I of Toa-Go (present day Togoville) and Dr Gustav Nachtigal, the German emissary, signed a treaty on 5 July 1884 making Togo (then known as Togoland) a Protectorate of Germany. The northern and eastern boundaries of the German Protectorate were established and ratified with France on 23 July 1897; the western border and those of a neutral zone were defined in the Anglo-German treaty of Zanzibar on 1 July 1890.

German rule ended soon after the start of the First World War. When the radio installation at Kamina was captured by a British and French invading force on 26 August 1914, von Döring, the acting German Governor, surrendered – the first Allied success of the war (Moberley 1931)! The British occupied western Togoland, including Lomé, Ho, Kpandu, Klouto and Bismarckburg, and the French retained

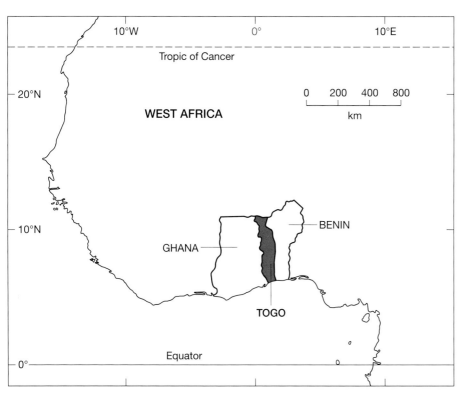

Figure 1.   The geographical position of Togo within West Africa.

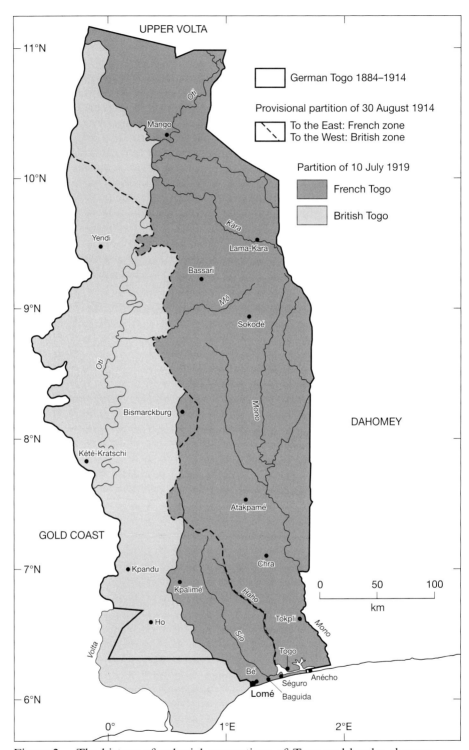

Figure 2.   The history of colonial occupations of Togo and border changes (adapted from *Atlas du Togo. Les Atlas Jeune Afrique*. Les Editions J. A., 1981, Paris).

Mango, Sokodé, Atakpamé and Anécho and the eastern part of Togoland. At the end of the war the treaty of Versailles (Article 119) required Germany to relinquish Togoland. The Anglo-French declaration of 10 July 1919 formally partitioned the territory (Fig. 2), and further modifications followed in the years 1927–1929. The partitioning split the land of the Ewé, who have always played a major role in Togolese history, and the repercussions are still felt today.

When in 1946, after the end of the Second World War, the Mandate system was replaced by a United Nations (UN) trusteeship, Ewé demands for reunification resurfaced. In May 1956, a plebiscite, controlled and monitored by the UN, indicated that people living in British Togoland wished to become part of Ghana, despite Ewé opposition. A separate plebiscite (28 October 1956) in French Togoland indicated that 72% of voters wished to be a self-governing Republic within the French community.

From 1956 until 1958, Nicolas Grunitzky was Prime Minister of an autonomous government. His brother-in-law, Sylvanus Olympio, became Prime Minister on 16 May 1958 and presided over the birth of the independent Republic of Togo on 27 April 1960; regrettably he was assassinated on 13 January 1963 during a coup. This was led by Sergeant (later General) Etienne (Gnassingbe) Eyadéma, who invited Grunitzky to return to form a Government. However, on 13 January 1967 Eyadéma, by then a Lieutenant-Colonel, seized power which he has retained ever since but not without opposition. This erupted in violent clashes and these led to the establishment of a national conference, followed by a general strike, in 1991 and multi-party elections in 1993.

THE HISTORY OF ORNITHOLOGICAL WORK IN TOGO

The colonial history of Togo is important in an ornithological context. As already described, the extent of German "Togoland" was greater than the present-day Republic of Togo, as it encompassed what are now parts of Ghana. This has occasionally led to confusion. Thus, many of the specimens referred to as being from "Togoland" by important authors such as Reichenow and Bannerman were collected at sites such as Kété Kratschi and Yendi which are now in Ghana.

The first records of birds from Togo were obtained from collections made by German colonists at the end of the 19th. century. Dr. Richard Büttner was based at Bismarckburg, a newly established outpost situated near present-day Katchanké in the Adélé hills, and his collection of 133 species was identified and described by Reichenow (1891a,b, 1892, 1893). Büttner took much interest in the local people, their surroundings, living conditions and social life and parts of his most interesting account (Büttner 1893) appear in Appendix 1.

The name Bismarckburg also arouses some confusion ornithologically. There are some specimens in the Berlin Museum, mostly collected by Fromm, labelled as from Bismarckburg and without further information on locality, but these were collected at a second town named Bismarckburg by German colonists. This other Bismarckburg was at the south-eastern tip of Lake Tanganyika in what is now Tanzania.

In February 1893 Ernst Baumann travelled to Togo and was stationed at Misahöhe (Anon 1893, 1895). He sent specimens to the Berlin Museum and his first series added 6 species to Büttner's list, bringing the total for the territory to 139 (Reichenow 1894a). Further specimens from him and Böder's donation (see p. 53) of a *Dryotriorchis spectabilis* (Anon 1894a), brought the total to 162 (Reichenow 1894c). He published a note on the Black Kite *Milvus migrans*, describing how they fly with their legs stretched out horizontally, only to bring them forward when they strike (Baumann 1894a), but he is more famous for the discovery of a nest of *Picathartes gymnocephalus* (Baumann 1894b). Reichenow named in Baumann's honour a warbler *Eremomela baumanni*, which is now considered to be synonymous with *E. pusilla*, and a greenbul *Phyllostrephus* (now *Phyllastrephus*) *baumanni* (Reichenow 1894c, 1895). For many years, Mt. Agou was known as "Pic Baumann" and a tree-frog endemic to the Akwapim-Togo Range and known from only 3 sites, of which Misahöhe is the type locality, is *Hyperolius baumanni* (Ahl 1931, Schiotz 1967).

From Reichenow's (1897) account it seems that Baumann returned to Germany with additional collections made by Büttner in the Bismarckburg area, together with others from Misahöhe and Kété Kratschi (in present-day Ghana). Sadly, Baumann died of malaria (black water fever) in hospital in Cologne shortly after returning to Germany for a brief holiday (Anon 1895, von Schalow 1896, Gebhardt 1964). There is a plaque in his memory at the German cemetery at Misahöhe and the English translation of the inscription reads "Dedicated to the memory of the meritorious Togo explorer E. Baumann who died in the Service of his Fatherland on 4 September 1895." This date is consistent with Anon (1895) but conflicts with that (5 August 1895) given by von Schalow (1896) and Gebhardt (1964).

In 1895 Lieutenant Klose collected birds at Kété Kratschi, and so did 1st. Lt. Count von Zech (Reichenow 1897). The latter, Count Julius von Zech auf Neuhofen (1868–1914), was a Bavarian Catholic nobleman who collected birds whenever he could. After Kété Kratschi (1895–1900), he was in charge of Anécho on the coast (1901–1902), then Chancellor of Togo (1902), acting Governor (1903–1905), and finally Governor from 1905 to 1910 (Gann & Duignan 1977).

Whilst at Kété Kratschi, von Zech mounted an expedition (January 1896) to counter an incursion by a French detachment, which had set up posts at Aledjo and Kirikri (Cornevin 1987), and reached Djougou (now in Benin). The following year he went to Tchamba via Bismarckburg and set up various treaties with local chiefs to counter, once again, a French presence. Unlike some of his immediate predecessors, von Zech was a popular and humane Governor. He took his responsibilities seriously and Cornevin (1987) considered him to be the most important legislator of Togo. He was able to maintain good relationships with his political masters in Berlin, whilst, at that time, being passionately concerned for the needs of the people. He spent much time trekking into the bush and mountains to meet them and became an authority on their laws and customs (Gann & Duignan 1977).

Apart from von Zech, others, also famous for their military and exploratory exploits, supplied Reichenow with specimens. 1st. Lt. G. Thierry found time to collect 180 skins of 121 species in the Mango area (Reichenow 1899) whilst coping with an insurrection there in 1897, and 3 separate revolts in 1898. The accessions record kept at the Museum für Naturkunde, Berlin, and started in 1900 by Reichenow, shows that Thierry sent a further 106 skins (55 from Yendi, now Ghana) to Berlin between 1900 and 1902. At least one of his specimens, a *Ptilopachus petrosus petrosus*, was sold by O. Neumann to H. Boardman Conover and is now in the Field Museum of Natural History, Chicago (Conover's accession number B143.02 of 7 May 1929, D. Willard, pers. comm.).

Dr. Kersting, commander of the Sokodé and Bassar areas, collected many birds at Kirikri after travelling northwards to pacify the Kara area. Most of his skins were described by Reichenow (1902a) together with those in the following collections, which raised the species total to 355: one by Kurz, who worked on the coast; another from the Mango region by Dr Rigler, an active protagonist in Togolese military history; one from Bassar by Lieutenant Klose; one from Sokodé by F. Schröder; one by Dr H. G. von Döring. The latter, a medical man, who later took charge of Atakpamé until 1901, was a member of Dr Gruner's expedition in 1894–95 from Misahöhe to Kété Kratschi, Salaga, Yendi, Mango and as far as Say on the Niger river in Niger. It was the same von Döring, acting as Governor in the absence of the Duke of Mecklenburg (see below), who surrendered German Togoland to the invading British and French troops in 1914.

On 15 January 1914, the Berlin Museum received from Adolf Friedrich Duke of Mecklenburg, the only specimen from Togo of the Great White Pelican *Pelecanus onocrotalus*. Other bird specimens were also received there from G. Schmidt, 1st Lt. Smend, Richers, Metzger, A. Mischlich and Keilhack. The museum also has skins marked "Togo Expedition" but no dates are given on these labels.

After the departure of the Germans in 1914, no ornithological work took place until mid 1919. Dr. Millet-Horsin, a medical officer already decorated with the Croix de Guerre and a Chevalier de la Légion d'Honneur (Anon 1918a,b), spent four months at Anécho (Bouet 1955). He was certainly there on 5 June 1919 but had already left on 16 August to travel to Benin, Senegal and Mali (Millet-Horsin 1921a). Apart from some anecdotal accounts of birds in Togo including a discussion of the differentiation of *Centropus monachus* from *C. senegalensis* (Millet-Horsin 1921a, b, c, 1922), he described two new subspecies (*Phalacrocorax africanus menegauxi* and *Halcyon torquatus pontyi*, both now suppressed) and a variety of nests (Millet-Horsin 1921d), before producing a valuable summary of his observations (Millet-Horsin 1923).

A much longer gap then followed before ornithological work recommenced in the 1950s. Villiers (1951b) provided a very general account of birds in Togo, and his collections from both Togo and Benin were deposited at the I.F.A.N. Museum at Dakar and fully described by Dekeyser (1951). Joseph Douaud, a Catholic priest, made valuable observations during his stay in Togo (Douaud 1955, 1956a,b, 1957), and noted the importance of the country for wintering House Martins *Delichon urbica*. J. Brunel also visited Togo in the 1950s as he referred to sightings at Atakpamé in his account of birds in Benin (Brunel 1958).

Between 1962 until 1965, Jeremy R. Davidson, visited Togo regularly in summer and winter and netted and ringed birds in a swamp near the international airport at Lomé. The birds were ringed with C.R.M.M.O. rings (J. R. Davidson, pers. comm.) but no details are traceable in Paris (G. Jarry, pers. comm.).

In the late 1960s and early 1970s, a series of Belgian expeditions made collections (4807 specimens of 304 species) comparable with those of the Germans (De Roo 1970, De Roo *et al.* 1969, 1971, 1972 and Louette 1975). Feather mites were also collected and some have been described (e.g. Gaud 1989, 1990 a,b, 1993). Other data on avian parasites in Togo are given in Cheke (1982b) and Quentin *et al.* (1986).

Netta Robinson observed birds at Lomé from September 1970 until the summer of 1972 and has published her data (Robinson 1972, 1973, 1974). She mentions (Robinson 1973) that John A. Broadbent and P. J. Broadbent visited Lomé from December 1970 to January 1971, and caught and ringed 758 birds of 32 different species. These data were not published and unfortunately very little information has been traced. P. W. P. Browne lived at Lomé from 19 January 1976 to 30 May 1977 and published his findings (Browne 1980).

In June 1977, M. Bougat and Mme Salami were tape-recording amphibian vocalizations at Kovié and, whilst doing so, inadvertently recorded the calls of *Sarothrura rufa*. These were identified by Erard & Vielliard (1977).

J. Frank Walsh first visited Togo in 1972 when working for the World Health Organization Onchocerciasis Control Programme in West Africa (WHO/OCP). He made frequent visits and lived permanently at Kara from February 1986 until June 1990. Robert A. Cheke also worked for the WHO/OCP in Togo from 5 May until 25 July 1979, and then for 3 month periods (almost annually) until April 1990. Apart from 2 visits during 1985, when Cheke was based at Lomé, both authors were based in Kara, and became more familiar with savanna birds than those of the forest. However, both Cheke and Walsh regularly travelled throughout the country, and often into otherwise inaccessible places when using a helicopter to search for and spray immature stages of the onchocerciasis vector *Simulium damnosum* s.l. During many of these visits, a WHO/OCP colleague, Sammy A. Sowah of Ghana, accompanied them but also contributed many independent bird records.

In the 1980s some important surveys were conducted. F. Roux and G. Jarry conducted a waterbird survey of Lake Togo on 26 January 1984 (IWRB via C. Perennou, pers. comm.). The Keran Park and the Fazao Park reserves were surveyed in March and April 1984 by a team from Minster Agriculture Limited which included Dr. and Mrs. Patrick Duncan and Dr J. Michael Lock. Although their main task was to give advice on the management of the reserves, their final report listed the birds seen (Minster Agriculture Limited 1984). Unfortunately, the team's sojourn in Togo was marred by a fatal road accident.

Henning Lege traversed Togo from south to north, 11–29 December 1984, and made a number of valuable observations. Similarly, Dr. David T. Holyoak and his wife Mary Seddon noted many birds of interest when making the same journey in the reverse direction, 22–25 November 1988. Mrs Joanna B. Taylor, wife of the U. S. A. Ambassador to Togo, was in Togo from February 1988 until August 1990 and on several occasions accompanied the authors in the field. She also obtained valuable records, principally from the forested areas in the Kpalimé region, and made them available to us.

Other data for the check-list have been provided by Patrick M. Claffey, who lived in the Bassar area in the early 1990s, and by T. Crisler, who was based at Mango during 1993 and 1994.

GEOGRAPHY

Togo is a long narrow rectangular-shaped country, extending 570 km northwards from the Atlantic Ocean at latitude 06°10'N to latitude 11°06'N, and shares borders with Ghana, Benin and Burkina Faso (Fig. 3). Its width varies from a minimum of 50 km at 10°22'N, (parallel with Mango) to a maximum of 135 km at 8°42'N, (parallel with Fazao). The coastline runs approximately from west to east for 70 km.

Togo (area 54,390 km^2, population of 3.7 million in mid 1990s) is the third smallest West African state (The Gambia and Guinea-Bissau being smaller) and with Ghana is the third most densely populated country (68 persons per km^2) after Nigeria and The Gambia. As in all West African coastal states, Togo's population is concentrated in coastal areas; 15% live in the capital, Lomé, and there are heavily populated rural districts at Kpalimé, Badou, Kara and Dapaon (Fig. 3).

Figure 3.   The main towns and rivers of Togo.

GEOLOGY AND TOPOGRAPHY

Togo is composed of five broad geological zones (Fig. 4). In the north, the Dapaon plateau area (3040 km^2) consists of Precambrian crystalline rocks, with a region of granite intrusions at its southern boundary. The striking topographical feature is the eastern extension of the Gambaga escarpment, cut by the main highway (RN1) near the Fosse aux Lions National Park (Plate 5). South of the plateau, the Oti, Koumongou and western half of the Kara river basins (total area 7280 km^2) are comprised of Palaeozoic sediments of the Voltaian series, and consist of uniform gently dipping sandstones, shales and mudstones. In this zone the main rivers present a relatively mature aspect, and there are numerous meanders and oxbow lakes throughout the Oti valley and in the lower reaches of the Koumongou and Kara rivers.

Further south, the Voltaian series is replaced by the upper Precambrian rocks of the Buem formation and slightly older Togo series. Both consist largely of shales, sandstones and basalt, but those of the Buem formation are derived from ancient volcanoes, and those in the Togo series are usually metamorphosed to quartzites and phyllite. Both the Buem and Togo series, especially the latter, are highly folded and form the spectacular Atakora-Togo mountain chain which extends northwards from Kpalimé to Fazao and then north-northeast to the Natitingou district of the Republic of Benin. Despite their age, erosion has not destroyed their grandeur, and a very considerable portion of this mountainous zone (6500 km^2) exceeds 400 m a.s.l., the highest point being Mt. Agou (986 m) just east of Kpalimé. As a result, Togo and northwestern Benin look much more rugged than their neighbours Ghana and Nigeria (Fig. 5).

East and southeast of the mountain chain lies the central plain (c. 20,000 km^2) of the Mono river basin and the upper Sio and Haho valleys. The rivers are fairly narrow and straight, and long stretches have gravel/sand bottoms which are interrupted every few km by barriers of metamorphic rocks. This plain, half of which lies below 200 m a.s.l., is covered by the lower Precambrian Dahomeyean series of gneisses and schists, the oldest rocks in Togo, and is low and undulating. There are a few, faunistically important, inselbergs near the Benin frontier with elevations above 350 m a.s.l.

The coastal plain (3700 km^2), which is covered by tertiary sedimentary rock formations with recent deposits in the valleys, extends some 35–55 km inland and is flat and low-lying. The widths of the Sio, Haho and Mono rivers increase as each meanders through the coastal plain, and their flood plains, which are seasonally inundated, are attractive to birds.

The coastline consists mostly of low lying sandy beaches often lined with coconut trees, and backed by tidal flats and shallow lagoons, the largest being L. Togo. There is a normal west to east drift of sand along the coast, which in western Nigeria is estimated at 1 to 1.5 million tons per annum, and this forms deposition beaches on the western side of any man-made breakwater. Such a deposition beach has formed west of the large breakwater at Lomé Port which juts out 1200 m from the original shoreline, and was constructed between 1964 and 1967. During the first seven years post-construction, the shore line, west of the breakwater, extended nearly 300 m seaward (John & Lawson 1972). In the 1980s this actively accreting shore was rich in birdlife, despite a great deal of human activity, including sand digging. Unfortunately most of the pools immediately adjacent to this and other parts of the shoreline, which harbour waders and roosting terns, are rapidly being re-claimed.

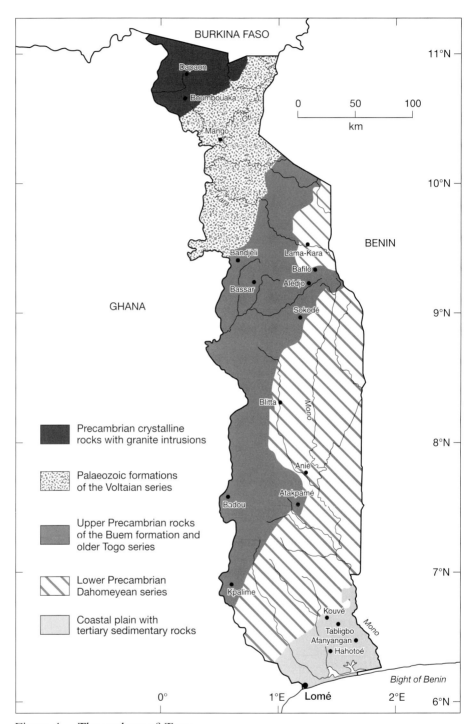

Figure 4.   The geology of Togo.

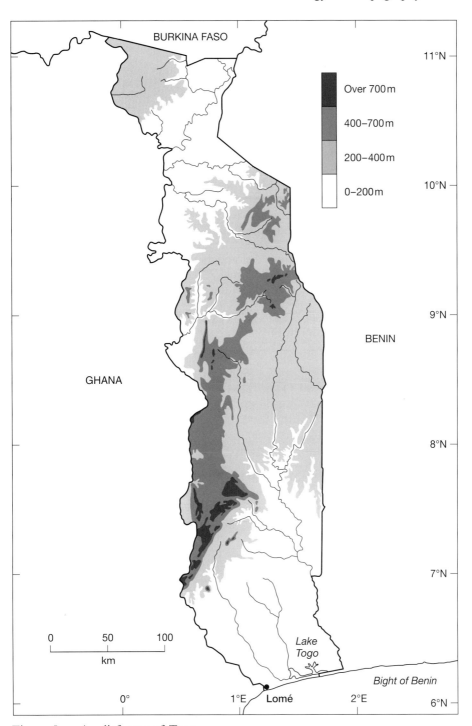

Figure 5.   A relief map of Togo.

DRAINAGE (Hydro-electricity and Fisheries)

The drainage of Togo is relatively simple. The frontier between the Republic of Benin and Togo runs along the watershed between the Ouémé river system in Benin and the Volta and Mono river systems in Togo. In addition, the whole of the northern two-thirds of the country and a strip that extends south along the Ghana border to within 100 km of the coast (the total covering nearly 24,000 km² (44%) of Togo), is part of the Volta basin in which rivers flow southwest and westwards into the man-made Volta Lake of Ghana (Fig. 6).

The Mono basin includes the central, southern and eastern parts of the country, and covers 42% (22,600 km²) of Togo. In 1987 a large hydro-electric dam, built across the Mono river at Nangbeto 35 km southeast of Atakpamé, was completed. Little concern was paid to the environment during the final phases of its construction, when the flow of the river was stopped, until the reservoir was filled.

Although at its maximum extent the Nangbeto lake only stretches 40 km north of the dam site, its formation has drowned 75 km of the main river channel and parts of the Anié river – the main tributary of the Mono. Routine operation of the hydro-electric station has resulted in a fairly constant river flow below the dam, which had previously been highly seasonal.

Since 1990, the seasonal flow of the Oti river has been modified and controlled by the construction (in Burkina Faso) of a large dam across the Oualé river, its main tributary.

The remaining southwestern part of the country, covering 7800 km² (14%) of Togo is drained by the Sio and Haho rivers. These coalesce, near Abobo, to form L. Togo, a large lagoon which extends 25 km eastwards along and just inland of the coast, and opens into the sea at Anécho.

The larger rivers of Togo are extensively fished. The Oti, where it forms the frontier with Ghana, is grossly overfished and catches have declined throughout the last 20 years (Levèque et al. 1988). This probably is also the case for the lower Mono, but data are not available.

Inshore fishing, in which fishermen use huge dugout canoes and shore-based seine netting, is a major industry which is probably still at a sustainable level. The upwellings of water from June to October, and a weaker upwelling from December to March, bring cold nutrient-rich water to the surface which greatly increases the production of phytoplankton (Ansang 1979) and, consequently, fish such as the sardine *Sardinella* sp. (Mensah 1969).

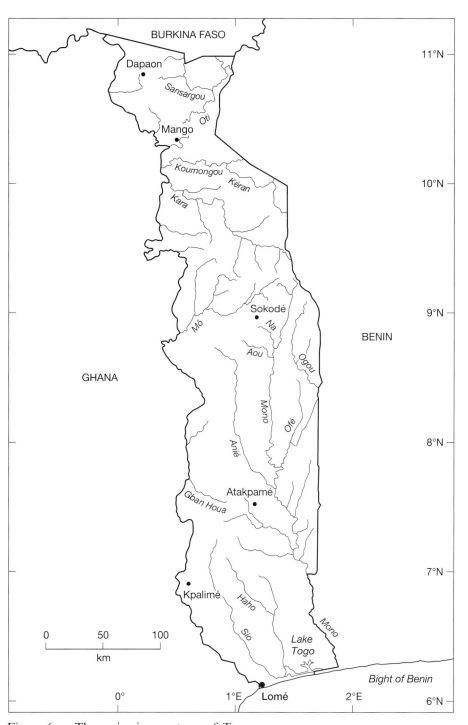

Figure 6.   The main river systems of Togo.

CLIMATE AND THE SEASONS

The climate of Togo as in other West African states, is controlled mainly by the Intertropical Convergence Zone (ITCZ) which oscillates north and south in phase with the apparent movement of the sun, though with a lag of 1–2 months. From November–February (the dry season) the ITCZ usually lies over the Atlantic Ocean to the south of Togo, while in August, the height of the wet season, it lies well to the north of the country, deep into the Sahara. The ITCZ is formed by the convergence of 2 air masses; the northeast trade winds to the north, and the southeast trade winds of the Southern hemisphere to the south. The southeast trade winds are modified by a belt of moist westerly winds, the southwestern monsoon, which flow over Togo from May–September bringing cloud cover and showers, which advance and retreat with the movement of the ITCZ. During the dry season, the northeast trades from the Sahara bring hot, dry, dust-laden air (the Harmattan) over the whole of Togo.

Winds are usually light throughout the country, apart from sea breezes in coastal areas and winds that blow in the north at the height of the dry season, but may reach Force 10 when line squalls, ferocious and spectacular electric storms, move westwards through the country.

Rainfall is the most important climatic factor throughout West Africa. In general, rainfall is high in the south and declines northwards – see Fig. 3 in *The Birds of Nigeria* by Elgood *et al.* (1994). In Togo, this south-north pattern is disrupted by the orographic effect of the Togo and Atakora mountains. As a result most rain falls in a band which runs north-northeast across the centre of Togo from 7°N to 10°N, and decreases both north and south of this region (Table 1). In addition, Togo's coastal plain is protected from the monsoon, which sweeps in parallel to the Ghana and Togo coastlines, by Cape St. Paul in eastern Ghana, which effectively produces a rainshadow. This results in the coastal strip of Togo receiving the least rainfall (Table 1). Cold upwelling water off the eastern Ghana and Togo coasts during July, August and September probably also contributes to the existence of this dry coastal zone (Trewartha 1962). The highest rainfall occurs in the forested areas, e.g. the annual mean rainfall at Kpalimé is 1800 mm.

The length of the dry season is of major importance as regards vegetation cover (Figs. 7 and 8). Consequently, the region north of Mango, which has a mean annual rainfall of 1000 to 1100 mm and a 5 month dry season (November–March), has a much drier aspect than the coastal plain where mean annual rainfall is less than 950 mm but there are only 2 dry months (December and January). Although the rainfall patterns in West African states, including Togo, are fairly predictable, there can be considerable annual variation. This variability increases in the lower rainfall areas of the north, and reinforces the effects of the longer dry season on the vegetation. Southern Togo experiences a "little dry season" in August when there is a reduction in rainfall compared with that in July and September (Table 1). A similar rainfall pattern occurs in coastal districts of Benin, Ghana and Nigeria.

The amplitude of monthly mean temperatures varies between c. 3°C at Lomé and 4.5°C at Mango (Tables 2 and 3), but these figures are easily surpassed by typical diurnal amplitudes. Although annual mean temperatures everywhere fall between 25°C and 28°C (Table 2), an absolute maximum of 41°C was recorded at Mango in April and a minimum of 12°C at Sokodé in November.

The vegetation and zoogeography of Togo and Benin are anomalous when compared with those of Ghana and Nigeria, their neighbours to both west and east (see section on vegetation). This "Togo-Benin Gap", formerly referred to as the "Dahomey Gap", experiences higher radiation values with increased sunshine hours (Table 4), lower mean cloudiness and far fewer thunderstorm days per year, than its neighbours (Hayward & Oguntoyinbo 1987).

Table 1. Mean monthly rainfall (in mm) recorded at 4 stations in Togo. Data for this table and Tables 2, 3, and 4 are taken from World Climate Disc Global Climatic Change Data CD-ROM, Chadwyk-Healey Ltd., Cambridge and Hayward & Oguntoyinbo (1987). Means derived from data for 1951–1990.

Station	Latitude	Alt. m asl	Jan	Feb	Mar	Apr	May	Jun	Jul	Aug	Sep	Oct	Nov	Dec	Total mm
Lomé	06°08'N	20	11.3	28.3	64.7	98.5	144.2	251.7	92	28.1	63.7	91.3	25.1	9.7	923.8
Atakpamé	07°32'N	400	9.1	36.2	96.1	117.9	132.1	201.2	217.8	178.9	201.5	132.1	31	17.6	1401.4
Sokodé	08°59'N	386	5.8	20.6	61.6	105.9	135.4	200.2	239.6	259.7	255.2	113	19.3	15	1441.3
Mango	10°21'N	145	0.2	4.4	27.4	61.7	108.6	142.9	194.2	238.5	249.5	74.4	9.4	3.9	1136.7

Table 2. Mean monthly temperatures (°C) and their averages at 4 stations in Togo (data for 1951–1990).

Station	Jan	Feb	Mar	Apr	May	Jun	Jul	Aug	Sep	Oct	Nov	Dec	Average
Lomé	26.8	27.8	27.9	27.9	27.2	25.9	25.0	24.8	25.5	26.2	27.0	26.8	26.6
Atakpamé	26.8	27.6	27.4	26.6	25.9	24.6	23.6	23.5	23.9	24.8	26.1	26.2	25.6
Sokodé	25.8	27.2	28.3	27.6	26.6	25.3	24.3	24.2	24.5	25.4	25.4	25.1	25.8
Mango	26.7	28.5	29.6	29.5	28.2	26.5	25.4	25.1	25.6	26.8	27.3	26.7	27.2

Table 3. Mean monthly values of maximum and minimum values of temperature (°C) and of relative humidity (expressed as a %) at Atakpamé, Togo.

	Jan	Feb	Mar	Apr	May	Jun	Jul	Aug	Sep	Oct	Nov	Dec	Year Mean
Maximum Temperature	34	35	35	34	33	31	29	28.5	30	31	33	33.5	
Minimum Temperature	20.5	21	22	22	21	21	21	20	21	21	21	21	
Maximum RH	77	82	86	83	84	89	92	93	93	92	86	76	86
Minimum RH	42	48	59	62	64	73	75	76	73	69	58	49	63

Table 4. Mean monthly sunshine and mean daily sunshine (both in hours) at Lomé and Sokodé in Togo for the years 1955–58.

	Jan	Feb	Mar	Apr	May	Jun	Jul	Aug	Sep	Oct	Nov	Dec	Range
Lomé Monthly	192	200	211	204	194	153	139	148	151	198	234	226	95
Lomé Daily	6.2	7.1	6.8	6.8	6.2	5.1	4.5	4.8	5	6.4	7.8	7.3	
Sokodé Monthly	263	251	238	224	233	178	123	115	130	200	236	273	158
Sokodé Daily	8.5	9	7.7	7.5	7.5	5.9	4	3.7	4.3	6.4	7.9	8.8	

VEGETATION

The vegetation of West Africa has been classified on a number of occasions, most notably by Aubréville (1938), Chevalier (1900), Keay (1959) and White (1983). Possibly the most influential has been the classification of Nigerian vegetation by Keay (1953). In essence the vegetation zones occur as a series of bands, whose positions relative to the coast are directly related to the decreasing rainfall and increasing severity of the dry season at progressively more northern latitudes. Keay's (1953) vegetation zones or types, as applied to Togo, are lowland rainforest, derived savanna, Guinea savanna and Sudan savanna, terms which we have used in the systematic list of bird species. However, in this section we have used Vanpraet's (1980) classification of Togo's vegetation based largely on satellite imagery taken between December 1975 and February 1976. He divided the vegetation into 5 eco-floristic zones (Table 5) and 15 subzones. As far as possible, we have related Vanpraet's classification to that of Keay (1953).

Despite the small size of Togo, the original vegetation cover, although predominantly dense semi-evergreen or deciduous forest, was quite varied. This is mainly due to the range of latitude covered by the country (c. 5°) but also to the mountainous nature of much of the terrain. Although no detailed study has been made, at least 2,300 species of plants, of which 20 or more are endemic, are known to occur in Togo (Davis *et al.* 1986, quoted in Sayer *et al.* 1992). Regrettably, however, the most distinctive feature of Togo's vegetation today is its extremely degraded state which is a result of the high density of the rural population. This degradation is especially noticeable along the border between Ghana and Togo that runs through the existing forest zone. Although the forest in the Volta Region of Ghana is itself seriously degraded, it survives in a much better state than that of Togo, and the contrast in the amounts of forest which exist on each side of the border is most marked.

Owing to the low rainfall associated with the Togo-Benin Gap (see section on climate), the coastal plain of Benin and Togo has much lower rainfall than the countries to the east and west, except for the anomalous Accra Plains in Ghana. In addition, the Togo-Atakora mountain chain, despite its relatively low elevation, exerts a strong orographic effect. The vegetation zones reflect this relief and rainfall pattern and the wettest, most heavily wooded area occurs in a band running SW to NE across the centre of the country from 6°15'N to 10°00'N. Both north and south of this band lies more open, drier country.

Table 5. The vegetation zones of Togo based on Vanpraet's (1980) study and the corresponding names used by Keay (1953).

Zone	Name	Surface Area km²	%	Keay's Classification
I	Dry continental at low altitude	33,390	61.4	Guinea savanna
II	Dry coastal at low altitude	8,800	16.2	Derived savanna
III	Very dry continental at low altitude	3,600	6.6	Sudan savanna
IV	Sub-humid at medium altitude	3,900	7.2	Lowland rainforest
V	Dry sub-humid at medium altitude	4,700	8.6	Guinea savanna

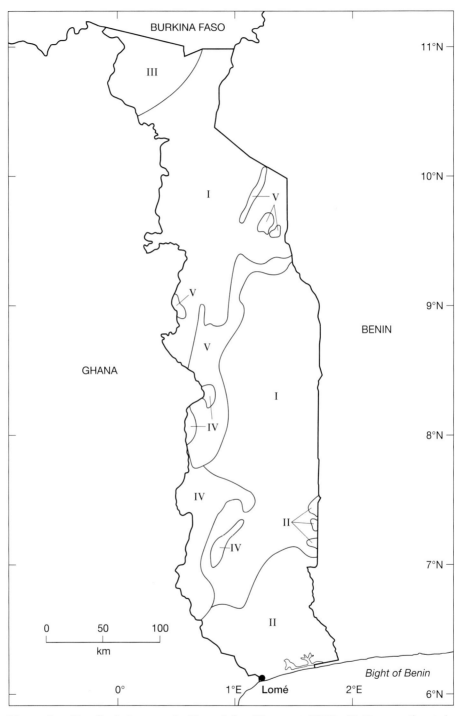

Figure 7.   Eco-floristic zones in Togo (after Vanpraet 1980). (I) Dry continental
at low altitude (Guinea savanna); (II) Dry coastal at low altitude
(Derived savanna); (III) Very dry continental at low altitude (Sudan
savanna); (IV) Sub-humid at medium altitude (Lowland rainforest);
(V) Dry sub-humid at medium altitude (Guinea savanna).

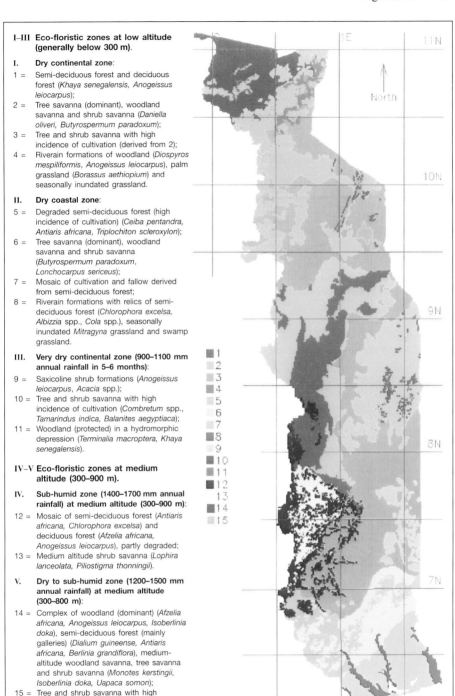

I–III Eco-floristic zones at low altitude (generally below 300 m).

I.   Dry continental zone:

1 =   Semi-deciduous forest and deciduous forest (*Khaya senegalensis, Anogeissus leiocarpus*);

2 =   Tree savanna (dominant), woodland savanna and shrub savanna (*Daniella oliveri, Butyrospermum paradoxum*);

3 =   Tree and shrub savanna with high incidence of cultivation (derived from 2);

4 =   Riverain formations of woodland (*Diospyros mespiliformis, Anogeissus leiocarpus*), palm grassland (*Borassus aethiopium*) and seasonally inundated grassland.

II.   Dry coastal zone:

5 =   Degraded semi-deciduous forest (high incidence of cultivation) (*Ceiba pentandra, Antiaris africana, Triplochiton scleroxylon*);

6 =   Tree savanna (dominant), woodland savanna and shrub savanna (*Butyrospermum paradoxum, Lonchocarpus sericeus*);

7 =   Mosaic of cultivation and fallow derived from semi-deciduous forest;

8 =   Riverain formations with relics of semi-deciduous forest (*Chlorophora excelsa, Albizzia* spp., *Cola* spp.), seasonally inundated *Mitragyna* grassland and swamp grassland.

III.   Very dry continental zone (900–1100 mm annual rainfall in 5–6 months):

9 =   Saxicoline shrub formations (*Anogeissus leiocarpus, Acacia* spp.);

10 =   Tree and shrub savanna with high incidence of cultivation (*Combretum* spp., *Tamarindus indica, Balanites aegyptiaca*);

11 =   Woodland (protected) in a hydromorphic depression (*Terminalia macroptera, Khaya senegalensis*).

IV–V Eco-floristic zones at medium altitude (300–900 m).

IV.   Sub-humid zone (1400–1700 mm annual rainfall) at medium altitude (300–900 m):

12 =   Mosaic of semi-deciduous forest (*Antiaris africana, Chlorophora excelsa*) and deciduous forest (*Afzelia africana, Anogeissus leiocarpus*), partly degraded;

13 =   Medium altitude shrub savanna (*Lophira lanceolata, Piliostigma thonningii*).

V.   Dry to sub-humid zone (1200–1500 mm annual rainfall) at medium altitude (300–800 m):

14 =   Complex of woodland (dominant) (*Afzelia africana, Anogeissus leiocarpus, Isoberlinia doka*), semi-deciduous forest (mainly galleries) (*Dialium guineense, Antiaris africana, Berlinia grandiflora*), medium-altitude woodland savanna, tree savanna and shrub savanna (*Monotes kerstingii, Isoberlinia doka, Uapaca somon*);

15 =   Tree and shrub savanna with high incidence of cultivation (derived from 14).

1
2
3
4
5
6
7
8
9
10
11
12
13
14
15

Figure 8.   Vegetation map of Togo based on satellite imagery recorded 1972–76; adapted from Vanpraet (1980) and prepared by Dr. M. Packer. Colour codes refer to vegetation types as in Fig. 7.

I.   Dry continental zone
(= Guinea savanna) (Figs. 7 and 8)

This varied zone (area c. 33,390 km^2) covers 60% of the land surface, and is divided into two large blocks by the Togo-Atakora mountain chain. The division of this zone into Southern and Northern Guinea savanna, as occurs in Nigeria, is not strictly possible in Togo for there is a lack of important populations of *Isoberlinia* spp. which are used as key indicators in this subdivision. However, the terms are used in the species accounts in the systematic list, where they refer to the appropriate vegetation type found either north or south of the Bafilo mountain ridge, which acts as an ecological barrier.

There is not a large quantitative difference in the mean annual rainfall from south to north of this zone, e.g. 1150 mm at Notsé (6°57'N) and 1050 mm at Mango (10°20'N), but the increasing harshness of the dry season (2–3 dry months in the south, 5–6 dry months in the north) means that the two blocks have differences which parallel those of the adjacent Guinea savanna belts of Nigeria.

South of the Togo mountains, this zone is mainly drained by the Mono river system. In this subzone there are some patches (covering an area c. 200 km^2) of semi-deciduous forest containing a variety of tree species, e.g. *Afzelia africana, Antiaris africana* and *A. welwitschii, Ceiba pentandra, Chlorophora excelsa, Khaya senegalensis* and *Triplochiton scleroxylon*. This semi-deciduous forest mainly occurs in the upper Mono and Ogou valleys, but the best lies in the Forest of Abdoulaye centred on 8°40'N, 1°20'E. In the adjacent riverine forest of the Mono R. forest hornbill species have frequently been recorded.

Much of the remaining area south of the Togo mountains, together with the Mo valley and the Keran National Park area in the north (total area c. 12,640 km^2), consists of savanna woodland with *Daniella oliveri* and shea butter *Butyrospermum paradoxum* among the dominant tree species. This woodland is especially well developed in the Keran Park. Riverine forest with abundant *Berlinia grandiflora* is found throughout the Mo valley, but the finest tracts occur in the Koumongou valley near Naboulgou (Keran Park) where a number of forest birds have been recorded, including Narina's Trogon *Apaloderma narina*, Red-chested Cuckoo *Cuculus solitarius* and African Emerald Cuckoo *Chrysococcyx cupreus*, and reach their northernmost range in Togo. This forest also harbours an important population of Hadada *Bostrychia hagedash*, a species which is almost absent from the Kara valley where riverine forest has been completely destroyed downstream of Kara town.

What remains of this zone (c. 20,000 km^2) occurs south of the Bafilo ridge in the vicinity of Sokodé and in the headwaters of the Mono basin, and extends north of the Bafilo ridge to the upper Koumongou R. near Kandé. It consists of tree and shrub savanna and extensive areas of cultivation derived from the woodland savanna, and among important crops grown are yam *Dioscorea* spp., maize *Zea mays* and sorghum *Sorghum bicolor*. Degradation is extreme and a virtually treeless landscape occurs in some areas just north of Kara town where population densities exceed 60 persons/km^2. Much of this sub-zone supports a very impoverished avifauna, which became noticeably more depleted between 1980 and 1990.

A small (area c. 550 km^2) but very important sub-division of this zone is the riverine vegetation of the Oti valley where *Mimosa pigra* and *Mitragyna inermis* are important riverine plants. Within this region there is an extensive area of seasonally flooded grassland on deeper soils consisting mainly of *Andropogon* spp., *Hyparrhenia* spp. and *Heteropogon* spp. This is especially important for a small, probably resident, breeding population of Crowned Cranes *Balearica pavonina* and for migratory flocks of cranes, storks and bustards, and at the height of the dry season, Denham's Bustard *Neotis denhami* breeds in the parched grasslands. Patches of forest thicket and groves of *Borassus aethiopum* also occur, the latter of importance to Red-necked Falcons *Falco chicquera* and Grey Kestrels *F. ardosiaceus*. In the vicinity of Mango, and downstream of the town, there are extensive rice fields which support substantial wintering populations of egrets and waders and important numbers of wildfowl.

II. Dry coastal zone
(= Derived savanna in part) (Figs. 7 and 8)

As a result of the low rainfall, Guinea savanna almost reaches the coast in the extreme west of Togo. Near Agou there is an extensive plantation of oil palm *Elaeis guineensis*, but further east the natural vegetation is forest. Aubréville (1937) showed that even in the early part of the 20th century there were substantial vestiges of ancient forest remaining, although much had been destroyed long before. The German colonial authorities planted c. 13,000,000 trees during a reforestation programme begun in 1907. They planted mostly teak trees *Tectona grandis* (Martin 1991) but included indigenous species such as *Anogeissus leiocarpus*, *Chlorophora excelsa*, *Erythrophleum guineense* and *Khaya ivorensis* (Unwin 1920). Sacred groves, containing forest trees, still existed in the 1930s, but today the coastal plain consists of largely degraded forest and tree savanna (area c. 5,300 km^2), and short grassland and scrub. Much of the zone is under intensive cultivation (area c. 3,000 km^2), the principal crop being cassava *Manihot esculenta*. Most large trees are the exotic *Ceiba pentandra*, but there are a few baobabs *Adansonia digitata*. Some small plantations of teak *Tectona grandis* occur, and neem *Azadirachta indica* and *Cassia siamea* are commonly planted near buildings. The latter 2 species and the cactus *Opuntia robusta* are sometimes used as field boundaries. Some fine riverine forest, with relict semi-deciduous forest of *Chlorophora excelsa*, *Albizia* spp. and *Cola* spp., occurs in the Sio, Haho and Mono valleys whose lower reaches are all seasonally flooded and contain extensive inundated *Mitragyna inermis* and swamp grasslands. This riverine forest and seasonally inundated area, which in the late 1970s still covered an area of 500 km^2 (Vanpraet 1980), is extremely important for both resident and migratory birds. Although mangroves *Rhizophora* spp. are found in Togo (Keay 1954), there are no mangrove swamps surviving today which are of significance to birds. Coconut palm *Cocos nucifera* groves are found along the coastal strip and flourish on impoverished sandy soil but they support a very poor bird fauna.

III. Very dry continental zone at low altitude
(Sudan savanna in part) (Figs. 7 and 8).

This zone coincides almost exactly with the Dapaon plateau. The two important factors which influence its vegetation are the hot dry harmattan wind from the NE and the dense population of 60–100 persons/km^2. The area is heavily cultivated with millet *Pennisetum americanum*, cotton *Gossypium* spp. and groundnut *Arachis hypogaea*, and grazed by livestock; rice *Oryza sativa* is grown extensively in the better watered areas. Close to settlements the only trees in much evidence are those of economic importance such as shea butter *Butyrospermum paradoxum*, locust bean *Parkia biglobosa*, *Acacia albida*, *Ficus* spp., *Lannea acida*, and baobab *Adansonia digitata*. In some places there is open orchard woodland consisting almost entirely of shea butter trees. Away from population centres, open tree-shrub savanna occurs (area c. 3356 km^2) and the prominent tree species include *Combretum* spp., *Tamarindus indica*, *Balanites aegyptiaca* and baobabs. A small proportion of the area is escarpment and rock pavement (area c. 232 km^2) where *Acacia* spp.

predominate, and acacia scrub also occurs in the extreme northwest of Togo. Within this zone there is a small alluvial plain (area c. 12 km^2), the Fosse aux Lions National Park, with a rich and varied vegetation which includes an extensive swampy grassland (mainly *Andropogon* spp.) with small thickets of *Rhaphia* spp. In drier parts there is rich forest containing *Ficus* spp., *Daniella oliveri, Afzelia africana, Terminalia macroptera* and *T. indica*, while in the gallery forest *Khaya senegalensis, Syzygium guineense* var. *guineense, Cassia sieberiana, Rhaphia* spp., *Diospyros mespiliformis* and *Vitex* spp. occur. The Park, which is located close to a spectacular section of the Gambaga scarp, was extremely rich in birds and mammals prior to the extensive damage to the national park system in the early 1990s. It is probably still important ornithologically.

IV. Sub-humid zone at medium altitude
(= Lowland rainforest in part) (Figs. 7 and 8)

Although much of Togo was originally well forested, this had been reduced, by the late 1980s, to scattered pockets as a result of human pressure and the relatively dry conditions. Most remaining forest patches are found in an area that stretches from just south of Kpalimé to the west of Blitta which is located on the Precambrian mountain chain. The best developed forests are found on the Plateaux Region in the valleys of the Dayi R. and Gban-Houa R. (= the Wawa R. in Ghana) and their tributaries, in the extreme west along the uplands of the Togo-Ghana border, and on the Danyi Plateau and the Kloto, Akposso and Haito mountains. These relict forest patches are similar floristically to those of the adjacent Volta Region of Ghana which have been classified as Dry Semi-deciduous forest by Hall & Swaine (1976), and the characteristic tree species are *Antiaris africana* and *Chlorophora excelsa*. In the vicinity of Badou there are small areas of the exotic bamboo *Bambusa vulgaris*. At the forest / savanna boundary there are occasional ground fires which kill saplings and reduce the prevalence of trees with small girth and those with thin bark. Nevertheless, forest cover can persist if fires are sufficiently infrequent, and in these areas facultative savanna trees such as *Anogeissus leiocarpus* and *Afzelia africana* occur as well as abundant oil palm *Elaeis guineensis*, but *Hymenostegia afzelia* and other thin barked trees are absent. The relative openness of the forest canopy allows a profuse growth of forbs. In the heart of the forest 54% of large trees are evergreen, whereas in the peripheral areas affected by occasional fires only 26% are evergreen. The predominant tree fruits are fleshy and presumably adapted to animal dispersal.

Based on 1975–76 data, Vanpraet (1980) considered that the remaining moist semi-deciduous forest only covered an area of c. 2630 km^2. In contrast, a survey by FAO (1988) estimated that closed broadleaved forest covered c. 3040 km^2 in 1980, of which 470 km^2 was undisturbed. Both these surveys were considered to be over-optimistic by Sayer *et al.* (1992) who estimated that in 1989/90 only c. 1360 km^2, or 2.5% of the land area of Togo was forested. Despite this, forests remain immensely important as they are the prime habitat of 180 species (29%) of the recorded Togo avifauna. Of 233 species of forest birds recorded in the outstanding Tai forest in Côte d'Ivoire (Thiollay 1985a), 155 (67%) have been recorded in the fragmented forests of Togo since 1980. These include 84 species listed as "species either restricted to or regularly seen well inside primary forest and therefore probably originating from this habitat" (Thiollay 1985a).

In the north, the uplands (area c. 1270 km^2), which mainly lie above 800 m, are drier and only support medium altitude shrub savanna. Jenik & Hall (1966) have studied this vegetation in the Djebobo Massif (8°15'–8°20'N) just inside the Ghana border. They found that the dry harmattan winds had resulted in the development of a very sparse vegetation on windward slopes. The main trees found (*Lophira lanceolata*, *Piliostigma thonningii* and *Syzygium guineense* var. *macrocarpum*) are stunted and some hilltops are grass-covered and devoid of trees. It is on such open hilltops that the Long-billed Pipit *Anthus similis* was found in Ghana and may one day be found on similar hilltops in Togo. Leeward slopes have much deeper soils with more humus and leaf litter, and the vegetation is markedly denser and taller. Montane plants occur on the uplands at surprisingly low altitudes and sheltered ravines retain densely wooded vegetation including *Antiaris-Chlorophora* forest.

V.   Dry sub-humid zone at medium altitude
(= Guinea Savanna woodland) (Figs. 7 and 8)

Further north, well developed savanna woodland (area c. 4350 km^2) covers the Atakora-Togo mountains which run NE from the Togo-Ghana border at c. 8°30'N. At the southern end, the Fazao-Malfakassa National Park contains relict forest patches, which grow on steep hillsides, and some fine riparian forest. In the more mature forest patches are found *Antiaris africana, Chlorophora excelsa* and *Elaeis guineensis*. An important tree in the riparian woodland is *Berlinia grandiflora* which is a major source of food for sunbirds. In more open, drier woodland are found *Isoberlinia* spp, *Monotes kerstingii, Uapaca togoensis, Detarium microcarpum, Daniella oliveri, Lophira lanceolata* and *Burkea africana*. The shrub *Adenodolichos paniculatus* is typical of the plateau areas in this zone, and on heavily burnt areas the characteristic plants are *Maytenus senegalensis, Hymenocardia acida* and *Combretum* spp. The forest at Aledjo, in which *Uapaca* spp. are abundant, and the headwater streams of the Mono R., which rise in broken rocky country on the southern side of the Bafilo ridge, contain some dense riverine forest, and *Berlinia grandiflora* and native bamboo *Oxytenanthera abyssinica* thickets are abundant. It is here that several forest birds reach their northernmost limits in Togo. The northern forests of the Kara hills and the Defale ridge (total area c. 350 km^2) had been entirely destroyed by the mid-1980s, but Sirka peak just east of Kara, was still well wooded in 1990.

MIGRATION

No specific study of bird migration has been conducted in Togo and there has been little ringing, although many birds ringed elsewhere have been recovered in Togo (Appendix 2). Nevertheless, general field observations at regularly visited sites, e.g. Landa-Pozanda, have enabled us to assess the likely migratory status of some species. In most cases, however, the data do not permit confident separations into species which migrate within Togo and those that are sometimes absent from the country. As expected, migratory activity in Togo is similar to that recorded in Ghana and Nigeria, where more detailed studies have been made.

Migrants include: (a) birds which breed in the Palaearctic and spend the northern winters (the dry season) in Togo; (b) Palaearctic migrants on passage through Togo to destinations further south; (c) intra-African migrants, e.g. Abdim's Stork *Ciconia abdimii* and Lesser Striped Swallow *Hirundo abyssinica*, which visit Togo from the south or south-east of the country, mostly in the wet season; (d) intra-African migrants, e.g. Namaqua Dove *Oena capensis* and Bush Petronia *Petronia dentata*, which travel to Togo from the north in the dry season; (e) intra-African migrants, e.g. Rosy Bee-eater *Merops malimbicus*, which migrate to Togo from unknown areas, perhaps east or west of the country; (f) birds which migrate within the borders of Togo, usually from forest to savanna and *vice versa*, e.g. Red-shouldered Cuckoo-Shrike *Campephaga phoenicea*. Of the birds in categories c-f, some come to breed (Tables 6 and 7) and others are non-breeding visitors. Complications arise when some species have both sedentary and migratory populations. A few rare species, mostly marine birds, e.g. Sooty Tern *Sterna fuscata*, but also some waders, may be involved in transatlantic crossings.

The percentage of Palaearctic migrant species that occur in Togo is 17% (109 species, Appendix 3) of its total avifauna, and this is similar to the percentages for Ghana (19%, Grimes 1987) and Nigeria (18%, Elgood *et al.* 1994). Of the Palaearctic migrants, 17 non-passerine species probably also have Afrotropical populations in Togo.

Studies in other West African countries, especially Nigeria (Elgood *et al.* 1994), have clearly shown that Afrotropical forest birds are relatively sedentary while some savanna species and many aquatic species show well marked seasonal movements. In Togo, there is little evidence of migratory movement among Afrotropical forest species. Of 67 species of non-passerines living in non-aquatic forest habitats only 5 show definite signs of being migratory: the Black Cuckoo *Cuculus clamosus*, Red-chested Cuckoo *C. solitarius*, African Emerald Cuckoo *Chrysococcyx cupreus* and 2 aerial feeders – Mottled Swift *Tachymarptis aequatorialis* and White-throated Bee-eater *Merops albicollis*. Of the 91 species of forest-dwelling passerines none are known to be migratory. Of 54 Afrotropical aquatic non-passerines, 17 (31%) are known or suspected to be migratory in Togo, while none of the 9 passerines in this category migrate. Among savanna inhabiting Afrotropical species, 43 (33%) out of 130 non-passerines are suspected migrants while only 32 (20%) of 160 passerines are. Thus the overall picture is not very different from that of Nigeria (see Table 4 of Elgood *et al.* 1994).

Several migratory non-passerines appear to have resident populations in the south but are present only during the wet season in the northern savannas. Among these are Black Kite *Milvus migrans*, Red-chested Cuckoo *C. solitarius*, Diederik Cuckoo *Chrysococcyx caprius*, Klaas's Cuckoo *C. klaas*, Woodland Kingfisher *Halcyon senegalensis* and Broad-billed Roller *Eurystomus glaucurus*, together with a number of aquatic species including Cattle Egret *Bubulcus ibis*, Dwarf Bittern *Ixobrychus sturmii*, Allen's Gallinule *Porphyrio alleni* and Greater Painted-Snipe *Rostratula benghalensis*. The only passerine showing a similar pattern seems to be the Copper Sunbird *Nectarinia cuprea*.

In Ghana and Nigeria the Black Coucal *Centropus grillii* is considered to be an intra-country migrant. In Togo, however, there is clear evidence of an obvious influx in April (presumably from countries further south) of non-breeding birds into coastal swamp grassland.

The Yellow-breasted Apalis *Apalis flavida* is one of very few Afrotropical warblers in West Africa for which there is some evidence of migration. It is usually considered a resident, but it may be migratory in Togo and is almost certainly so in Burkina Faso. All records in Togo, except one in January, fall between 3 March and 4 November. The earliest sighting (3 March 1990) at Landa-Pozanda coincided with an influx of Willow Warblers *Phylloscopus trochilus*, probably from the south. In Burkina Faso, the only sighting of it (14–18 March 1978) in a woodland near Ouagadougou, which was regularly surveyed, followed the first movement northwards through Ouagadougou of the Inter-tropical Convergence Zone (ITCZ), which was accompanied by stormy conditions on 10–11 March (Thonnerieux *et al.* 1989).

BREEDING

No detailed or exhaustive studies of breeding birds in Togo have been conducted and there are none on moult. Most information on breeding has come from the authors' incidental observations, supplemented by those of others, and from a survey of the literature. In general, the breeding regimes of species in Togo are similar to those found in neighbouring countries such as Ghana (Grimes 1987) and Nigeria (Elgood *et al.* 1994). However, it is difficult to reach firm conclusions, e.g. most raptors are dry season breeders, in most cases because of the surprising paucity of information from all three countries.

Of the 411 resident species suspected of breeding in Togo, confirmation is available for only a quarter (112 species) and for only 18 of the 47 intra-African migrants suspected of nesting. Nevertheless, the Togolese data include confirmed breeding (or very strong evidence for breeding) for the following species for which data are lacking in Ghana: Hamerkop *Scopus umbretta*, Woolly-necked Stork *Ciconia episcopus*, African White-backed Vulture *Gyps africanus*, Grasshopper Buzzard *Butastur rufipennis*, Helmeted Guineafowl *Numida meleagris*, Stone Partridge *Ptilopachus petrosus*, Denham's Bustard *Neotis denhami*, Senegal Thicknee *Burhinus senegalensis*, Spotted Thicknee *B. capensis*, Egyptian Plover *Pluvianus aegyptius*, White-headed Lapwing *Vanellus albiceps*, Spur-winged Plover *V. spinosus*, Four-banded Sandgrouse *Pterocles exustus*, Western Bronze-naped Pigeon *Columba iriditorques*, Great Blue Turaco *Corythaeola cristata*, Blue-headed Coucal *Centropus monachus*, Spotted Eagle Owl *Bubo africanus*, Blue-bellied Roller *Coracias cyanogaster*, Speckled Tinkerbird *Pogoniulus scolopaceus*, Rufous-sided Broadbill *Smithornis rufolateralis*, Violet-backed Sunbird *Anthreptes longuemarei*, Pygmy Long-tailed Sunbird *A. platurus*, Yellow-bellied Sunbird *Nectarinia venusta*, Black-headed Weaver *Ploceus melanocephalus*, Grey-headed Oliveback *Nesocharis capistrata* and Red-winged Pytilia *Pytilia phoenicoptera*. The Rufous Scrub-Robin *Cercotrichas galactotes* also breeds in Togo but is as yet unknown in Ghana.

A similar list of species, known to breed in Togo but for which confirmation is lacking in Nigeria, includes Saddle-billed Stork *Ephippiorhynchus senegalensis*, Western Bronze-naped Pigeon *Columba iriditorques*, Blue-bellied Roller *Coracias cyanogaster*, Black-casqued Wattled Hornbill *Ceratogymna atrata*, Rufous-sided Broadbill *Smithornis rufolateralis* and Red-chested Swallow *Hirundo lucida*.

In view of the lack of data, generalisations about breeding should be treated with caution. The usual and simplest approach is to place the breeding species into those which breed in the dry season, those which breed in the wet season and those with a protracted breeding season (Tables 6 and 7). These tables provide information on breeding seasonality according to family for both resident and intra-African migrant species which are either suspected of nesting or are known to nest. Of the 49 resident non-passerines (Table 6), which are known to breed in Togo, more than half (26) are dry season breeders. In marked contrast, 44 of the 63 passerine residents, which are known to breed in Togo, do so in the wet season. Of the migrant breeders, 10 out of 13 non-passerines and 3 out of 5 passerines breed in the dry season.

The above analyses assume that each species is only considered once and is placed in one of the 3 divisions (dry, wet, protracted), and ignores any differences in breeding times due to habitat differences and sub-specific variation. In addition, what constitutes the beginning or end of the dry and wet seasons is somewhat arbitrary as their timings vary from one year to the next. Thus ubiquitous species may breed throughout the year in the forest but only in the wet season in the savanna, and an Afrotropical subspecies may co-exist during its breeding season with its relative from the Palaearctic, e.g. Black Kite *Milvus migrans*. The likelihood of

Table 6. The breeding data for Non-Passerines in Togo.

Summary of data on numbers of species of different avian families recorded as breeding, B, or suspected of breeding (B) in Togo, according to season of breeding and resident or intra-African migratory status. Palaearctic species are omitted. NB each species is only categorised once, even if, for instance, it has populations which are both resident and migratory.

D – Dry season; W = Wet season; P = Protracted breeding.

Family	RESIDENTS					INTRA-AFRICAN MIGRANTS			
	B+(B)	B	D	W	P	B+(B)	B	D	W
Podicipedidae	1								
Phalacrocoracidae	1	1		1					
Anhingidae	1								
Ardeidae	10	2		2		1			
Scopidae	1	1		1					
Ciconiidae	2	2	1	1		1	1	1	
Threskiornithidae	1								
Anatidae	3	1	1						
Accipitridae	29	8	7	1		2	2	1	1
Falconidae	6								
Phasianidae	8	3	1		2	1			
Turnicidae	2								
Rallidae	8	2	1		1				
Heliornithidae	1								
Otididae	1					2	1	1	
Jacanidae	1	1			1				
Burhinidae	1	1	1			1	1	1	
Glareolidae	1	1	1			4	1		1
Charadriidae	6	3	2	1		1			
Pteroclidae						1	1	1	
Columbidae	13	7	2	3	2	1			
Psittacidae	5								
Musophagidae	4	2	2						
Cuculidae	10	2		2		4	1		1
Tytonidae	1								
Strigidae	7	1	1						
Caprimulgidae	2					2	1	1	
Apodidae	6	2			2	1			
Trogonidae	1								
Alcedinidae	6	1		1		3	2	2	
Meropidae	4	2	2			1	1	1	
Coracidae	2	1		1		1			
Phoeniculidae	2								
Bucerotidae	10	2	2			1	1	1	
Capitonidae	13	2	1		1				
Indicatoridae	6								
Picidae	9	1	1						
Totals for non-Passerines	185	49	26	14	9	28	13	10	3

there being many varied and complex breeding patterns in Togolese birds is exemplified by a study of 4 forest species in Liberia by Chapman (1995). She found that each had a different breeding regime: the Fiscal Shrike *Lanius collaris* both bred and moulted in the wet season; the Chestnut and Black Weaver *Ploceus nigerrimus* moulted in the dry season but bred throughout the year; the Common Bulbul *Pycnonotus barbatus* moulted in the wet season but bred in nearly all months; and the Little Greenbul *Andropadus virens* had a protracted moult and a protracted breeding season.

Table 7. The breeding data for Passerines in Togo.

Summary of data on numbers of species of different avian families recorded as breeding, B, or suspected of breeding (B) in Togo, according to season of breeding and resident or intra-African migratory status. Palaearctic species are omitted. NB each species is only categorised once, even if, for instance, it has populations which are both resident and migratory. D = Dry season; W = Wet season; P = Protracted breeding.

| Family | RESIDENTS | | | | | INTRA-AFRICAN MIGRANTS | | | |
	B+(B)	B	D	W	P	B+(B)	B	D	W
Eurylaimidae	2	1	1						
Pittidae	1								
Alaudidae	3					2			
Hirundinidae	8	4		2	2	5	3	1	2
Motacillidae	3	2		2					
Campephagidae	3					1			
Pycnonotidae	19	1			1				
Turdidae	13	2		2					
Sylviidae	30	7	1	6		1			
Muscicapidae	10	1		1					
Platysteiridae	6	1	1						
Monarchidae	4	2		2					
Timaliidae	6	1	1						
Paridae	1								
Remizidae	1								
Salpornithidae	1								
Zosteropidae	1								
Nectariniidae	16	6		6		3	2	2	
Laniidae	2	2		2					
Malaconotidae	14	3		2	1				
Prionopidae	2	1			1				
Dicruridae	3	2	1	1					
Corvidae	2	2		2					
Oriolidae	3								
Sturnidae	10	2	1	1		2			
Passeridae	2	2		1	1	1			
Ploceidae	23	16	2	11	3	1			
Estrildidae	25	5	1	3	1	2			
Viduidae	7								
Fringillidae	3								
Emberizidae	2					1			
Totals for Passerines	226	63	9	44	10	19	5	3	2

Comparisons between the number of species breeding in Togo, Ghana (Grimes 1987) and Nigeria (Elgood *et al.* 1994) are not possible as the criteria used as evidence for breeding slightly vary between each. Those used in completing Tables 6 and 7 are as stated in the introduction to the Systematic List. In general, a species was classified as breeding only if a nest with eggs or young has been seen or documented, or if parent birds were seen with dependent young, but for a few species (raptors, hamerkop, and some weaver birds) breeding was accepted on the basis of other criteria, e.g. a raptor sitting close on the same nest on more than one occasion. Since these criteria are stricter than those used for Nigeria, which included, in addition, data on only nest building, copulation or the condition of the adults' gonads to provide dates for breeding and attribution of RB status (Elgood *et al.* 1994: page 45 and numerous species accounts), it is likely that the Togo data are under-stated in comparison.

ZOOGEOGRAPHY

The evolution and current distribution of African birds have been largely determined by changes in the climate and vegetation during the Pleistocene era. According to Moreau (1966), the evergreen forests of West Africa were reduced and fragmented, in comparison with their current extent, some 22,000 or more years ago. At this time the forest bird species retreated into the forest fragment refuges, which remained along the Guinea coast and in the Congo region, to emerge and spread again as the climate ameliorated and to retreat once again during the next dry period. It was such cyclic changes in the forest cover, and associated advances and retreats of the Sahara desert and the savanna vegetation to the south of it, which have shaped the West African flora and fauna. Moreau (1966) noted that a species need be only 20,000 years old to have experienced the full range of Africa's ecological vicissitudes since the last severe phase of the last glaciation. He also suggested that the current bird subspeciation in West Africa could have evolved within the last 10,000 years (Moreau 1969).

The total number of bird species recorded in Togo is about 100 less than the total for Ghana and about 260 less than the total for Nigeria. At present, a meaningful comparison between the birds of Togo and Benin is not possible since the latter's avifauna has been insufficiently studied. However, Benin and Togo are inextricably linked zoogeographically as together they form the "Togo-Benin Gap", formerly known as the Dahomey Gap, in which the intrusion of savanna into forest zones occurs much further south than in Ghana or Nigeria.

Of the 16 species recorded in Togo but not in Ghana (Table 8), 10 are not unexpectedly of northern or Sahelian origin (*T. leuconotus, G. fulvus, A. tracheliotus, F. coqui, P. exustus, C. aegyptius, M. cantillans, M. rufa, M. alba, C. galactotes*) and 2 are marine vagrants (*D. capense* and *S. longicaudus*). The remainder have all been recorded west of Ghana, although *S. hypopyrrha* and *M. vexillaria* (an intra-tropical migrant) have only occurred as vagrants, and *S. rufa* and *P. regulus* are, by their nature, likely to have been overlooked or under-recorded. Thus, in terms of species, the avifauna of Togo, although poorer largely because of its less extensive forest and smaller size, is similar to that of Ghana. It is significant that all forest species found in Togo also occur in Ghana.

In contrast, 5 of the 10 species known from Togo but not from Nigeria (Table 9) are forest species which occur in Upper Guinea only, the exceptions being the marine *D. capense*, the Sahelian *M. rufa*, and the 2 species of *Vidua*. Togo lies at the easternmost extremity of the ranges of 5 forest species (*C. maculosa, A. sharpii, I. rufescens, T. lagdeni, L. cupreocauda*) which means that they have not traversed the Togo-Benin Gap. Therefore, on the basis of species differences, the conclusion is that most of the Togolese avifauna have a western origin.

The identifications of sub-species are less comprehensive and more subjective than those of species, and confirmation of the occurrence of some forms in Togo is needed. However, on the basis of current knowledge there are about 14 sub-species recognised in Togo which do not occur in Ghana (Table 10), and about 25 sub-species known from Togo which are absent from Nigeria (Table 11). An analysis of these differences supports the hypothesis of a western origin for most Togolese birds, but is less convincing and reveals some interesting anomalies. For instance, both western and eastern forms of some species (e.g. *C. cristata, T. purpuratus, N. olivacea*) occur in Togo, but only the eastern forms of others (e.g. *C. aberrans, C. chloronota, N. adelberti, S. haematina*) and for these the Togo-Benin Gap has not been a barrier.

The evidence reviewed by Livingstone (1975) indicates that the Togo-Benin Gap, in its present form, may have only existed for about 5,000 years (the Holocene period). This is about half the time that was considered likely when Moreau was preparing his synthesis (Moreau 1966). Even during the Holocene it is thought that there was usually continuous forest vegetation across the Gap until human interference changed the landscape (D. E. Livingstone in Robbins 1978). This interpretation is strongly supported by Aubréville (1937) who provided convincing evidence of substantial forest cover of the coastal plain of Benin (Dahomey), and to a lesser extent of Togo, into the early 1900s. He concluded that in historical times the northern limit of the coastal forest in Togo was at Tsevié, about 40 km inland, and was up to 80 km inland in eastern Benin. He later concluded, using data on the distribution of isolated large trees characteristic of equatorial high forest, that the edge of the forest occurred substantially further north than he previously had thought (Aubréville 1949).

Robbins (1978) examined satellite images taken in 1973 and 1976 and confirmed the presence of patches of high forest within the Togo-Benin Gap. Our own extensive experience of surveying by helicopter in the mid 1980s showed that such forest relics

Table 8. Species recorded in Togo but not in Ghana.

Scientific Name	English Name	Check-list Species No
Daption capense	Pintado Petrel	1
Thallassornis leuconotus	White-backed Duck	41
Gyps fulvus	European Griffon	62
Aegypius tracheliotus	Lappet-faced Vulture	63
Francolinus coqui	Coqui Francolin	111
Sarothrura rufa	Red-chested Flufftail	120
Stercorarius longicaudus	Long-tailed Skua	187
Pterocles exustus	Chestnut-bellied Sandgrouse	209
Streptopelia hypopyrrha	Adamawa Turtle Dove	225
Caprimulgus aegyptius	Egyptian Nightjar	265
Macrodipteryx vexillaria	Pennant-winged Nightjar	268
Prodotiscus regulus	Wahlberg's Honeyguide	333
Mirafra cantillans	Singing Bush-lark	351
Mirafra rufa	Rusty Bush-lark	353
Motacilla alba	White Wagtail	377
Cercotrichas galactotes	Rufous Scrub-Robin	416

Table 9. Species recorded in Togo but not in Nigeria.

Scientific Name	English Name	Check-list Species No
Daption capense	Pintado Petrel	1
Gyps fulvus	European Griffon	62
Campethera maculosa	Little Green Woodpecker	340
Mirafra rufa	Rusty Bush-lark	353
Apalis sharpii	Sharpe's Apalis	448
Illadopsis rufescens	Rufous-winged Akalat	90
Telophorus lagdeni	Lagden's Bush-shrike	532
Lamprotornis cupreocauda	Copper-tailed Glossy Starling	548
Vidua larvaticola	Black-faced Firefinch Indigobird	615
Vidua togoensis	Togo Paradise Whydah	617

Table 10. Subspecies recorded in Togo but not in Ghana. Those in square brackets require confirmation. Data based on subspecies recognised in volumes 1–4 of *The Birds of Africa* and in Howard & Moore (1991).

Scientific Name	Check-list Species No
Glareola nuchalis nuchalis	145
Halcyon malimbica torquata	282
Corythornis cristata cyanostigma	287
[*Pogoniulus subsulphureus flavimentum*]	323
Trachyphonus purpuratus togoensis	331
Hirundo daurica kumboensis	366
[*Myrmecocichla cinnamomeiventris cavernicola*]	423
Cisticola aberrans petrophila	437
Camaroptera brevicaudata brevicaudata	449
Camaroptera chloronota chloronota	451
Nectarinia olivacea cephaelis	504
Nectarinia adelberti eboensis	510
Pyrenestes ostrinus frommi	593
Spermophaga haematina togoensis	594

Table 11. Subspecies recorded in Togo but not in Nigeria. Those in square brackets require confirmation. Data based on subspecies recognised in volumes 1–4 of *The Birds of Africa* and in Howard & Moore (1991).

Scientific Name	Check-list Species No
Columba livia gymnocyclus	220
Halcyon malimbica torquata	282
Corythornis cristata galerita	287
Tockus albocristatus macrourus	309
[*Ceratogymna cylindricus cylindricus*]	316
Trachyphonus purpuratus goffini	331
Galerida cristata senegallensis	356
Criniger barbatus barbatus	404
Alethe diademata diademata	413
Hyliota violacea nehrkorni	460
Muscicapa caerulescens nigrorum	476
Platysteira castanea hormophora	483
Terpsiphone nitens reichenowi	486
Terpsiphone rufiventer nigriceps	487
[*Anthreptes fraseri idius*]	499
Nectarinia seimundi kruensis	503
Nectarinia olivacea guineensis	504
Prionops caniceps caniceps	536
Oriolus brachyrhynchus brachyrhynchus	544
Lamprotornis splendidus chrysonotis	553
Malimbus scutatus scutatus	572
Malimbus rubricollis bartletti	575
Nigrita bicolor bicolor	585
Nigrita canicapilla emiliae	587
[*Pholidornis rushiae ussheri*]	611

were still in existence, though the most important forest block in southern Benin, the Lama forest, was at that time being destroyed. These observations support the findings of Diamond & Hamilton (1980) that many West African endemic species are not concentrated on either side of the Togo-Benin Gap, but rather are concentrated in Sierre Leone, eastern Côte d'Ivoire and western Ghana, and their ranges do not conform to the present-day distribution of lowland forests.

It may be that in more recent times the R. Volta to the west and the R. Niger to the east have been more important obstacles to animal movements than the Togo-Benin Gap. This was the suggestion of Booth (1958) and Robbins (1978) on the basis of their analyses of the distributions of mammals. In addition to the 4 species of birds whose eastern races occur in Togo, some mammals (Booth 1958) and grasshoppers (Jago 1964) of eastern origin are known to survive in refuges in the forests of the Togo highlands. More recently, it has been found that the Psocoptera of Togo and Benin are much more akin to those of Nigeria than to those of Côte d'Ivoire (Turner & Cheke 1983). However, the Togo-Benin Gap is considered to be an obstacle for tree-frogs, with only 4 of the 23 species of the West African fauna occurring on both sides (Schiotz 1967).

When the birds of Benin have been documented more thoroughly, more meaningful zoogeographical comparisons for this sub-region of West Africa would, perhaps, be between the birds west of the Volta R. but east of the Sierre Leone forest block, those between the Volta R. and the Niger R., and those east of the Niger R.

CONSERVATION

During the 1950s–1980s, numerous parts of Togo were designated as protected areas, the total area amounting to 14% of the country (IUCN 1991, World Bank 1993). The most important were the 3 National Parks of Fazao-Malfakassa (1920 km²), Fosse aux Lions (17 km²) and Keran (1,636 km²), and the 9 faunal reserves at Aboulaye (300 km²), Akaba (256 km²), Aledjo (8 km²), Djamdé (17 km²), Galangashie (75 km²), Haho-Yoto (180 km²), Kpéssi (280 km²), Oti Mandouri (1478 km²), and Togodo (310 km²) (Fig. 9). In addition, there are a few hunting reserves and 54 classified forests. A modern hotel, built for tourists, is sited at Fazao, rest-houses are available at Naboulgou in the Keran Park, and the Fosse aux Lions reserve is within easy reach of Dapaon.

Whenever dams are built, there is an inevitable loss of habitat, such as gallery forest, through submersion. This occurred in 1987 in Togo when L. Nangbeto was formed following the building of a dam across the Mono R. In February 1986 the lower reaches of the Mono R. supported up to 53 hippopotamus *Hippopotamus amphibius*. These had attracted tourists to a viewing point at Atchinedji which was inundated, with a subsequent loss of both habitat and large game. A similar loss of habitat will result if a second planned dam is built on the Mono at Adjarala near Tététou.

Another consequence of building dams is the control of water flow in the rivers that are fed from the dam. A dam, built in Burkina Faso during 1989, controls the flow of water in the tributaries of the Oti river in Togo. This may have caused the cessation of breeding of the Yellow-billed Storks at Mango in 1993, the first time in 30 years. This may also result in the inundation of a substantial part of the wintering area of an important population of Crowned Cranes, and may threaten the population of Hippopotamus in the Oti-Mandouri reserve. For future comparison, it is worthy of note that in the late 1980s Elephants *Loxodonta africana* were seen regularly at Fosse aux Lions, e.g. 44 on 9 Apr 1988, and were not uncommon in the Keran Park.

During the 1970s and 1980s, birds and other wildlife benefited from President Eyadéma's hegemony. He banned firearms but maintained the system of game reserves and National Parks, partly to provide himself and his guests with a hunting facility! Poachers caught in restricted areas suffered very severe penalties. However, once Eyadéma's authority waned in the early 1990s, firearms became abundant, the guarding of reserves became impossible, and wildlife suffered as a result (A. Opoku, 29 Jan 1992, pers. comm., Poncelet 1993, T. Crisler, 26 Aug 1993 pers. comm., S. A. Sowah, 7 Sep 1993, pers. comm., Walsh & Chardonnet 1995). Indeed by November 1991, the Keran and other National Parks were virtually disestablished.

The near destruction of the National Park / Faunal Reserve systems in the north continues and, if it persists, will result in the loss of most of the remaining wild herbivore species (Walsh & Chardonnet 1995). It is also likely to have a catastrophic effect on populations of large non-passerine birds, in particular, storks, bustards and diurnal raptors. In addition, the well developed riverine forest of the Keran basin is threatened and may well be destroyed in the future, and this will result in a retraction of the northerly range of a number of species, e.g. Narina's Trogon *Apaloderma narina* and Moho *Hypergerus atriceps*.

Another major threat to conservation is de-forestation. Only about 7.6% of Togo's original moist tropical forest, with a closed canopy, remains (World Conservation Monitoring Centre 1992). In 1980 there were 3040 km² of closed broadleaved forest, of which only 470 km² was considered to be undisturbed (FAO/UNEP 1981). Barnes (1990) working on deforestation trends for 1976–80 (FAO/UNEP 1981) predicted

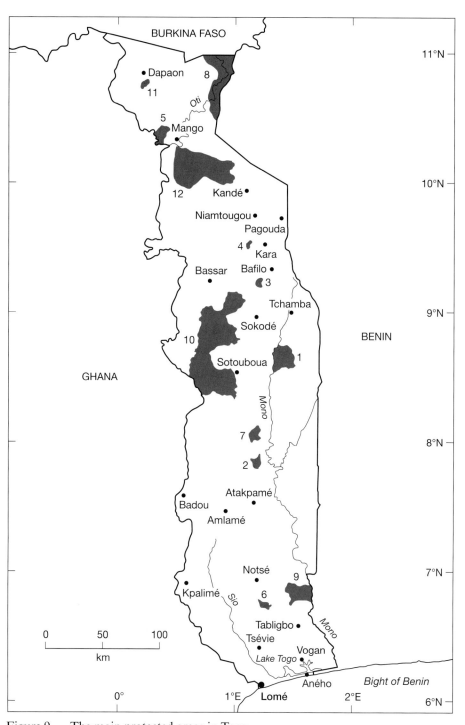

Figure 9.   The main protected areas in Togo.
Faunal Reserves: 1. Aboulaye; 2. Akaba; 3. Aledjo; 4. Djamdé;
5. Galangashie; 6. Haho-Yoto; 7. Kpessi; 8. Oti-Mandouri; 9. Togodo.
National Parks: 10. Fazao-Malfakassa; 11. Fosse aux Lions; 12. Keran.

that this would have been reduced to 2239 km² by the year 2000. The figures from FAO/UNEP (1981) are considered to give an excessively favourable picture of the situation according to Sayer *et al.* (1992) who state for Togo and Benin "there are only tiny areas of forest in either country where there is even a remote chance of retaining the full range of natural flora and fauna". Using UNEP/GRID (satellite imagery) data for 1989–90, Sayer *et al.* (1992) consider that only 1360 km² of Togo's lowland rain forest remained in 1990, and that based on FAO (1988) figures the annual net loss of forest between 1981 and 1985 was 21 km² per year. The impression of the authors, based on numerous helicopter flights, was that the annual rate of deforestation, in particular clear-felling, was even greater in 1988–90.

Forests at Misahöhe, those remaining near Badou in the Plateaux region, and gallery forests along the major rivers are in urgent need of preservation. The amount of tree-felling at Misahöhe is probably too far advanced, and the rate of felling too fast, to save specialised forest species such as the Blue Cuckoo-Shrike *Coracina azurea*, last recorded there by Dekeyser (1951).

Over and above these considerations, the greatest threat to all wildlife in Togo is the high density and rapid growth (3.6% per year) of the human population (Sayer *et al.* 1992). This is the highest in West and Equatorial Africa, with the exception of Cote d'Ivoire which has a much lower population density. Thus, even during the period when firearms were banned and reserves strictly and rigorously protected, catapults were abundant and very effective in killing a variety of birds. Another invidious activity is the snaring of waders and terns, including the rare Damara Tern *Sterna balaenarum*, on the beach front at Lomé.

The recent expansion and development of Lomé have resulted in both the loss of most of the shore-line habitat and saline pools and marshy areas that lie behind. Thus, the numbers of waders reported in this Check-list may well exceed those recorded in future years.

The urgency for conservation measures in Togo is apparent from the 28 bird species recorded in the country which also appear in the species lists included in *The ICBP/IUCN Red Data Book* (Collar & Stuart 1985). These are: (a) Rare and listed in the main text of the *Red Data Book* – *Sterna balaenarum*; (b) Threatened and listed in Appendix D – *Ciconia ciconia, Falco peregrinus, Sterna dougalli*; (c) Near-threatened and listed in Appendix C – *Illadopsis rufescens, Lamprotornis cupreocauda*; (d) Candidate species to be treated as threatened and listed in Appendix G – *Sula capensis, Tigriornis leucolophus, Gorsachius leuconotus, Ephippiorhynchus senegalensis, Urotriorchis macrourus, Hieraaetus dubius, Spizaetus africanus, Francolinus ahantensis, Balearica pavonina, Vanellus superciliosus, Rynchops flavirostris, Streptopelia hypopyrrha, Pachycoccyx audeberti, Merops malimbicus, Ceratogymna elata, Campethera maculosa, Apalis sharpii, Hyliota violacea, Muscicapa ussheri, Platysteira blissetti, Illadopsis puveli, Telophorus lagdeni.*

One hindrance to conservation in Togo is the lack of precise knowledge of the Togolese fauna, although Villiers (1951a) wrote a general account and Roure (1967) provided an inventory of large mammals and reptiles. Apart from birds, little is known about vertebrates other than antelopes (Fischer 1923, Baudenon 1952, Chardonnet *et al.* 1990), bats (De Vree *et al.* 1969, 1970, De Vree & Van der Straeten 1971) and reptiles (Werner 1898, Sternfeld 1909, Villiers 1951a), and only a few insect groups have been studied in detail, e.g. butterflies (Karsch 1893), aquatic bugs (Poisson 1951), Odonata (Karsch 1893, Fraser 1951), Neuroptera (Fraser 1951), Orthoptera (Karsch 1893, Fishpool & Popov 1984, Popov 1985), Psocoptera (Turner & Cheke 1983) and horseflies (Chainey & Cheke 1994).

SYSTEMATIC LIST

The sequence of families and species, species names, subspecific classification, and English and French vernacular names follow volumes 1–4 of the *Birds of Africa* (BOA) (Brown *et al.* 1982, Urban *et al.* 1986, Fry *et al.* 1988, Keith *et al.* 1992) and unpublished lists prepared in May 1991 for future volumes in preparation (A. Richford, pers. comm.). In a few cases, the BOA nomenclature has been updated as a result of subsequent research, and these new recommendations are indicated clearly in the text where and when they occur, but it is likely that some names published eventually in BOA will differ from the 1991 list. Subspecific names of species not covered by published volumes of BOA are those recognised by Howard & Moore (1991) unless otherwise stated.

The geographical coordinates of localities mentioned in the check-list are listed in the Gazetteer. Many names have alternative spellings on different maps and these inconsistencies are perpetuated in publications. Some places have also changed their names since colonial times, and some even more recently, e.g. Lama-Kara is now officially referred to as Kara. Where different spellings or alternative names for the same town are known, these have been listed in the Gazetteer, but one preferred form has been used consistently in the text.

Each species account includes information on status, abundance, habitat, distribution and, when applicable, breeding in Togo. In general, a species was classified as breeding only if a nest with eggs or young has been seen or documented, or if parent birds were seen with dependent young, but for a few species (raptors, hamerkop, and some weaver birds) breeding was accepted on the basis of other criteria, e.g. a raptor sitting close on the same nest on more than one occasion.

Many records mentioned in the text are based on the authors' own, previously unpublished, observations and are not accredited in the text to avoid unnecessary repetition. All other records are acknowledged through the use of either a published reference or an acronym of the name of the observer who supplied the information (see below). The willingness and generosity of these observers (see Acknowledgements) are much appreciated.

Species are placed in square brackets if there is any doubt about their occurrence in Togo, are unnumbered, and are given no status. Reasons for the uncertainty are given.

Categories used to record status and abundance are the same as those used in the check-list for Ghana (Grimes 1987). These are listed below:

ABBREVIATIONS & ACRONYMS

RB	Resident breeder
R(B)	Resident, but breeding not proved
PM	Palaearctic migrant
Afm	Migrates within Togo
AfM/B	Migrates to and from Togo to breed in Togo
AfM/NB	Migrates to and from Togo to spend non-breeding season in Togo
V	Vagrant
?	Indicates a doubt over the status immediately preceding the question mark, but not of occurrence.

If more than one category is applicable, the more important is stated first.

The five categories for abundance are the same as those used in the Ghana checklist (Grimes 1987). These, somewhat loose definitions, are

Abundant	invariably encountered without much effort in large numbers in their preferred habitat.
Common	invariably encountered singly or in small numbers in their preferred habitat.
Not uncommon	often, but not invariably, met within their preferred habitat.
Uncommon	infrequent and sporadic in preferred habitat.
Rare	rarely seen or heard, often implying less than a dozen records.

Museum Collections

BMNH	Natural History Museum [formerly British Museum (Natural History)], Tring, UK
BMNHL	Natural History Museum [formerly British Museum (Natural History)], London, UK
FMNH	Field Museum of Natural History, Chicago, USA
IFAN	Museum of the Institut Fondamental d'Afrique Noire, Dakar, Senegal
MNB	Museum für Naturkunde der Humboldt-Universität, Berlin, Germany
MNHN	Muséum National d'Histoire Naturelle, Paris
MRAC	Musée Royale de l'Afrique Centrale, Tervuren

Observers

AA	A. Alvarado
A&W	A. Arne and C. Warneker
P&JB	P. J. & J. A. Broadbent per British Trust for Ornithology
PMC	P. M. Claffey
TC	T. Crisler
JRD	J. R. Davidson
H&S	D. T. Holyoak & M. B. Seddon
UK	U. Kaiser
HL	H. Lege
JML	J. M. Lock
PM	P. Michelsen
FAO	Food and Agriculture Organisation
DP	D. Partridge
R&J	F. Roux & G. Jarry (per International Waterfowl and Wetlands Research Bureau).
SAS	S. A. Sowah
JBT	J. B. Taylor
RWT	R. W. Taylor

NON-PASSERINES

STRUTHIONIDAE

[STRUTHIO CAMELUS
Ostrich
Autruche d'Afrique

In Jun 1903 Dr. Kersting gave a skeleton from "the hinterlands of Togo" to the MNB. It is unlikely that it was obtained within the current boundaries of Togo, but not impossible. Ostriches occur at Biu (10°40'N) in Nigeria and may have been found as far south as Jebba (9°8'N) in 1899 (Elgood 1982). On 3 Feb 1902, A. Mischlich, the chief of the German station at Kratshi (= Kété Kratschi, Ghana), presented to the Berlin zoological gardens a young ostrich which had been obtained at Libtako (= Liptako) which is in present-day Burkina Faso. The bird died on 23 May 1902 and was given to the MNB in whose registration book is written (entry 118), "Libtako is in very arid country. The natives there catch the ostriches and tame them. Herds of 20–30 birds came to Kratshi. Likewise the ostriches occurring in Hausaland are said to come from Libtako." Bouet (1913) also noted that Hausa from Kano and Sokoto travelled to Niger and Mali to purchase domesticated ostriches from those living on islands in the Niger R. between Timbuctoo and Niamey and elsewhere, including Liptako.

There is an ostrich egg on the pinnacle of the chief's hut in Fazao.]

PROCELLARIIDAE

1.   DAPTION CAPENSE   V

Pintado Petrel
Pétrel damier

Coastal vagrant. Seen off Anécho, date unknown (Millet-Horsin 1923). Record considered acceptable owing to known reliability of the observer (W. R. P. Bourne, pers. comm.).

HYDROBATIDAE

2.   HYDROBATES PELAGICUS   V, PM

British Storm-Petrel
Océanite tempête

Coastal vagrant. Seen off Anécho, date unknown (Millet-Horsin 1923).

PODICIPEDIDAE

3.   TACHYBAPTUS RUFICOLLIS   R(B)

Little Grebe
Grèbe castagneux

Rare resident. One on the Mono R. 25 km east of Sotouboua, Nov (Cheke 1982b); in 1989 singles present on pond beside L. Togo at Agbodrafo, Jul and Dec, and 2 there Sep (JBT); 3 at Anié, May; 1 at Mango, date unknown (TC).

SULIDAE

4.   SULA CAPENSIS   V

Cape Gannet
Fou du Cap

Coastal vagrant in wet season only, no dates given (Douaud 1957). The species used to be common in the Gulf of Guinea during the 1950s and 1960s (the period of Douaud's stay in Togo) but has since declined, probably because of excessive culling by the fishing industry (T. B. Oatley, pers. comm.). Now listed as a candidate species to be treated as threatened in Appendix G of Collar & Stuart (1985).

Many birds ringed on the breeding grounds in South Africa have been recovered in Cameroon and Gabon and a few in Ghana and Nigeria, but none have been reported from Togo (T. B. Oatley, pers. comm.).

5.   SULA LEUCOGASTER   V

Brown Booby
Fou brun

Coastal vagrant (*S. l. leucogaster*), but may be a regular visitor. Young birds more common than adults, end Jun to early Aug (Douaud 1955).

PHALACROCORACIDAE

6.   PHALACROCORAX AFRICANUS   RB

Long-tailed Cormorant
Cormoran africain

Resident (*P. a. africanus*) and common on water-courses and lakes in the northern savanna. Most southern records in dry season, suggesting local movements. Millet-Horsin (1921d) described *P. a. menegauxi* (considered synonymous with *africanus*), from the lagoons of Togo and Dahomey (= Benin), and considered it very common throughout the lagoon (Millet-Horsin 1923). Occasional in forest, e.g. Djodji, Feb. Group of 50, mostly juveniles, Nangbeto, Apr (JBT), and at least 58 there, Jun.

Breeding. Breeds annually together with *A. melanocephala* at Mango, but usually fledges later than the herons, mainly during the late rains; may also breed opportunistically. Mango records include: recently fledged bird, Sep 1987, and fully fledged nestling, Oct 1986 (Walsh *et al.* 1990); up to 11 birds sitting on nests in *Ceiba pentandra* trees, Oct 1988; 1989 records suggest double-brooding as 3 sitting tight, 6 Aug 1989, when herons had well-grown young, and 12 sitting in same trees but in different nests, one with 2 young, 5 Nov 1989, when herons had left. May also breed in Kara area, where seen flying with food, Jun.

ANHINGIDAE

7.   ANHINGA MELANOGASTER   R(B)

Darter
Anhinga

Now rare resident (*A. m. rufa*), but formerly not uncommon in the Lomé area, 1963–65 (JRD); also common along water-courses in Benin, 1955–56 (Brunel 1958).

No records since mid 1960s until July 1989 when one was sighted over the lower Sio R. near Lomé. In 1990, 8 at Anié, Feb, one L. Nangbeto, Apr (JBT) and 16 there, Jun. The reappearance in the south may be associated with the creation of the lake caused by the damming of the Mono R. at Nangbeto in 1987. No records from the north despite intensive surveys in recent years.

Breeding. A bird with nesting material flying over dam at Nangbeto, Jun 1990.

PELECANIDAE

| 8. | PELECANUS ONOCROTALUS | V |

Great White Pelican
Pélican blanc

Vagrant, only one record. On 15 January 1914, the Duke of Mecklenburg, the Governor of Togo, presented the MNB with a skin collected at Lomé, date unknown. The species may not have been uncommon in the past (see below under *P. rufescens*) as it has been recorded in flocks of more than 400 from coastal regions in southeast Ghana (Grimes 1987). The specimen was originally identified by Reichenow in the MNB (register entry 921) as *P. sharpei* Bocage 1871, but later he considered that it was probably only an extreme case of colour variation within *P. onocrotalus* (Reichenow 1915), a view supported by Chapin (1932).

| 9. | PELECANUS RUFESCENS | V |

Pink-backed Pelican
Pélican roussâtre

Vagrant. There is a specimen labelled "Togo" (date unknown) in the MNB, which was collected by G. Thierry who was active in the Mango area. The only other record is one soaring over Domaine Gravillou, 7 Apr 1990. Robinson (1972) saw a pelican at Lomé, 13 Nov 1970, which she thought was this species. According to Piraux (1987) "Grey Pelicans" occur on L. Togo, and Villiers (1951a) reported *Pelecanus* to be numerous in some regions, but these reports may refer to either *P. rufescens* or to *P. onocrotalus* (see above).

Bouet (1914) reported the species as rare in the lagoons of Benin and saw a captive bird at Ouidah, which had presumably been taken in one of the lagoons.

ARDEIDAE

Botaurinae

| 10. | IXOBRYCHUS MINUTUS | R(B), PM |

Little Bittern
Blongios nain

Not uncommon, probably resident (*I. m. payesii*), in the Lomé area, where birds in breeding condition occur Sep. Collected in north at Mango by G. Thierry, date unknown (Reichenow 1902a). Presence of Palaearctic migrants confirmed by collection of *I. m. minutus* at Niamtougou, Jul (De Roo *et al.* 1971). Other northern records (subspecies unknown) from Landa-Pozanda and Naboulgou, Feb–May.

11.   IXOBRYCHUS STURMII   Afm/(B), R?(B)

Dwarf Bittern
Blongios de Sturm

Not uncommon wet season visitor, Jul–Sep, to the Dapaon and Mango areas in the north. One beside the Anié R. at 07°55'N, 18 May 1990, was probably migrating northwards. Status in the south less clear. Browne (1980) recorded no marked seasonal fluctuations in numbers at Lomé. His and other records there, Jan–Apr (including an immature in Jan), suggest it may be resident in coastal areas.
   Breeding. Territorial behaviour (involving a pair and a third bird) Tantigou, Aug.

Ardeinae

12.   TIGRIORNIS LEUCOLOPHUS   R(B)

White-crested Tiger Heron
Onoré à huppe blanche

Rare resident. The only recent record is 2 singles beside the Koué R. in the Fazao mountains, Feb 1988 (Walsh *et al.* 1990). Collected by E. Baumann at Akposso, 25 Dec 1894 (Reichenow 1897, Chapin 1932), and by Kurz at Anécho, date unknown (Reichenow 1902a). Listed as a candidate species for treatment as threatened in Appendix G of Collar & Stuart (1985).

13.   GORSACHIUS LEUCONOTUS   R(B)

White-backed Night Heron
Bihoreau à dos blanc

Rare resident, known only from collected specimens: a juvenile, Bismarckburg, date unknown (Reichenow 1891a); Atakpamé, 20 Mar 1969 (De Roo *et al.* 1971); Borgou, 9 Dec 1969 (De Roo *et al.* 1972). Listed as a candidate species to be treated as threatened in Appendix G of Collar & Stuart (1985).

14.   NYCTICORAX NYCTICORAX   R(B), PM?

Black-crowned Night Heron
Bihoreau gris

Not uncommon resident (*N. n. nycticorax*) from Lomé north to Dapaon. Numbers probably supplemented by Palaearctic visitors, mostly juveniles, as more common in the dry season.

15.   ARDEOLA RALLOIDES   PM, R(B)

Squacco Heron
Crabier chevelu

Locally common Palaearctic migrant, Sep–Apr, to rivers, lakesides and marshes throughout. Also resident from the Keran Park northwards and at the coast, where recorded Nov–May, Jul and Sep (Robinson 1972), and at L. Togo, Jun (JBT). Also seen Nangbeto, Jun (JBT).
   Breeding. Bird in full breeding condition Domaine Gravillou, Aug.

16.   **BUBULCUS IBIS**   AfM/NB, R(B)

    Cattle Egret
    Héron garde-boeufs

Abundant dry season visitor (*B. i. ibis*) throughout except forests, Oct–May.
Occasionally roosts communally in trees in towns such as Atakpamé and Kara. Locally
common resident in coastal areas and perhaps occasionally elsewhere, e.g. 11 roosting
in a Baobab tree at Ketao, Jul.
    Breeding. No evidence of breeding in north, although one in breeding dress Tantigou,
4 Jun 1990. 2 birds in full breeding condition lower Sio R., near Lomé, Aug. Has bred
in coastal Ghana (Grimes 1987).

17.   **BUTORIDES STRIATUS**   RB

    Green Heron
    Héron vert

Common resident (*B. s. atricapillus*) throughout, preferring well-wooded riversides in
both savanna and forest. Usually solitary.
    Breeding. Bird incubating C/4 Fosse aux Lions swamp, Aug. Nest building Domaine
Gravillou, Aug.

18.   **EGRETTA ARDESIACA**   V

    Black Heron
    Aigrette ardoisée

Rare, status uncertain. One at Zébé marsh, date unknown (Millet-Horsin 1923), and
12 at L. Togo, 26 Jan 1984 (R&J).

19.   **EGRETTA GULARIS**   R(B)

    Western Reef Heron
    Aigrette gorge blanche

Uncommon resident (*E. g. gularis*) along shore at Lomé. No inland records.

20.   **EGRETTA GARZETTA**   PM, R(B)

    Little Egret
    Aigrette garzette

Common resident (*E. g. garzetta*) throughout and abundant after influx of Palaearctic
migrants in Aug. Flocks of up to 200 occur at L. Nangbeto.

21.   **EGRETTA INTERMEDIA**   R(B)

    Yellow-billed Egret
    Aigrette intermédiaire

Not uncommon resident (*E. i. brachyrhyncha*) throughout. Usually single birds beside
dams or rivers, but 6 at Domaine Gravillou, Apr.

22.   **EGRETTA ALBA**   R(B)

    Great Egret
    Grande Aigrette

Not uncommon resident (*E. a. melanorhynchos*) in marshland, and at margins of wide rivers and lakes from the coast north to Dapaon. Frequent in lagoons at the coast during the wet season (Douaud 1955). Usually solitary, but 10 at Domaine Gravillou, Apr, and 12 at Panseni, Aug.

Breeding. A black-billed bird (breeding condition) Panseni, Jul. Douaud (1955) stated that *E. alba* probably bred in Togo.

| 23. ARDEA PURPUREA | PM, ?R(B) |

Purple Heron
Héron pourpré

Common Palaearctic migrant throughout (*A. p. purpurea*) at margins of lakes, rivers and marshes, mostly Oct–Jun; a few present in all months.

A bird ringed at the Sea of Azov, Russia, recovered 3.5 km from Lomé, just west of the Togo/Ghana border, in Aug.

Breeding. No records. Adult carrying stick, Ghana (Macdonald 1979).

| 24. ARDEA CINEREA | PM, R(B) |

Grey Heron
Héron cendré

Common Palaearctic visitor (*A. c. cinerea*) to rivers, lakes, marshes and coastal areas in dry season, mid Oct to Apr. Up to 250 counted along the length of the Oti R., Jan 1988 and 1989. Some, presumably residents, present during the wet season, e.g. at least 56 at Nangbeto dam, 24 Jun 1990.

Birds recovered in Togo ringed in Hungary (1), Switzerland (1) (Brown *et al.* 1982), Germany (1) (Cramp & Simmons 1977) and the U.S.S.R. (Rydzensky 1956).

| 25. ARDEA MELANOCEPHALA | RB, Afm?/(B) |

Black-headed Heron
Héron mélanocéphale

Common resident in the Oti valley area and not uncommon dry season visitor as far south as Nangbeto.

Breeding. Records at Mango, where birds were present at 2 colonies in *Ceiba pentandra* trees Apr–Oct, include the following: 27 nests, some with young almost ready to fly, Oct 1986; 2 colonies, one of 56 the other of 70 nests mostly still being built, Jul 1987; 10 fledglings standing in the crowns of 2 nest trees, Sep 1987; 102 nests, Jul 1988; many nests with well grown young, Oct 1988; 81 nests, Jul 1989; 12 part-built nests with attendant adults, 22 Apr 1990. In a second colony in an *Acacia* tree beside the Oti R. near Panseni, 10 nests contained eggs and the other a sitting bird, Oct 1988, 6 nests contained young in early Nov, and the colony was deserted by 16 Nov.

| 26. ARDEA GOLIATH | R(B) |

Goliath Heron
Héron goliath

Rare resident. Millet-Horsin (1923) rated the species as rare but recorded singles around the shoreline of L. Togo, and in marshes and amongst semi-flooded tall grasses. Only 6 recent records, all singles: Anécho, Mar (Cheke *et al.* 1986); near Mango, Jan; Oti-Toutionga, Jun; Panseni, Feb; and beside the Oti R. at 10°33'N, 00°41'E, and at 10°40'N, 00°46'E, Dec.

SCOPIDAE

27.   SCOPUS UMBRETTA   RB

Hamerkop
Ombrette du Sénégal

Common resident, especially north of Atakpamé.

Breeding. Nests beside most major rivers in north and as far south as the upper Sio
and Notsé dam (3 nests). Nest-building: Fosse aux Lions, Aug; Naboulgou, Oct;
Tantigou, Feb. Copulation: Mango, Nov; Naboulgou, Aug; Nangbeto, Aug (JBT).

CICONIIDAE

28.   MYCTERIA IBIS   AfM/B

Yellow-billed Stork
Tantale ibis

Breeding visitor to the north, apparently absent mid Jul to mid Sep. Population is centred
around a colony in Mango town. Birds return in mid Sep and after breeding disperse along
the Oti and Koumongou valleys. One at Akposso in the south, Dec (Reichenow 1897).

Breeding. Colony in large Baobab tree at Mango occupied from mid Sep to mid
Feb, though most young fledge by mid Jan; colony consisted of 20–25 pairs during
1987–89. Local inhabitants reported the colony was at least 30 years old in 1988 and
the same tree was used during the previous decade. In 1986, there were 8 nests in *Ceiba*
trees, but these were not used in subsequent years. No birds returned to breed in 1993
(TC). This may have been a result of a modified flow pattern in the Oti R. which was
caused by the damming of the Oualé R. in Burkina Faso during 1989.

An isolated nest (C/2 on 9 Dec 1987) in a riverine tree beside the Oti R., near
Mango, failed.

29.   ANASTOMUS LAMELLIGERUS   AfM/NB, R?(B)

African Open-bill Stork
Bec-ouvert africain

Not uncommon visitor (*A. l. lamelligerus*) to the Oti basin, Dec–Apr, with highest
numbers in Feb. Rare at other times, but some may be resident as records in all months
except Sep. No evidence of breeding. Largest flock (60 birds) at Koumongou, Apr.
Most southern records are near Kara: 8 birds in Feb, one in Jul.

30.   CICONIA NIGRA   PM

Black Stork
Cigogne noire

Rare Palaearctic migrant to protected areas in northern savannas, Jan–Mar (Walsh
1991). 6 records of singles or pairs in the Koumongou valley, Feb–Mar; one in the Oti
valley at 10°40'N, 00°46'E, Jan.

31.   CICONIA ABDIMII   AfM/NB

Abdim's Stork
Cigogne d'Abdim

Regular transequatorial migrant seen on passage, Apr–Jun. Largest flock (250 birds) at Kandjo, Apr. Birds returning southwards seldom seen, but 2 at Mango, 25 Nov 1987.

32.   CICONIA EPISCOPUS   RB, AfM?/(B)

Woolly-necked Stork
Cigogne épiscopale

Not uncommon resident (*C. e. microscelis*) in the Oti basin, possibly augmented by influx of intra-African migrants, Oct–Jun. Most southern record in Mo valley: 2 pairs, during wet season.

Breeding. 4 nest sites located in the Oti and Koumongou valleys in the years 1987–89. Eggs probably laid Aug; adults incubating, Sep; fledglings, end Nov.

33.   CICONIA CICONIA   PM

White Stork
Cigogne blanche

Not uncommon Palaearctic visitor (*C. c. ciconia*), mid Nov to mid Feb, to the Oti basin in some years (Walsh 1989); flocks up to 200. Northbound birds over Lomé, early 1988 (AA) and 1990 (RWT). One collected Atakpamé, Mar (De Roo 1970); a pair at Kara, Apr (UK). Listed as threatened in Appendix D of Collar & Stuart (1985).

34.   EPHIPPIORHYNCHUS SENEGALENSIS   RB

Saddle-billed Stork
Jabiru du Sénégal

Rare resident in the Oti reserve and Keran Park. Aerial surveys suggest there are unlikely to be more than 4 pairs in the country. Listed as a candidate species for treatment as threatened in Appendix G of Collar & Stuart (1985).

Breeding. Nested in Baobab trees in the Keran Park, 1986–89, and in the Oti reserve near Panseni, 1987–89. Nest-building, Aug; egg-laying, early Oct (two C/4 and one C/5); young fledged, end Jan.

35.   LEPTOPTILOS CRUMENIFERUS   AfM/NB

Marabou Stork
Marabout d'Afrique

Rare visitor: one at Mandouri, Jun and Oct; another beside the Oti at 10°35'N; a pair in the Keran Park, Feb (Walsh *et al.* 1990). One collected at Bismarckburg, Jan (Reichenow 1891a).

THRESKIORNITHIDAE

36.   PLEGADIS FALCINELLUS   PM

Glossy Ibis
Ibis falcinelle

Rare Palaearctic migrant (*P. f. falcinellus*): one at Mango, Dec 1984 (HL); Tantigou and Ayengré, Apr 1988 (Walsh *et al.* 1990); 4 at Domaine Gravillou, 7 Apr 1990, and 5 there 2 days later.

37.   BOSTRYCHIA HAGEDASH   R(B)

Hadada
Ibis hagedash

Not uncommon resident along wooded streams in savanna areas, common in Keran Park. Numbers are declining in unreserved areas where riverine forests are being destroyed. Present in Fazao mountains but not seen in forested valleys of the southwest, although collected Bismarckburg, date unknown (Reichenow 1892).

[BOSTRYCHIA RARA

Spot-breasted Ibis
Ibis vermiculé

Roure (1967) included the Spot-breasted Ibis in his list of species deserving special protection in Togo, but on what basis is unclear as there are no apparent records. There are only 2 confirmed records from Ghana (Grimes 1987) and none from Nigeria (Elgood *et al.* 1994). In Côte d'Ivoire it is restricted to the primary rain forest at Tai (Thiollay 1985b).]

38.   THRESKIORNIS AETHIOPICA   AfM/NB

Sacred Ibis
Ibis sacré

Rare visitor to north: one in the Keran Park, Apr 1979 (Cheke & Walsh 1980); singles at Domaine Gravillou, Feb 1988 and May 1990.

[PLATALEA ALBA

African Spoonbill
Spatule d'Afrique

Togo is included in the distribution map of Brown *et al.* (1982) but no records have been traced. Occurs as a vagrant in coastal areas of eastern Ghana (Grimes 1987).]

PHOENICOPTERIDAE

[PHOENICONAIAS MINOR

Lesser Flamingo
Petit Flamant

Togo is included in the distribution map of Brown *et al.* (1982) but no records have been traced. There have been no records in Ghana since before 1870 (Grimes 1987).]

ANATIDAE

Dendrocygninae

39.   DENDROCYGNA BICOLOR   V

Fulvous Whistling-Duck
Dendrocygne fauve

Vagrant, only 2 records: Millet-Horsin (1923) saw one for sale, which was said to have been captured on L. Togo; one amongst a flock of *D. viduata*, Tantigou, 7–9 Apr 1990.

40.   DENDROCYGNA VIDUATA   RB, AfM/(B)

White-faced Whistling-Duck
Dendrocygne veuf

Common resident throughout, except in forest. Especially common in the Oti basin
and the flood plain of the lower Mono R., and generally more numerous in the dry
season, when flocks of more than 1000 may occur in the Oti valley, but 2000 Tantigou,
4 Jun 1990. An albinistic duck (white body feathers and black primaries) was sighted
at Domaine Gravillou, Jul 1988 and Oct 1989; another, possibly the same bird, sighted
Oti-Toutionga, Jan 1990. Sharland (1975) reported two partial albinos (white on the
wings only) near Jos, Nigeria.
    Breeding. A pair with 6 small downy ducklings and 15 flightless young (from 4
broods) near Mango, Oct. An adult with 7 young Domaine Gravillou, Dec.

41.   THALASSORNIS LEUCONOTUS   V

White-backed Duck
Erismature à dos blanc

Vagrant (*T. l. leuconotus*), only 2 records: one on the Mono R. at 07°09'N, 01°27'E,
17 Nov 1981 (Cheke & Walsh 1984); a pair at Anié, Apr 1990 (JBT). Not recorded in
Ghana (Grimes 1987), and rare in Benin, where recorded on the banks of the Niger R.
at Bodjécali (Bouet 1914).

Tadorninae

42.   ALOPOCHEN AEGYPTIACUS   V

Egyptian Goose
Oie d'Egypte

Vagrant, one record only: one collected at Mango by G. Thierry, date unknown
(Reichenow 1902a).

Anatinae

43.   PLECTROPTERUS GAMBENSIS   R(B), AfM?(B)

Spur-winged Goose
Plectroptère de Gambie

Common resident in north, especially along the Oti R. upstream of Mango. Possible
influx there in the dry season as flocks of 300 or more Mango, Feb. Occasional as far
south as 9°N.
    Breeding. A pair with well-grown young 8 km north of Mango, Oct.

[PTERONETTA HARTLAUBII

Hartlaub's Duck
Ptéronette de Hartlaub

The southern third of Togo is included in the distribution map of Brown *et al.* (1982),
but no records have been traced. Given the extent of the authors' flights over Togolese
rivers, it is unlikely the species would have been missed if it was present.]

44.   SARKIDIORNIS MELANOTOS   AfM/NB

Knob-billed Duck
Canard casqué

Not uncommon visitor (*S. m. melanotos*), Dec–Apr, to northern river valleys, e.g. Oti and Koumongou. Sometimes forms large loose flocks, e.g. more than 100 near Mango, Feb. Once recorded, a female, as far south as Sara-Kawa, Feb.

45.   NETTAPUS AURITUS   R(B), AfM?/(B)

African Pygmy Goose
Sarcelle à Oreillons

Not uncommon resident in north, where recorded in all months except Sep. Max. count (11) at Domaine Gravillou, Apr. Occasional in south, where it may be migratory; Brunel (1958) recorded it in southern Benin, Oct–Dec, but a pair Sio R., near Lomé, Apr.

[ANAS SPARSA

African Black Duck
Canard noir

Dowsett (1993) and Dowsett & Forbes-Watson (1993) included it in their list of species for Togo, but acknowledged that its "occurrence requires proof". This resulted from a mis-reading of Walsh (1985), who did not claim that the species occurred in Togo but simply pointed out that habitat suitable for the species was available there.]

46.   ANAS ACUTA   PM

Northern Pintail
Canard pilet

Not uncommon Palaearctic migrant (*A. a. acuta*), Nov–Mar, to Oti and Koumongou valleys and Tantigou. Largest flock (53 birds) Tantigou, Jan 1988.

47.   ANAS QUERQUEDULA   PM

Garganey
Sarcelle d'été

Not uncommon Palaearctic migrant, Oct–Apr, to northern third of country, although Togo is excluded from the distribution mapped in Brown *et al.* (1982). Flock of at least 100 Tantigou, 28 Feb 1988, 67 of which still present 8 Mar. 6 pairs as far south as L. Alago near Sika-Kondji, Feb 1988. A female at Domaine Gravillou, 5 Jul 1987.

[ANAS CLYPEATA

Northern Shoveler
Canard souchet

Brown *et al.* (1982) include the northern third of Togo in their distribution map for the Northern Shoveler but no records have been traced.]

48.   AYTHYA NYROCA   PM

Ferruginous Duck
Fuligule nyroca

Rare Palaearctic migrant. Douaud (1957) stated that it occurred in Togo, presumably at L. Togo, but gave no details. There are no other records, although northern Togo is included in the distribution map in Brown *et al.* (1982).

[AYTHYA FULIGULA

Tufted Duck
Fuligule morillon

Brown *et al.* (1982) include the northern half of Togo in their distribution map for this species but no records have been traced.]

ACCIPITRIDAE

Pandioninae

49.   PANDION HALIAETUS   PM

Osprey
Balbuzard pêcheur

Not uncommon Palaearctic migrant (*P. h. haliaetus*) throughout, mainly Nov–Mar but a few records Jun–Oct.
   Birds recovered in Togo from Finland (2) and Sweden (2) (Saurola 1994).

Accipitrinae

50.   AVICEDA CUCULOIDES   R(B), Afm?/(B)

African Cuckoo Falcon
Baza coucou

Not uncommon in well-wooded savanna from near the coast as far north as the Keran Park. Status uncertain. Lack of records, Oct–Dec, and party of 6 Keran Park, Jun, suggest it may be migratory. *A. c. cuculoides* collected Tchonou (De Roo *et al.* 1969), but no confirmed records of *A. c. batesi.*

51.   PERNIS APIVORUS   PM

Honey Buzzard
Bondrée apivore

Uncommon Palaearctic passage migrant in the savanna, Sep–Oct, and Mar–Apr. Records additional to those in Walsh *et al.* (1990) are: an immature at Kara, Oct; one at Landa-Pozanda, Mar; a Finnish-ringed bird recovered near Kpalimé, Aug; and a Belgium-ringed bird recovered on the western side of L. Togo, Nov. Probably overwinters in the forest but only one record other than the one near Kpalimé: 2, which could have been on passage, Misahöhe, Apr.

52.   MACHAERHAMPHUS ALCINUS   R(B)

Bat Hawk
Milan des chauves-souris

Not uncommon resident (*M. a. anderssoni*) throughout savanna woodlands north to Tantigou; many records from Kara and Landa-Pozanda. Also present in forest clearings: Badou, Jan–Feb 1987, and Yégué (Douaud 1956b).

Breeding. Nuptial display Landa-Pozanda, Jul (Cheke & Walsh 1980).

53.   ELANUS CAERULEUS   R(B)

Black-shouldered Kite
Elanion blanc

Common resident (*E. c. caeruleus*) of savannas throughout, especially on the coastal plain.

Breeding. Territorial display Kara, Jun.

54.   CHELICTINIA RIOCOURII   AfM/NB

African Swallow-tailed Kite
Milan de Riocour

Rare intra-African migrant, only 5 records: G. Thierry collected 2 (neither with dates but both in the MNB), one in "Togo", the other at Mango (Reichenow 1902a). One sighted at Mango, Dec 1981 (Cheke 1982b) and 2 there, Dec 1984 (HL); one at Bafilo, Oct 1981 (Cheke 1982b).

55.   MILVUS MIGRANS   Afm/B, PM

Black Kite
Milan noir

Abundant intra-African migrant (*M. m. parasitus*) and Palaearctic visitor (*M. m. migrans*) throughout, late Sep to late Apr. Migratory flocks include: 44 flying southeast over Kara, 23 Sep 1987; 22 *parasitus* flying southeast over Kara, 29 Sep 1988; group of 16 *parasitus* at Notsé, 19 Apr 1990. Small populations of *parasitus* present in all habitats throughout the year.

91 birds roosted in a Kapok tree *Ceiba pentandra* at Kpalimé, 27 Jan 1988.

Palaearctic birds ringed in Germany (3), Switzerland (2) and France (2) have been recovered in Togo (Anon 1957, Douaud 1957, Jokele 1974). One of the German birds was found 29 years after ringing (Jokele 1974).

Breeding. Nest in *Acacia* tree with 2 young 10 km southwest of Koumongou, Mar; nest with well-grown young Kara, 4 May, and ready to fly 19 May. Sitting birds: on nest in *Ceiba pentandra* tree Agbatitoe, Dec, another at Kpalimé, Jan; Atakpamé, Jan; Tovegan, Jan; Agadji, Feb; Tététou, Feb; Tokpli, Feb; Mango, Apr. Copulation: Anié, Jan; Agomé-Glouzou, Nov. Courtship feeding: Kpaya, Feb. Building: Fosse aux Lions, Jan; Kara, Mar.

56.   HALIAEETUS VOCIFER   R(B)

African Fish Eagle
Pygargue vocifer

Uncommon resident along margins of large rivers and dams, occurs throughout the north and as far south as Notsé. Said to have once been common on the lagoon near Anécho, but was already rare in the 1920s (Millet-Horsin 1923).

57.   GYPOHIERAX ANGOLENSIS   RB

Vulturine Fish-Eagle
Palmiste d'Angola

Common resident of well wooded valleys with an abundance of oil palms *Elaeis guineensis*, especially in the Fazao area. Most northerly record at Naboulgou; most southerly at Nyivé.

Breeding. Adult at a newly-lined, empty nest in the Kamasse R. valley, Nov 1988; this contained 1 downy young, 17 Feb 1990. 1 young in nest beside the Kewa river, on same day.

58.   NEOPHRON PERCNOPTERUS   V

Egyptian Vulture
Percnoptère d'Egypte

Vagrant, recorded Fazao, date unknown but during Mar–Apr 1984 (Minster Agriculture Limited 1984); no other records.

59.   NECROSYRTES MONACHUS   RB

Hooded Vulture
Vautour charognard

Abundant resident (*N. m. monachus*) throughout, except coastal area. A total of 60+ was regularly counted at Badou in the forest zone; one roost tree at Atakpamé was used by 45 individuals.
Breeding. Adult beside nest in *Ceiba pentandra* tree 8 km south of Kara, Mar. Pair building in a *Borassus* palm 5 km south of Kara, Oct–Nov; one bird attending this nest, Nov; one sitting, Dec, and a single chick in this nest, Jan.

60.   GYPS AFRICANUS   RB

African White-backed Vulture
Vautour africain

Not uncommon, widespread resident in the north, occasionally recorded as far south as Blitta.
Breeding. Sub-adult sitting, apparently incubating, in an abandoned nest of a Saddle-billed Stork *Ephippiorhynchus senegalensis,* Koumongou valley, Keran Park, 10 and 27 Jan 1989; this nest had contained stork eggs in Dec 1988. Bannerman (1930) stated that birds in immature plumage may breed.

61.   GYPS RUEPPELLII   AfM/NB

Rüppell's Griffon
Vautour de Rüppell

Rare dry season visitor (*G. r. rueppellii*), Jan–Apr, to northern areas. Influx of 30 or more to the Keran Park, Mar 1990, may have been in association with arrival of wandering lion (*Panthera leo*).

62.   GYPS FULVUS   V, PM

European Griffon
Vautour fauve

Vagrant, only one record: one in the north of Keran Park, 21 Feb 1988. No records from Ghana or Nigeria but observed in the W National Park, Niger (Shull *et al.* 1986) and several records, including a Spanish-ringed bird, in Senegal (Morel & Morel 1990).

63.   AEGYPIUS TRACHELIOTUS   V

Lappet-faced Vulture
Vautour oricou

Vagrant, only 2 records: one at a buffalo (*Syncerus caffer*) carcass beside the

Oti R. at 10°35'N on 21 Feb 1987; 2 at 10°34'N 00°36'E resting with a flock of 25 African White-backed Vultures and 4 Ruppell's Griffons, 3 Mar 1989.

64.   AEGYPIUS OCCIPITALIS   V

White-headed Vulture
Vautour à tête blanche

Vagrant. Collected at Sokodé, date unknown, by Dr. Kersting who donated it to the MNB on 15 May 1903. One beside the Mono R. at 08°43'N, 01°16'E, 20 Oct 1981 (Cheke 1982b); recorded on the Ghana-Togo border at 08°30'N, 00°20'E (Grimes 1987).

65.   CIRCAETUS GALLICUS   PM, R?(B)

European and Beaudouin's Snake Eagles
Circaète Jean-le-Blanc ou Circaète de Beaudouin

Occurs throughout the year but influx in the dry season suggests that the European race (*C. g. gallicus*) is a not uncommon Palaearctic migrant, Sep–Apr. Occurs frequently in northern savannas but occasional as far south as Anié. The resident race (*C. g. beaudouini*) is difficult to distinguish from *gallicus* but all wet season records, e.g. one in the Keran Park, 12 Aug, and those involving breeding activity probably refer to *beaudouini*. One Landa-Pozanda, 15 Apr 1990, was in full wing moult and unlikely to have been able to migrate.
Breeding. One carrying a stick Landa-Pozanda, 19 Mar 1988.

66.   CIRCAETUS CINEREUS   R(B)

Brown Snake Eagle
Circaète brun

Common resident, usually in savanna but also seen in forest, e.g. Idifiou and Misahöhe. Noted as far south as Adédakopé, Feb.
Breeding. One, of 4 birds together, carrying a stick Naboulgou, Mar. No published records for West Africa but now known to breed in Côte d'Ivoire and Ghana, Feb (J. F. Walsh).

67.   CIRCAETUS CINERASCENS   R(B)

Smaller Banded Snake Eagle
Circaète cendré

Not uncommon resident in northern savanna. Occasional as far south as the Mo valley and once as far south as 11 km north of Wahala, Sep.

68.   TERATHOPIUS ECAUDATUS   R(B), AfM?/(B)

Bateleur
Bateleur à queue courte

Locally not uncommon resident, but numbers declining. Occurs in reserves such as Fazao and Keran Parks. Possible influx to northern areas in the dry season, e.g. Oti valley.

[DRYOTRIORCHIS SPECTABILIS

Congo Serpent Eagle
Serpentaire du Congo

One was presented alive to the Berlin Zoological garden by Böder, who was the

"Customs Director" at Sebbe, Togoland (Anon 1894b). In the Atlas of Reichenow (1900–1904), Sebbe was sited north of Klein Popo so very probably refers to Zébé (the site of the first German official residence erected in 1884), which is situated on the Benin border near Anécho. Thus, it is probable that the bird was imported from Nigeria, where it is known to occur, and without further details the record must remain dubious. Reichenow (1902a) listed the Berlin zoo bird but stated that no information was available on its place of capture. Bannerman (1930) stated that the specimen "cannot now be found in the Berlin Museum. It is probably in a provincial museum in Germany."]

69.   POLYBOROIDES TYPUS   RB, AfM?/(B)

African Harrier Hawk
Serpentaire gymnogène

Common resident (*P. t. pectoralis*) in both forest and well-wooded savanna from the coast as far north as Fosse aux Lions. Possible migratory behaviour suggested by 6 separate birds moving southwest over Kara, during a 3 minute spell, 4 Aug 1986.
   Breeding. Nest 10 m up in a young Baobab *Adansonia digitata* at Landa-Pozanda and used in consecutive years 1988–1990; 2 fledglings seen in the nest, Jul 1988. Other records were only of birds at the nest and sitting, Apr–Jul. Display flight above gallery forest fringing the Mono R. at 08°33'N, 01°16'E, Oct.

70.   CIRCUS MACROURUS   PM

Pallid Harrier
Busard pâle

Rare Palaearctic migrant, Nov–Mar. The authors' records were all in the northern savannas but there are 3 records from the south: collected by E. Baumann at Misahöhe, Nov (Reichenow 1897); Douaud (1957) saw the species in fields of cassava and maize near Lomé; an immature male near Lomé, Feb 1989 (JBT).

71.   CIRCUS PYGARGUS   PM

Montagu's Harrier
Busard cendré

Uncommon Palaearctic migrant, Nov–Mar. All records in northern savannas except a male 10 km from Lomé, Nov 1953 (Douaud 1957).

72.   CIRCUS AERUGINOSUS   PM

Marsh Harrier
Busard des roseaux

Common Palaearctic migrant (*C. a. aeruginosus*) throughout, late Sep to mid Apr, but especially common in the Oti basin. Earliest arrivals tend to be females, which also winter further south.

73.   MICRONISUS GABAR   R(B)

Gabar Goshawk
Autour gabar

Not uncommon resident of well-wooded savanna and forest edges. Melanistic birds Bénali, May, Dapaon, Apr, Landa-Pozanda, Apr, Kara, Aug, and Kpessidé, Aug.

Breeding. Carrying nesting material Kara, Jun. Display flights Landa-Pozanda, Aug.

74. MELIERAX METABATES   R(B)

Dark Chanting Goshawk
Autour-chanteur sombre

Not uncommon presumed resident (*M. m. metabates*) in northern savanna. Most southern record: 3 at Ketao, Aug.

75. ACCIPITER TACHIRO   R(B)

African Goshawk
Autour tachiro

Uncommon resident (*A. t. macroscelides*) of forest, and gallery forest in the savanna as far north as Naboulgou.

76. ACCIPITER BADIUS   RB

Shikra
Epervier shikra

Common resident (*A. b. sphenurus*) throughout, especially in well-wooded savanna.
    Breeding. A pair nested unsuccessfully Kara, Jan–Feb (Walsh *et al.* 1990). Adult sitting on nest: 40 km south of Notsé, Feb; Barkoissi, Apr; Mandouri, Apr. Carrying nesting material: Kara, Feb; Péwa, Mar. Copulation: Fosse aux Lions, Nov; Kara, Mar. Display: Kara, Mar.

77. ACCIPITER ERYTHROPUS   R(B)

Western Little Sparrowhawk
Epervier de Hartlaub

Not uncommon resident (*A. e. erythropus*) restricted to forest and riverine woodland in formerly forested country. Collected Bismarckburg, Aug and Nov (Reichenow 1891a), Ahoué-houé, Jul (De Roo *et al.* 1969) and Misahöhe, Aug (De Roo *et al.* 1971). Observed Lomé, date unknown (Browne 1980), Djodji, Oct, Kpimé-Tomegbé, Oct (Cheke *et al.* 1986), Oga, Feb, Atchinedji, Mar and Anonoe, Mar.

78. ACCIPITER OVAMPENSIS   AfM?/NB

Ovampo Sparrowhawk
Epervier de l'Ovampo

Uncommon, mainly in savanna areas, but status uncertain. Usually considered an intra-African migrant but may be resident in Togo (Brown *et al.* 1982). A juvenile male collected Bismarckburg, Apr, was ascribed to *A. rufiventris* by Reichenow (1891a, 1902a) and by Sclater (1930) but Bannerman (1930) noted it under *A. ovampensis* and wrote, "This specimen is a young bird, and has been wrongly recorded as the South African Sparrow-Hawk (*A. r. rufiventris*)." Recent records (all singles) are: Avétonou, Oct (Cheke *et al.* 1986); Oualé R., Oct; Naboulgou, Jan and Apr; Oti-Toutionga, Jan; Ayengré and Landa-Pozanda, Mar and Apr. Thus, apart from the Oct records, all data for Togo fall in months outside the period May to Dec when it is usually recorded in West Africa, e.g. Côte d'Ivoire (Thiollay 1985b), Ghana (Grimes 1987), Mali (Lamarche 1980), Nigeria (Elgood 1982) and Senegal (Morel & Morel 1990). Grimes mentioned a May record which, being early, he said was "consistent with migration from the south."

79.   ACCIPITER MELANOLEUCUS   R(B)

Black Sparrowhawk
Autour noir

Uncommon forest resident (*A. m. temminckii*). Collected by R. Büttner at Bismarkburg, Apr (Reichenow 1897). Singles sighted at Idifiou and Kpété Béna, Mar, and near Tchébébé, Jul (Cheke & Walsh 1984), 2 at Misahöhe, Feb (JBT) and one at Badou, Jul (JBT).

80.   UROTRIORCHIS MACROURUS   R(B)

Long-tailed Hawk
Autour à longue queue

Very rare forest resident, only 2 records (both singles): Djodji, Oct (Cheke *et al.* 1986), and near Tinkiro, Feb. Listed as a candidate species for treatment as threatened in Appendix G of Collar & Stuart (1985).

81.   BUTASTUR RUFIPENNIS   AfM/B

Grasshopper Buzzard
Buse des sauterelles

Abundant intra-African migrant to northern savannas, late Oct to early Jun. Not uncommon south to Notsé.

Breeding. A pair building near Naboulgou and sitting in the nest to form the cup, 7–8 Apr 1990. Another bird sitting on a very small nest in a bunch of mistletoe *Tapinanthus* sp. in a tree 6 km west of Sagbiabou in the Keran Park, 22 Apr – 4 Jun 1990. Breeds in Mar in northern Nigeria, (Elgood 1982) and in Jun in Mali (Millet-Horsin 1921d, Cheke 1995).

82.   KAUPIFALCO MONOGRAMMICUS   R(B)

Lizard Buzzard
Buse unibande

Common resident (*K. m. monogrammicus*) especially in degraded forest and well-wooded savannas.

Breeding. One uttering "song" Djamdé, Aug. According to Brown *et al.* (1982), "song" is only heard when adults are territorial. E. Baumann collected downy young Leglebi, Apr (Reichenow 1902a), but this site is in Ghana.

83.   BUTEO BUTEO   V, PM

Common Buzzard
Buse variable

Vagrant, one record only: one (likely to be Steppe Buzzard *B. b. vulpinus* but *B. b. buteo* also possible) ringed Norrby, Sweden, recovered Atakpamé, 28 Feb 1968. Grimes (1987) ascribed this bird to *B. b. vulpinus* but it was not identified to race by the ringer (B.-O. Stolt, pers. comm.).

84.   BUTEO RUFINUS   V, PM

Long-legged Buzzard
Buse féroce

Vagrant. An immature (*B. r. rufinus*) Naboulgou, 17 Mar 1990.

85. BUTEO AUGURALIS   RB, Afm?/(NB)

Red-necked Buzzard
Buse d'Afrique

Common resident in forest areas and not uncommon in southern savannas. Occasional
in coastal areas (Browne 1980). Apparently dry season migrant to northern savannas,
where all records Oct to early Jul.
     Breeding. A pair attending a nest Misahöhe, Jan 1988 (Walsh *et al.* 1990).

86. AQUILA RAPAX   RB

Tawny Eagle
Aigle ravisseur

Not uncommon resident (*A. r. belisarius*), frequenting well-wooded savanna such as
the Fazao reserve. Recorded from Tokpo in the south to Mandouri in north.
     Breeding. Sitting on nest in gallery forest beside the Keran R., Feb.

87. AQUILA WAHLBERGI   R(B)

Wahlberg's Eagle
Aigle de Wahlberg

Not uncommon in savanna south to Bafilo. Both colour phases occur.

88. HIERAAETUS SPILOGASTER   R(B)

African Hawk Eagle
Aigle autour fascié

Not uncommon resident throughout the savanna regions. Collected Kamé and
Misahöhe (Reichenow 1894b, 1902a).

89. HIERAAETUS PENNATUS   PM

Booted Eagle
Aigle botté

Uncommon Palaearctic migrant (*H. p. pennatus*), Sep–Apr, mostly to northern
savannas. Both dark-phased and light-phased birds occur.

90. HIERAAETUS DUBIUS   R(B)

Ayres' Hawk Eagle
Aigle d'Ayres

Rare resident, only 2 records: an adult male collected by E. Baumann at Misahöhe,
1 Apr 1895 (Stresemann 1924); one in forest fringing the Koué R. at 08°21'N,
00°43'E, 7 Mar 1988 (Walsh *et al.* 1990). Listed as a candidate species for treatment as
threatened in Appendix G of Collar & Stuart (1985).

91. LOPHAETUS OCCIPITALIS   R(B)

Long-crested Eagle
Aigle huppard

Not uncommon resident throughout, including forest.
     Breeding. No records; breeds Nigeria, Mar (Brown *et al.* 1982).

92.   SPIZAETUS AFRICANUS   R(B)

Cassin's Hawk Eagle
Spizaète de Cassin

Rare resident of forests and well-wooded savanna habitats such as in the Fazao and Pagala regions. Collected by E. Baumann at Kamé, 24 Feb 1893 (Stresemann 1924). Only 6 records, 1988–90: one near Idifiou, 6 Feb 1988 (Walsh *et al.* 1990); 3 at 08°19'N, 00°44'E (Koué R.), 7 Mar 1988; singles at Tasso, 11 May 1988 (Walsh *et al.* 1990), Dzogbégan, 12 May 1988, Bénali, 13 May 1988 and near Pagala, 20 Mar 1990. Listed as a candidate species for treatment as threatened in Appendix G of Collar & Stuart (1985).

93.   STEPHANOAETUS CORONATUS   RB

Crowned Eagle
Aigle blanchard

Not uncommon resident of forest and densely wooded savanna; occurs north to the Mo valley.
   Breeding. Adult sitting on nest in Mo valley at 08°57'N, 00°37'E, Nov 1988. Nest with chick at same location but different tree, Feb–Mar 1990.

94.   POLEMAETUS BELLICOSUS   R(B)

Martial Eagle
Aigle martial

Not uncommon resident, especially in the Keran reserve. All records north of Bagan except one at Badou, Oct.

SAGITTARIIDAE

95.   SAGITTARIUS SERPENTARIUS   AfM/NB

Secretary Bird
Messager serpentaire

Rare dry season visitor to far north including Keran Park (Walsh *et al.* 1990 and FAO *in* Robinson 1973).

FALCONIDAE

Falconinae

[FALCO NAUMANNI

Lesser Kestrel
Faucon crécerellette

Brown *et al.* (1982) include the whole of Togo in their map of the distribution of the Lesser Kestrel, but no records have been traced.]

96.   FALCO TINNUNCULUS   PM, R?(B), AfM?/(B)

Common Kestrel
Crécerelle des clochers

Not uncommon Palaearctic migrant (*F. t. tinnunculus*), Jan–Apr, to savannas throughout;

principally from Bafilo northwards, but also Lomé (Douaud 1957). A Tunisian ringed bird has been recovered near Kandé, Apr. Also common Afrotropical resident (*F. t. rufescens*) in all habitats, including towns and cities (Atakpamé, Kara, Kpalimé, Lomé), but may be subject to local movements, e.g. all forest records fall in the dry season.

Breeding. All records refer to *rufescens*. A pair regularly attended a nest in a tree at Badou, Mar, but were not seen entering it (Cheke *et al.* 1986). A pair regularly roosted on the roof of the Kara Hotel, Kara, 1987–1990. Probably bred there each dry season, but only evidence was copulation in a nearby *Borassus* palm, Mar.

97.   FALCO ALOPEX   R(B)

Fox Kestrel
Faucon renard

Not uncommon resident of escarpments and rocky hills from Défalé northwards. Regular as far south as the Faille d'Aledjo, Feb–Jun, and occasionally there, Oct–Nov. Most southern record is at Fazao (Minster Agriculture Limited 1984).

Thierry collected one at Tuntundi, near Mango, 14 Mar 1899, and a female at Mantje (? = Mankie), 22 Jan 1902. The Tuntundi specimen was used by Reichenow (1899) for the description of *Cerchneis alopex deserticola*.

Breeding. Territorial pair Faille d'Aledjo, May.

98.   FALCO ARDOSIACEUS   R(B)

Grey Kestrel
Faucon ardoisé

Common resident in well-wooded savanna in the north, uncommon in the south. Recorded Klein-Popo (= Anécho) (Reichenow 1902a), Haho, Lomé and Tsévié.

Breeding. One making repeated journeys along same flight path (once carrying a snake) Landa-Pozanda, Jun. Breeds Ghana, Jan–Mar; dependent young, mid May (Grimes 1987).

99.   FALCO CHICQUERA   R(B)

Red-necked Falcon
Faucon chicquera

Not uncommon resident (*F. c. ruficollis*) most frequently met in northern savannas with abundant *Borassus* palms, e.g. Mandouri, Mango, and Tantigou, but also 4 records from the Kara area and singles at Anié, May, and Lomé, Jul (JBT).

Breeding. A bird carrying food (as if to a nest) Tantigou, Apr.

100.   FALCO VESPERTINUS   PM

Red-footed Falcon
Faucon kobez

Vagrant from Palaearctic. A male and 3 females Landa-Pozanda, 5 Apr 1988 (Walsh *et al.* 1990). Mass movement of c. 300, in groups of 20–30, over Kara between 1630 and 1700 hrs, 3 Jun 1987 (SAS). Only one record in Ghana (Helsens 1996).

[FALCO CONCOLOR

Sooty Falcon
Faucon concolore

Reichenow (1902a) lists this as being collected by Dr. Rigler at Mango, date unknown, but the specimen is *F. ardosiaceus.* The skin is in MNB and the error was noted on the label by Stressemann.]

101.   FALCO SUBBUTEO   PM

Hobby
Faucon hobereau

Rare Palaearctic migrant. Recorded Lomé, date unknown (Browne 1980), Bafilo, Dec (Cheke & Walsh 1980), Badou, Jan (Walsh *et al.* 1990), Kandé, Apr (Walsh *et al.* 1990), Klouto, Apr and Sotouboua, Apr.

102.   FALCO CUVIERI   R(B)

African Hobby
Faucon de Cuvier

Not uncommon resident of forests and well-wooded savanna from Landa-Pozanda south to the coast. Once recorded as far north as Mango, date unknown (TC).

103.   FALCO BIARMICUS   R(B), AfM

Lanner Falcon
Faucon lanier

Not uncommon, presumed resident (*F. b. abyssinicus*) throughout, especially in northern savanna. *F. b. abyssinicus* was collected by Richers at Lomé, date unknown, and *F. b. tanypterus* was collected by G. Thierry at Mango, date unknown (Reichenow 1902a), and by the Togo Expedition at Gurnia (? = Kourniéré), date unknown. Some intra-African migration probably takes place, therefore, and this is suggested by the preponderance of records from Jan to Apr; there are only 4 records outside this period (2 in Jul, 1 in Oct, 1 in Nov).

104.   FALCO PEREGRINUS   PM, R?(B)

Peregrine Falcon
Faucon pèlerin

Not uncommon resident (*F. p. minor*) in savanna and in coastal districts. Probably a dry season visitor also (*F. p. peregrinus* or *F. p. calidus,* but *F. p. minor* also a possibility) as most records occur Oct–Apr. Listed as threatened in Appendix D of Collar & Stuart (1985).
   Breeding. Copulation at Fosse aux Lions, Jan. One carrying prey at Kara, Mar.

PHASIANIDAE

Numidinae

105.   GUTTERA PUCHERANI   R(B)

Crested Guineafowl
Pintade de Pucheran

Rare resident (*G. p. verreauxi*) of forest and gallery forest in savanna. Collected Bismarckburg, date unknown (Reichenow 1891a), and Misahöhe, Nov (Reichenow 1897). One seen near Pagala, 25 Jul 1953 (Douaud 1956b). Recent records all from near Fazao: 2 Apr 1984 (JML and Minster Agriculture Limited 1984); a flock of at least 10, 22 Dec 1984 (HL); 8 or more, 14 Apr 1989; at least 2, 27 Jun 1989.

106.   NUMIDA MELEAGRIS   RB

Helmeted Guineafowl
Pintade sauvage

Abundant resident (*N. m. galeata*) of well-wooded savanna from Dapaon in the north to as far south as 40 km from the coast. Especially common in protected areas such as the Keran and Fosse aux Lions reserves where, on open ground at the southern edge of the reserve, an extraordinary pre-roost gathering of more than 500 birds was observed, 9 Apr 1988.

Breeding. A half-grown chick with 11 adults at Mango, Jan; an adult with a small flightless chick Naboulgou, Jul (Cheke & Walsh 1980); a pair with 3 very small chicks 5 km north of Mango, Oct; 4 adults with 4 chicks Fosse aux Lions, Nov; juvenile bird in party of 50 birds Naboulgou, Dec (HL).

Gallinae

107.   COTURNIX COTURNIX   PM

Common Quail
Caille des blés

Rare Palaearctic migrant. One collected Kirikri, Feb (Reichenow 1902a). Millet-Horsin (1923) described the species as rare in "Bas-Togo", occasionally reaching the coast. A ringed bird, almost certainly this species, found near Kpéssi, date unknown (Douaud 1957). Captive birds Kara, 1984, were said to have been bred from wild stock.

108.   COTURNIX CHINENSIS   AfM/(B)

Blue Quail
Caille bleue

Status unknown, probably overlooked. One collected Ezimé, 2 Dec 1968 (De Roo 1970); one near Pasa, 23 May 1980.

[COTURNIX DELEGORGUEI

Harlequin Quail
Caille arlequine

Urban *et al.* (1986) include the whole of Togo in their map of the distribution of the Harlequin Quail, but no records have been traced.]

109.   PTILOPACHUS PETROSUS   RB

Stone Partridge
Poule de rocher

Abundant resident (*P. p. petrosus*) of rocky terrain in savanna areas. Occurs from Namoundjoga in the north, where collected Jul (De Roo *et al.* 1971), to at least as far south as Kpalimé. Also found in forest clearings, e.g. Badou, Kouniohou, Misahöhe, where collected Apr (Reichenow 1897, 1902a), and Oga. A specimen collected Mango by G. Thierry, date unknown, is in the FMNH.

Breeding. A half-grown chick amongst a flock of 10 birds Landa-Pozanda, Apr (Walsh *et al.* 1990). A brood of 3 downy chicks with an adult Klabé Apégamé, May. A pair behaving as if chicks present Atakpamé, Jan.

110.   FRANCOLINUS LATHAMI   R(B)

Latham's Forest Francolin
Francolin de Latham

Rare resident of forest and well-wooded savanna. One collected Bismarckburg, Apr (Reichenow 1891a, 1902a); one at Fazao, 22 Dec 1984 (HL).

111.   FRANCOLINUS COQUI   R(B)

Coqui Francolin
Francolin coqui

Rare resident (*F. c. spinetorum*), only one record: the francolin collected at Nanergou, 15 Aug 1968 (De Roo *et al.* 1969), and misidentified as *F. albogularis buckleyi* was *F. coqui* (Snow & Louette 1981).

112.   FRANCOLINUS ALBOGULARIS   R(B)

White-throated Francolin
Francolin à gorge blanche

Rare resident, only one record: a bird at Landa-Pozanda, Oct (Cheke 1982b). A francolin collected at Nanergou (De Roo *et al.* 1969) and ascribed to *F. albogularis buckleyi* was misidentified as *F. coqui* (Snow and Louette 1981).

113.   FRANCOLINUS AHANTENSIS   R(B)

Ahanta Francolin
Francolin d'Ahanta

Locally common resident restricted to forest and forest edge. Recent records from Misahöhe, Jan–Feb and Apr (Walsh *et al.* 1990 and JBT); Agbenohoué, Jul; Fazao, Jul; Nangbeto, Aug (JBT). Heard Pagala, Jul (Douaud 1956b), and noted by Millet-Horsin (1923) as occurring, but rare, near the coast. Collected Misahöhe, Jan (Reichenow 1897), Ahoué-houé, Jul (De Roo *et al.* 1969). Listed as a candidate species for treatment as threatened in Appendix G of Collar & Stuart (1985).

114.   FRANCOLINUS BICALCARATUS   RB

Double-spurred Francolin
Francolin à double éperon

Abundant resident (*F. b. bicalcaratus*) throughout savanna zones, forest/savanna edges and forest clearings, e.g. Badou, Djodji, and in coastal areas (Browne 1980).
   Breeding. Downy young Kirikri, Dec (Reichenow 1902a). Dead chick only a few days old near Oulita, Feb (Walsh *et al.* 1990). Flightless chick Sokodé, Jan. Adult with brood which could barely fly Landa-Pozanda, Jul. Brunel (1958) suggested they lay twice a year in southern Benin, where he found C/5–6, Feb and Oct, and juveniles, Dec–Feb and Jun.

TURNICIDAE

115.   ORTYXELOS MEIFFRENII   AfM?

Quail Plover
Turnix de Meiffren

Status unknown, only one record: one at Landa-Pozanda, 17 May 1988 (Walsh *et al.* 1990).

116.   TURNIX SYLVATICA   R(B)

Little Button-Quail
Turnix d'Afrique

Rare resident (*T. s. lepurana*), only recorded from northern savanna. Collected Nanergou, 15 Aug 1968 (De Roo *et al.* 1969). One at Tantigou, 5 Feb 1989 and 4 there, 12 Jan 1990.

117.   TURNIX HOTTENTOTTA   R?(B), AfM?

Black-rumped Button-Quail
Turnix nain

Rare, status unknown (*T. h. nana*). The only information is from Millet-Horsin (1923), who stated that the species occurred in the savanna but was rare.

RALLIDAE

Himantornithinae

118.   HIMANTORNIS HAEMATOPUS   R(B)

Nkulengu Rail
Râle à pieds rouges

Rare resident of forest, only one record: one collected by E. Baumann at Misahöhe, date unknown (Reichenow 1894a, 1902a).

Rallinae

119.   SAROTHRURA PULCHRA   R(B)

White-spotted Flufftail
Râle perlé

Rare resident (*S. p. pulchra*), but may be overlooked. Collected Kirikri, Feb, Misahöhe, Jun, and Podji, May (Reichenow 1902a). A male flushed Domaine Gravillou, 1 Jul 1989, was north of the species' usually recognised range but it has been noted further north in Mali (Lamarche 1980), Niger (Giraudoux *et al.* 1988) and Nigeria (Elgood 1982).

120.   SAROTHRURA RUFA   R(B), V?

Red-chested Flufftail
Râle à camail

Status unclear. *S. r. bonapartei* known from Togo on the basis of a song heard in the background of a recording of frog calls made at Kovié, 16 Jun 1977 (Erard & Vielliard 1977). The identity was confirmed by analysis of sonograms. Calls probably of this species, including antiphonal answers, heard Ayengré, 19 Jul 1989, and Kara, 22 Jul and 3 Aug 1989.

121.   CREX EGREGIA   R(B), Afm?

African Crake
Râle des prés

Not uncommon resident recorded from Lomé north to Tantigou. Frequents rank vegetation beside rivers, swamps and marshes. May be local migrant, as all northern records during the wet season. Two specimens of Miègemarque's in the MNHN from coastal Benin were both collected in the dry season: a male at Adjacin, 8 Feb 1895 (Oustalet 1898), and a female near Porto-Novo, 25 Jan 1895.

Breeding. No records. Breeds in Nigeria, Apr–Nov in south, Jun–Sep in central areas and Aug to mid Sep in north (Elgood *et al.* 1994).

122.   AENIGMATOLIMNAS MARGINALIS   Afm?/R?(B)

Striped Crake
Marouette rayée

Status uncertain, only one record: Lomé, Feb (Douaud in Bouet 1955). Occurs in coastal Ghana from Cape Coast to Keta (Grimes 1987).

123.   AMAURORNIS FLAVIROSTRIS   RB

Black Crake
Marouette noire

Common resident throughout, especially in rank grass beside rivers, lakes and dams. Abundant along the Sio R. near Lomé where more than 100 counted, Feb.

Breeding. An adult with a half-grown chick Tantigou, Feb; a recently fledged immature Fosse aux Lions, Feb; nest building Lomé, Mar (Robinson 1972).

124.   PORPHYRIO ALLENI   R(B), AfM?

Allen's Gallinule
Talève d'Allen

Uncommon resident and intra-African migrant. Recorded near Lomé, Jan–May (Browne 1980, Robinson 1972) and Jul–Sep. Inland records: Keran Park, Apr (Cheke & Walsh 1980); Kara, Jul (Cheke 1982b); 4 Domaine Gravillou, Jul; one Fosse aux Lions, Jul.

Breeding. Adult sitting on nest, Kara, 19 Jul 1980. Juvenile Lomé, Feb 1990. An adult carrying food and feeding another bird, which might have been its mate or a large chick, near Lomé, Aug 1989.

125.   PORPHYRIO PORPHYRIO   R(B)

Purple Swamphen
Talève poule-sultane

Uncommon resident (*P. p. madagascariensis*) occurring in 2 separate populations. The first occurs at L. Togo where recorded Nov (Robinson 1972), Aug–Sep and by Millet-Horsin (1923), date unknown; one for sale Lomé, Apr; one near Lomé beside the Sio river, Jul (JBT). The second population is in north; single birds Domaine Gravillou, Feb, Apr and Jul.

126.   GALLINULA CHLOROPUS   RB

Common Moorhen
Gallinule poule d'eau

Not uncommon resident (*G. c. meridionalis*) of marshes, lakes and riversides throughout. Usually found in small numbers but 9 at Dadja dam, Mar, and 8–10 at Lomé lagoon, Sep (PMC).

Breeding. Adult with juvenile Domaine Gravillou, Jul. Juveniles: Fosse aux Lions, Jan–Feb; Mango, Mar; Sotouboua, Mar.

127.   GALLINULA ANGULATA   AfM/NB

Lesser Moorhen
Gallinule africaine

Uncommon wet season visitor. Probably only passage migrant in the north where noted
Domaine Gravillou and Tantigou, July only; up to 8 noted each year 1987–89 at
Domaine Gravillou. Also occurs Lomé, May (Robinson 1972).

GRUIDAE

Balearicinae

128.   BALEARICA PAVONINA   AfM, R(B)

Black Crowncd Crane
Grue couronnée

Locally not uncommon resident (*B. p. pavonina*). Low numbers occur in northern
savannas during wet seasons but numbers increase dramatically in the dry season due
to an influx of migrants. Max. counts in the north: Keran R. valley – 180 in 1986
(26 Apr) and 430 in 1990 (18 Apr); Oti R. valley – 120 in 1987 and 251 in 1986 (Apr).
Collected as far south as Kirikri, Dec (Reichenow 1902a), and A. Villiers recorded it
at Kara in the wet season of 1950 (Dekeyser 1951), but there are no recent records
south of Naboulgou. Listed as a candidate species for treatment as threatened in
Appendix G of Collar & Stuart (1985).

HELIORNITHIDAE

129.   PODICA SENEGALENSIS   R(B)

African Finfoot
Grébifoulique du Sénégal

Common resident (*P. s. senegalensis*) in rivers in both savanna and forest, preferring
those with plenty of cover over-hanging their banks. Especially common along the
Mono R. from near its source (close to Pasa in the north), Jul, to as far south as
06°54'N, Dec. Most northern record: Tchanaga on Oti R., Nov. Also occurs in much
smaller rivers including the Akama, Amou, Anié, Aou, Domi, Gban-Houa, Gonobé,
Kara, Koué, Kpaza, Mo, Na, Ove and Pasa. Moves north as the wet season progresses,
recurs in impermanent rivers as they begin to flow, and retreats south, or into perennial
water-courses, in the dry season.

OTIDIDAE

130.   NEOTIS DENHAMI   AfM/B

Denham's Bustard
Outarde de Denham

Rare, dry season breeding visitor (*N. d. denhami*), Nov–Apr, to the Keran Park. Max.
count: 5 in open grassland plain east of the main road through the reserve, south of
Mango, 21 Feb 1988. No recent records elsewhere, but Brunel (1958) mentioned a dry
season sighting at Atakpamé.

Breeding. Male in display in the grassland plain, 10 km southeast of Mango, 18 Mar 1990. Adult female with chicken-sized flightless chick in nearby woodland, bordering the plain, 7 Apr 1990.

| 131. | EUPODOTIS SENEGALENSIS | R(B) |

White-bellied Bustard
Outarde de Sénégal

Not uncommon resident (*E. s. senegalensis*) of northern savannas. At least 5 pairs Tantigou, Jul 1989, where it is present all year. Also regular in the Mango area, including Domaine Gravillou. Southernmost record: a pair near Ketao, Jul and Aug 1989.

| 132. | EUPODOTIS MELANOGASTER | AfM/B? |

Black-bellied Bustard
Outarde à ventre noir

Not uncommon wet season visitor (*E. m. melanogaster*), Apr–Oct, to savannas as far north as Dapaon. Noted central Togo, e.g. Bafilo, Sep, Bagan, May, Fazao, Apr (Minster Agriculture Limited 1984), and Moretan, Aug. No records further south. A few may be resident as there are dry season records, e.g. males at Koumongou, 24 Jan 1989, Tantigou, 21 Jan 1990, in the Keran reserve, 15 Feb 1987, and at Landa-Pozanda, 31 Mar 1990.
Breeding. Territorial flights by 3 males Sara-Kawa, 31 Aug 1986.

JACANIDAE

| 133. | ACTOPHILORNIS AFRICANA | RB |

African Jacana
Jacana à poitrine dorée

Abundant resident of riversides, swamps, dams and pools throughout except forest. Flocks of more than 100 recorded in the north at Domaine Gravillou, Jun, and in the south, beside the Sio R. near Lomé, Feb.
Breeding. C/4 Domaine Gravillou, May–Jun, and Aug. Single downy chick Wahala, Aug, and Domaine Gravillou, Aug. Downy chicks: 3 lower Sio R., near Lomé, Sep; one there with many juveniles, Feb; 2 at Tantigou, Feb, and 3 in Sep and Nov.

ROSTRATULIDAE

| 134. | ROSTRATULA BENGHALENSIS | R?(B), AfM? |

Greater Painted-Snipe
Rhynchée peinte

Status unclear. Probably not uncommon resident (*R. b. benghalensis*) but undergoes local movements in search of suitable habitat; all records Nov–Aug. Usually found in rank grass beside dams in northern savanna as far south as Ayengré. Also recorded Lomé, Dec–Jan (P&JB; Browne 1980), the lower Sio R. near Lomé, May, and recorded southern Benin, Jan 1955 (Brunel 1958). Max. counts at Tantigou: 16 on 27 Apr 1987; 8 on 7 Apr 1990.

HAEMATOPODIDAE

135.   HAEMATOPUS OSTRALEGUS   V, PM

Eurasian Oystercatcher
Huîtrier pie

Vagrant from the Palaearctic (*H. o. ostralegus*). One on Lomé beach, 17 Nov 1985 (Cheke *et al.* 1986).

RECURVIROSTRIDAE

136.   HIMANTOPUS HIMANTOPUS   PM, R(B)

Common Stilt
Échasse blanche

Not uncommon Palaearctic migrant (*H. h. himantopus*) to coast, lakesides and edges of water-courses throughout. Present Lomé, Sep–May (Robinson 1972), and a few records there Jul–Aug; some may be resident therefore in coastal areas. All inland records, Nov–Apr. Max. counts: 40 at L. Togo, 26 Jan 1984 (R&J); 24 at Lomé, 15 May 1971 (Robinson 1972); 10 at Tantigou, 8 Apr 1990.

137.   RECURVIROSTRA AVOSETTA   PM

Eurasian Avocet
Avocette élégante

Rare Palaearctic migrant. Collected Anécho, Dec (Reichenow 1902a). More recent records at Lomé: 10 flew into Ghanaian waters, 27 Oct 1985 (Cheke *et al.* 1986); 5 on 2 Feb 1986 (Cheke *et al.* 1986); 5 on 27 Mar 1987 and 6 on 13 Dec 1987; singles on 1 Jan 1987, 5 Jan 1988 and 15 Sep 1989. These records and the lack of sightings by earlier coastal observers, including Browne (1980) and Robinson (1972), may reflect the increase in the western Palaearctic populations. Avocets are much more common now in Ghana (Hedenström *et al.* 1990) than in the 1970s (Grimes 1987). As many as 2,000 were recorded at the Keta lagoon, close to the Togolese border, Oct 1988. This is now recognised as an important site for Avocets (Ntiamboa-Baidu 1991).

BURHINIDAE

138.   BURHINUS SENEGALENSIS   RB

Senegal Thick-knee
Oedicnème du Sénégal

Common resident along riversides and beside dams and lakes throughout the savanna zones from the northern border to as far south as Sika-Kondji. Subject to local movements in response to changes in water levels. Largest flocks: 30 at Kpani, Feb; 19 at Domaine Gravillou, Jun; 16 at Landa-Pozanda, Mar.

   Breeding. A pair with 2 dependent young (about one-third grown) Naboulgou, 26 Apr 1987.

[BURHINUS VERMICULATUS

Water Thick-knee
Oedicnème vermiculé

Togo's coastal strip is included in the range of the Water Thick-knee by Urban *et al.* (1986) but no records have been traced.]

139.   BURHINUS CAPENSIS   AfM/B, R?(B)

Spotted Thick-knee
Oedicnème du tachard

Status uncertain. Probably intra-African migrant (*B. c. maculosus*) but might be resident. Bouet (1955) referred to records from Togo but gave no details. Present in the Landa-Pozanda area, Oct–Jun, but not in the wettest months. Max. count: 5, possibly 7, 20 Nov 1988; one Nangbeto, Apr (JBT).

Breeding. A pair with 2 downy young (about 2 days old) in a *Eucalyptus* plantation at Landa-Pozanda, 2 May 1988 (Walsh *et al.* 1990).

GLAREOLIDAE

Cursoriinae

140.   PLUVIANUS AEGYPTIUS   RB

Egyptian Plover
Pluvian d'Egypte

Not uncommon resident, usually encountered in low numbers beside large rivers such as the Koumongou, Mono and Oti, but also occurs at edges of dams. Subject to local movements in response to water level variations.

Breeding. C/2 in sand beside the Mono R. at Sika-Kondji, 25 Jan 1988 (Walsh *et al.* 1990). A pair behaving as if nesting Tchanaga, 16 Apr 1987.

141.   CURSORIUS TEMMINCKII   Afm?/(B)

Temminck's Courser
Courvite de Temminck

Not uncommon on burnt grassland and airstrips throughout the savanna areas, Dec–Sep. Nomadic but status uncertain: coastal birds may be resident, but only seen in the vicinity of Lomé, mid Jun to Sep (Douaud 1957), and 31 Dec. Largest flock: 17 at Sara-Kawa, 14 Feb 1988.

142.   CURSORIUS CHALCOPTERUS   AfM?/(B)

Bronze-winged Courser
Courvite à ailes violettes

Status uncertain, but probably intra-African migrant in dry season to northern savannas. Only 2 records: one Landa-Pozanda, 20 Nov 1988; 2 separate birds calling after dusk, 16 km NW of Mango, 22 Nov 1988 (H&S).

Glareolinae

143.   GLAREOLA PRATINCOLA   AfM/(B), PM?

Collared Pratincole
Glaréole à collier

Locally common dry season visitor to northern rice-paddies, lakesides and rivers
especially in the Mango area, Dec–Jul, where it may breed (pair performing greeting
display, May). Max. count: 100 at Domaine Gravillou, Mar 1990. Occasional in the
south: 22 at Anié, Apr 1990; a few coastal records at Lomé, including an immature,
Aug (Browne 1980).

144.   GLAREOLA NORDMANNI   V, PM

Black-winged Pratincole
Glaréole à ailes noires

Vagrant. A male collected by R. Büttner at Bismarckburg, 25 Oct (Reichenow 1892,
1893).

145.   GLAREOLA NUCHALIS   Afm/B

Rock Pratincole
Glaréole aureolée

Uncommon intra-African migrant (*G. n. liberiae*) to large rivers. Breeds locally in
north, where only recorded Landa-Pozanda, Apr–Nov. Records in south: sightings
along Mono R., near Tététou, May (Dekeyser 1951) and Jul–Nov; a pair Atchinedji,
Mar. Max. count: a migratory group of 23 at Landa-Pozanda, 25 Aug 1981 (Cheke
1982a). Bird with a white nuchal collar (identified as *G. n. nuchalis*) Landa-Pozanda,
Oct (Cheke 1982a).
   Breeding. All breeding data from Landa-Pozanda: C/1, Jun 1981 (Cheke 1982a);
C/2, May–Jun 1983; dependent young, Jul 1979 (Cheke 1980).

146.   GLAREOLA CINEREA   V

Grey Pratincole
Glaréole grise

Vagrant. One beside the Oti R. at Mango, 27 May 1983 (Cheke & Walsh 1984). A pair
was collected by E. Baumann, 27 Dec 1894 (Reichenow 1897, 1902a), but the locality is
in Ghana. In the earlier publication (and clearly marked on the specimens' labels in the
MNB) the location was given as Apasso, which is in Ghana and was beside the Volta R.
at 06°28'N 00°06'E before the creation of L. Volta. In the 1902 paper, Akposso, a forested
area in the Plateaux region of Togo, was stated to be the collection site.

CHARADRIIDAE

Charadriinae

147.   CHARADRIUS DUBIUS   PM

Little Ringed Plover
Petit Gravelot

Not uncommon Palaearctic visitor (*C. d. curonicus*) to lakesides and riversides throughout, Nov–Apr. Max. count: 18 Domaine Gravillou, 6 Dec 1987. One ringed in UK recovered near Lomé, Jan (Mead & Hudson 1985).

148.   CHARADRIUS HIATICULA   PM

Ringed Plover
Grand Gravelot

Common Palaearctic visitor to coast, Jul–May. Largest numbers occur Nov–Mar, when flocks of 200 are frequent at Lomé (Cheke *et al.* 1986) and occasionally reach 250 (6 Nov 1989). Scarce inland: 4 at Domaine Gravillou, Apr.

Birds ringed in Finland (2) and Orkney (1) (Corse 1990, Mead & Clark 1991) have been recovered in Togo (see Appendix 2).

149.   CHARADRIUS PECUARIUS   V

Kittlitz' Plover
Pluvier pâtre

Vagrant, only 5 records: one Lomé, 9 Mar 1985 (Cheke *et al.* 1986); one inland, at the edge of the dam at Kara, 5 Mar 1988; an adult in partial breeding dress Lomé, 14 Sep 1989 (JBT); an immature Lomé, 28 Sep 1989; 4 Anécho, 14 Jan 1995 (PMC).

150.   CHARADRIUS FORBESI   Afm/(B), R?(B)

Forbes' Plover
Pluvier de Forbes

Not uncommon throughout, frequenting riversides, fields and edges of lakes. Status uncertain, recorded in all months except Sep. In south occurs Lomé, Oct–Apr (Browne 1980, JBT), and in north mainly Mar–Jun. A possible wet season visitor, therefore, to northern savannas, where it may breed. Usually singles or pairs, but flocks of 12 and 8 at Landa-Pozanda, Jan and Mar respectively, and one of 22 at Domaine Gravillou, Apr.

151.   CHARADRIUS ALEXANDRINUS   PM

Kentish Plover
Pluvier à collier interrompu

Rare Palaearctic migrant (*C. a. alexandrinus*), only 4 records: one Lomé, 11 and 31 Mar, and 10 Nov 1985 (Cheke *et al.* 1986); an immature there 19 Aug 1989.

152.   CHARADRIUS MARGINATUS   R(B)

White-fronted Plover
Pluvier à front blanc

Common resident (*C. m. marginatus* (= *hesperius*)) of the shore-line, but in low numbers.

Breeding. Probably breeds Lomé beach, where paired off and behaving territorially during the dry season (Cheke *et al.* 1986). Breeds Ghana, Jan–Sep (Grimes 1987).

153.   PLUVIALIS DOMINICA   V

Lesser Golden Plover
Pluvier fauve

Coastal vagrant. A bird in winter plumage – considered the Nearctic *P. d. dominica* because of size, generally grey plumage and prominent white supercilium – Lomé,

19 Oct 1985 (Cheke *et al.* 1986). Another bird (either *P. d. dominica* or *P. d. fulva*) Lomé, 21 Aug 1987, was joined by a second, 26–28 Aug. Of 2 contrasting birds seen together at Lomé, 15 Sep 1989, one was a very grey bird, probably *dominica*, and the other, which was missing a leg and appeared very golden, was probably *fulva*. One at Lomé, 1–29 Mar 1990, was most likely *dominica*.

P. d. dominica and *P. d. fulva* are often regarded as separate species and both occur in West Africa (Fishpool & Demey 1991).

154.	PLUVIALIS SQUATAROLA	PM

Grey Plover
Pluvier argenté

Common Palaearctic visitor to the coast, Jul–May. Flocks at Lomé build up Aug–Oct. Max. count: 120, 6 Nov 1989. Most are in winter plumage but birds in summer dress noted Mar, Apr, Oct, and Nov.

A bird ringed in Denmark recovered near Anécho, Oct.

Vanellinae

155.	VANELLUS SENEGALLUS	RB

African Wattled Lapwing
Vanneau du Sénégal

Common resident (*V. s. senegallus*) of savanna north of the Bafilo ridge. Only one record further south: one along Mono R. at 7°10'N, Feb. Prefers riversides and edges of dams but occasionally seen in open grassland and croplands. Flocks occur in Oti R. valley in the dry season, especially near Mango: 40, 7 Dec 1981; 50, 26 Jan 1986; 80, 24 Jan 1987; 86, 17 Jan 1988; 60, 28 Feb 1988; 62, 8 Mar 1988; 50, 10 Apr 1988. Also 20 at Fosse aux Lions, 27 Feb 1988. Although Hayman *et al.* (1986) wrote that "parties rarely reach double figures", the Togolese flocks are consistent with the statement by Urban *et al.* (1986) that larger flocks form in the non-breeding season in newly available habitat.

Breeding. C/2 Ketao, Jul. A pair with 2 downy young Landa-Pozanda, May. Adult with 2 dependent young Naboulgou, Jul (Cheke & Walsh 1980).

156.	VANELLUS ALBICEPS	RB

White-headed Lapwing
Vanneau à tête blanche

Common resident of riversides and dams. More frequent in the northern savannas but occurs as far south as Notsé and Tététou.

Breeding. C/4, being incubated by an adult seen belly-wetting, on sandbank of the Oti R. at Kandjo, Mar. A pair behaving as if defending a nest or young Tététou, Mar. Pair with a small downy chick Naboulgou, Apr (Walsh *et al.* 1990).

157.	VANELLUS TECTUS	R?(B), AfM?/(NB)

Black-headed Lapwing
Vanneau coiffé

Rare. Only recorded in northern grassland with sparse cover. Status uncertain, may be resident or intra-African migrant. Most often seen Tantigou: flocks of 14, May 1988 (Walsh *et al.* 1990), and 12–15 birds, Jun 1990; a pair, Apr 1987 and Apr 1990, and 3, of which one was immature, 2 Jul 1989. Other records: a pair near Dapaon, Apr 1987; 2 in the north of the Keran Park, Feb 1987; 3 near Mango, Feb 1988 (Walsh *et al.* 1990), where also seen, date unknown (TC).

158.   VANELLUS SPINOSUS   RB

Spur-winged Plover
Vanneau éperonné

Not uncommon resident in northern savannas, especially from Mango northwards. Moves away from flooding rivers, especially the Oti and Koumongou, during the rains when flocks of up to 50 occur beside dams, e.g. at Domaine Gravillou. Occasional as far south as Notsé, Apr, Anié, Feb, Sara-Kawa, Mar, and Tokpli, where 6, Nov (JBT).
   Breeding. Eggs: C/2 Panseni, Jan (Walsh *et al.* 1990); C/3 at Domaine Gravillou, Apr and May; C/4, Domaine Gravillou, May. Adult with 2 downy young Domaine Gravillou, May. Behaving as if nesting near Panseni, Apr (Cheke & Walsh 1980).

159.   VANELLUS SUPERCILIOSUS   V

Brown-chested Lapwing
Vanneau caronculé

Vagrant. Known only from a specimen in the MNB collected by R. Büttner at Bismarckburg, 26 Jan (Reichenow 1891a). Listed as a candidate species for treatment as threatened in Appendix G of Collar & Stuart (1985).

160.   VANELLUS LUGUBRIS   R(B)

Lesser Black-winged Lapwing
Vanneau demi-deuil

Uncommon resident of open country on the coastal plain. Noted near Lomé by Browne (1980); 3 beside the Sio R. near Lomé, Aug 1989, and 2 there, May 1990.

SCOLOPACIDAE

Calidridinae

161.   CALIDRIS CANUTUS   PM

Red Knot
Bécasseau maubèche

Uncommon Palaearctic migrant (*C. c. canutus*) to the shore-line, Oct–Mar. Max. count: 16 at Lomé, Feb.

162.   CALIDRIS ALBA   PM

Sanderling
Bécasseau sanderling

Common Palaearctic migrant along coast, Aug–May. Flocks of 300–500 regular at Lomé, Nov–Mar. One of 10, 25 May 1989, was in full breeding plumage. A bird ringed in South Uist recovered Lomé, Dec (Mead & Clark 1989), and birds bearing rings, possibly of South African origin, noted Mar and Sep–Nov 1985 (Cheke *et al.* 1986). Although there have been no recoveries in West Africa of birds ringed in South Africa, a Ghanaian-ringed bird was recovered on the Namibian coast in May 1992

(T. B. Oatley, pers. comm.). Movement of birds between Togo and South Africa or Namibia is, therefore, likely.

One inland record: one in summer plumage Kara, May (Cheke *et al.* 1986).

163.   CALIDRIS MINUTA   PM

Little Stint
Bécasseau minute

Common Palaearctic migrant to coast and inland wetlands, Sep–May. Max. count at coast – 100 at Lomé, Feb (Cheke *et al.* 1986); max. count inland – 40 at Domaine Gravillou, Feb.

164.   CALIDRIS TEMMINCKII   PM

Temminck's Stint
Bécasseau de Temminck

Rare Palaearctic migrant, only 3 records: one at Domaine Gravillou, 25 Nov 1987, and 4 there, 9 Apr 1990; one at Lomé, 15 Apr 1988. A bird ringed in France has been recovered in Benin, Mar.

165.   CALIDRIS FERRUGINEA   PM

Curlew Sandpiper
Bécasseau cocorli

Uncommon Palaearctic migrant, mainly to the coast, Jul–May. Max. count: 19 at Lomé, Nov (Cheke *et al.* 1986). Inland records: 2 at Tantigou, 8 and 10 Apr 1988, and one there, 3 May 1989.

166.   CALIDRIS ALPINA   V, PM

Dunlin
Bécasseau variable

Vagrant from the Palaearctic (*C. a. alpina*), only 4 records: one at Lomé, 19 Oct 1985 (Cheke *et al.* 1986), 4 on 21 Aug 1987, and a fresh corpse there, 14 Sep 1989; one at Anécho, 14 Sep 1995 (PMC).

167.   PHILOMACHUS PUGNAX   PM

Ruff
Chevalier combattant

Common Palaearctic migrant to coast and inland wetlands, late Aug to May. Max. count: 300 at L. Togo, 26 Jan 1984 (R&J). Largest inland counts: 100 at Domaine Gravillou, Feb; up to 55 at Tantigou, Jan–Apr.

Gallinagininae

168.   LYMNOCRYPTES MINIMUS   PM

Jack Snipe
Bécassine sourde

Rare Palaearctic visitor, known only from Domaine Gravillou: one on 25 Nov 1987, and 2 on 6 Dec 1987 (Walsh *et al.* 1990).

169.   GALLINAGO GALLINAGO   PM

Common Snipe
Bécassine des marais

Not uncommon Palaearctic migrant (*G. g. gallinago*) to edges of dams and rivers and to marshlands throughout, Sep–Apr. Max. count: 37 at Domaine Gravillou, Dec. A bird ringed Agoueve, near Lomé, 1 Jan 1971, was shot in Sicily, 22 Feb 1972 (Sharland 1979).

170.   GALLINAGO MEDIA   PM

Great Snipe
Bécassine double

Uncommon Palaearctic migrant, recorded only from Domaine Gravillou in north, and the Lomé area in south. Possibly a passage migrant as all sightings (bar 2) occur Mar–Apr and Aug. The exceptions are one near Mango, 9 Oct 1988, and a bird trapped Agoueve, near Lomé, 2 Jan 1971 (P&JB); also recorded southern Benin, Feb (Brunel 1958). Max. count: 20 at Domaine Gravillou, Aug.

Tringinae

171.   LIMMOSA LIMMOSA   PM

Black-tailed Godwit
Barge à queue noire

Uncommon Palaearctic visitor (*L. l. limmosa*) to coast, Apr (JBT), Sep, (Cheke *et al.* 1986; JBT) and Dec, and to wetland sites in the north, Nov–Aug. Max. count: 18 at Domaine Gravillou, Dec.

172.   LIMMOSA LAPPONICA   PM

Bar-tailed Godwit
Barge rousse

Uncommon Palaearctic visitor (*L. l. lapponica*) to coast. Recorded Lomé in May (a bird in full breeding dress, 3 May 1989, and 2 in non-breeding plumage 25 May 1989), Jul (Browne 1980), Sep (two records), and Oct–Nov (Cheke *et al.* 1986, JBT). Max. count: 8 in Nov.

173.   NUMENIUS PHAEOPUS   PM

Whimbrel
Courlis corlieu

Common Palaearctic visitor in low numbers (*N. p. phaeopus*) to the coast, Aug–Apr. Max. count: 8 at Lomé, Oct (Cheke *et al.* 1986).
   A bird ringed in Denmark recovered near Sokodé, Sep – the only inland record.

174.   NUMENIUS ARQUATA   PM

Eurasian Curlew
Courlis cendré

Uncommon Palaearctic visitor to the coast, Aug–May, and rare inland (probably *N. a. arquata* but *N. a. orientalis* has been collected in Ghana (Grimes 1987)). Most records refer to singletons. One inland record: one at Kabou, date unknown (PMC).

175. **TRINGA ERYTHROPUS** PM

Spotted Redshank
Chevalier arlequin

Not uncommon Palaearctic passage migrant to wetlands in northern savanna as far south as Ayengré, Nov–Apr. Max. count: 30 at Tantigou, Feb. One of 2 birds at Tantigou, 7 Apr 1990, was in breeding dress. Only 2 coastal records: one trapped Agoueve, near Lomé, 2 Jan 1971 (P&JB); one Lomé, Apr.

176. **TRINGA TOTANUS** PM

Common Redshank
Chevalier gambette

Not uncommon Palaearctic migrant (*T. t. totanus*) to coast, Nov–Mar (Robinson 1972). Robinson reported flocks of up to 50 at Lomé, Mar 1971, but recently only singles or pairs there, Sep–Nov 1985 and Feb 1986 (Cheke *et al.* 1986), Aug and Sep 1987, Jan and Sep 1988 and May, Jul, Sep and Dec 1989. One Naboulgou, Dec (Cheke 1982b), is the only inland record.

177. **TRINGA STAGNATILIS** PM

Marsh Sandpiper
Chevalier stagnatile

Uncommon Palaearctic migrant to coast and inland. Robinson (1972, 1973) regularly recorded it at Lomé, 21 Oct 1970 – 28 May 1971, but subsequent records are sporadic: singles at Anécho and Lomé, Mar 1985 (Cheke *et al.* 1986); Lomé, 26–28 Aug, 24 Sep 1987 and 14 Sep 1989; Anécho, 14 Jan (PMC); 2 at Anécho, 12–14 Sep 1995 (PMC). Browne (1980) did not record it. Only 2 inland records: one at Tantigou, 17 Jan 1988, and one there, 8 Mar 1988.

178. **TRINGA NEBULARIA** PM

Common Greenshank
Chevalier aboyeur

Common Palaearctic migrant to the coast and wetlands from Kara northwards. Less frequent in the middle of the country but seen Anié, Agomé Seva, Atchinedji and Avégode. Mainly Oct–Apr, but small numbers present throughout the year at the coast and some spring stragglers in the north, May–Jun. Highest coastal count – 55 at Lomé, Aug; highest inland count – 50 at Tantigou, Apr.

179. **TRINGA OCHROPUS** PM

Green Sandpiper
Chevalier culblanc

Common Palaearctic migrant, Sep–Apr, to the coast and wetlands throughout, including forest riversides. Less common than both *A. hypoleucos* and *T. glareola*. Usually singles or pairs, but flock of 7 at Lomé, Mar.

180. **TRINGA GLAREOLA** PM

Wood Sandpiper
Chevalier sylvain

Common Palaearctic visitor, Sep–Apr, to wet habitats throughout, except thick forest; occasionally later, e.g. 2 Tantigou, 24 May 1988. All Jul records probably involve the return of early migrants, e.g. 3 Domaine Gravillou, 5 Jul 1987, and 20 there, 14 Jul 1988. Highest inland count – 100 Domaine Gravillou, Feb; highest coastal count – 33 Lomé, Jan. A ringed bird from Sweden recovered near Anécho, Feb.

181.   XENUS CINEREUS   PM

Terek Sandpiper
Bargette de Terek

Rare Palaearctic migrant to the coast at Lomé. Only recorded by Robinson (1972): singles, 21 Oct–9 Nov 1970, and 19–30 Mar 1971; 5 on 13 May 1971 and one on 21 Sep 1971; 3 on 19 Feb 1972 and one on 25 Feb 1972.

182.   ACTITIS HYPOLEUCOS   PM

Common Sandpiper
Chevalier guignetta

Abundant Palaearctic visitor to wetlands throughout, often at riversides and along forest streams. Recorded in all months, except Jun. Usually singles or pairs, but 10 at Lomé, 31 Mar 1985 and 24 Sep 1987. A bird ringed in Togo has been recovered in Finland.

Arenariinae

183.   ARENARIA INTERPRES   PM

Ruddy Turnstone
Tournepierre à collier

Common Palaearctic migrant (*A. i. interpres*) to coastal habitats, Aug–Mar. Max. count: 30 at Lomé, Sep (one in summer dress).
   A Namibian-ringed bird recovered Ghana, Oct (Oatley 1983, Grimes 1987).

Phalaropodinae

184.   PHALAROPUS FULICARIUS   PM

Grey Phalarope
Phalarope à bec large

Rare Palaearctic visitor to coast. A group of 3 on the sea off Lomé, 9 Mar 1985, and a dead bird on the beach there, 24 Mar 1985 (Cheke *et al.* 1986).

STERCORARIIDAE

185.   STERCORARIUS POMARINUS   V, PM

Pomarine Skua
Labbe pomarine

Vagrant. One off Lomé, 11 Mar 1985 (Cheke *et al.* 1986).

186.   STERCORARIUS PARASITICUS   PM

Arctic Skua
Labbe parasite

Rare Palaearctic migrant to coast: one ringed as a pullus Shetland, recovered Lomé, Jun (Spencer & Hudson 1981); 3 out to sea off Lomé, 17 Nov 1985 (Cheke *et al.* 1986); one Lomé, 25 Sep 1987.

187.   STERCORARIUS LONGICAUDUS   V, PM

Long-tailed Skua
Labbe à longue queue

Vagrant. One collected Kolokopé, along the Mono R., 28 Aug 1969 (De Roo *et al.* 1971).

LARIDAE

188.   LARUS SABINI   V, PM

Sabine's Gull
Mouette de Sabine

Vagrant. One Lomé, 2 Feb 1986 (Cheke *et al.* 1986).

189.   LARUS CIRROCEPHALUS   V, AfM

Grey-headed Gull
Mouette à tête grise

Vagrant (*L. c. poiocephalus*) to coastal areas (Millet-Horsin 1923); also recorded Benin, e.g. mouth of L. Ahémé (Brunel 1958). One inland record: single Tantigou, 27 Feb 1988 (Walsh *et al.* 1990).

190.   LARUS RIDIBUNDUS   V, PM

Black-headed Gull
Mouette rieuse

Vagrant. One beside the Oti R. at 09°53'N, 11 Jan 1989.

191.   LARUS FUSCUS   PM

Lesser Black-backed Gull
Goéland brun

Uncommon Palaearctic migrant (subspecies uncertain, either *L. f. fuscus* or *L. f. graellsii*) to coastal waters, Aug–Apr. Max. count: 16 at Lomé, Sep.

STERNIDAE

192.   GELOCHELIDON NILOTICA   PM

Gull-billed Tern
Sterne hansel

Uncommon Palaearctic migrant (*S. n. nilotica*) to shoreline, Oct–Mar, all singles except 5 Lomé, Oct 1985 (Cheke *et al.* 1986).

193. STERNA CASPIA   PM, AfM/NB
      Caspian Tern
      Sterne caspienne

Rare visitor, either Palaearctic or African origin, to the coast. Only 6 records: 14 Lomé,
Feb (JBT); 2 Anécho, Mar (Cheke *et al.* 1986); 3 Lomé, Mar; one Lomé, Aug; 25 Anécho,
Sep (PMC); a Finnish ringed bird has been recovered in Togo, date and place unknown.

194. STERNA MAXIMA   AfM/NB
      Royal Tern
      Sterne royal

Common non-breeding visitor (*S. m. albididorsalis*) to coast, Aug–Apr. Although there is
only one Jun record (4 at Lomé – see Cheke & Walsh 1984), some may prove to be present
all year. Numbers begin to increase from mid Aug; max. count – 300, 30 Dec 1989.

195. STERNA SANDVICENSIS   PM
      Sandwich Tern
      Sterne caugek

Common Palaearctic visitor (*S. s. sandvicensis*) to the coast, Aug–Apr, mainly
Jan–Mar (Browne 1980). Usually present in low numbers but sometimes in flocks of
more than 750 (Cheke *et al.* 1986).
      Birds ringed in Denmark (2), Eire (1), France (3), Germany (1), Netherlands (2), Sweden
(1) and UK (10) (Spencer & Hudson 1982) recovered on the coast, Oct–Feb and Apr.

196. STERNA DOUGALLII   PM
      Roseate Tern
      Sterne de Dougall

Uncommon Palaearctic migrant (*S. d. dougalii*) to the coastline, Sep–Jun. Probably
declining as only singles or pairs noted 1985–87, but 11 (2 of which were ringed) Lomé,
14 Apr 1988. Listed as threatened in Appendix D of Collar & Stuart (1985).
      Birds ringed Eire (9) and the UK (3) recovered on the coast (Spencer & Hudson 1982).

197. STERNA HIRUNDO   PM
      Common Tern
      Sterne pierregarin

Common Palaearctic migrant (*S. h. hirundo*) to the coast, mostly Sep and Feb–Apr
(Browne 1980); some ringing recoveries in every month so birds may be present at any
time. Occasionally abundant, e.g. flock of 500 Lomé, 10 Nov 1985 (Cheke *et al.* 1985).
      Birds ringed Denmark (2), Finland (7), France (1), Germany (10), Netherlands (6),
Norway (2), Sweden (2) and UK (11) recovered on the coast or in off-shore waters
(Spencer & Hudson 1982; Mead & Clark 1988; Schloss 1962; Neubauer 1973;
Holgersen 1969, 1974).

198. STERNA PARADISAEA   PM
      Arctic Tern
      Sterne arctique

Uncommon Palaearctic migrant to coast, all records from Lomé: 2, Aug 1987 (Walsh
et al. 1990), one, Aug 1989, and one, Apr 1990.

Birds ringed in Denmark – the Faeroes (1), Finland (1) and Germany (1) (Schloss 1968) recovered Lomé, Nov, Oct and Jan respectively.

199. STERNA ANAETHETUS   V
Bridled Tern
Sterne bridée

Vagrant. One in non-breeding plumage Lomé, May–Aug 1976 (Browne 1980).

200. STERNA FUSCATA   V
Sooty Tern
Sterne fuligineuse

Vagrant (*S. f. fuscata*), only one record: an adult Lomé, 17 Aug 1989. No chicks ringed on islands off Florida, U.S.A, and recovered in West Africa, have been found in Togo although 7 were obtained in Ghana (Robertson 1969).

201. STERNA BALAENARUM   AfM/NB
Damara Tern
Sterne des baleiniers

Uncommon transequatorial migrant to the coast, Jul–Jan. First noted in Togo by Browne (1980), who saw birds in non-breeding plumage in flocks of up to 75 from Jul to Oct. Subsequent observations have included many birds in breeding plumage. Proportions of birds in full breeding dress to totals observed as follows: Jan 0/3; Jul 0/51; Aug 3/32, 21/21, 28/39; Sep 3/6, 41/51; Oct 1/1, 2/2; Nov 2/2. Flocks in the 1980s did not exceed 51. 2 were trapped by snares Lomé, Aug 1989 – an additional hazard to those encountered on its breeding grounds in southern Africa (Collar & Stuart 1985). The world population was thought to be as low as 7,000 birds by Braby *et al.* (1992) but, on the basis of further surveys, Simmons (1993) estimated it as 13,000.

202. STERNA ALBIFRONS   R?(B), PM
Little Tern
Sterne naine

Uncommon presumed resident and probable breeder (*S. a. guineae*) and Palaearctic visitor (*S. a. albifrons*) to coastal districts. Records of the latter (black-billed adults) Lomé, Nov.
    Breeding. A pair of *S. a. guineae* courtship feeding Lomé, 20 Jul 1989. A population of *S. a. guineae* was thought by Browne (1980) to be breeding 35 km east of Lomé.

203. CHLIDONIAS HYBRIDUS   PM
Whiskered Tern
Guifette moustac

Rare Palaearctic migrant (*C. h. hybridus*) to shoreline. One Lomé, date unknown (Browne 1980), and 5 in summer plumage Lomé, 19 Apr 1990.

204. CHLIDONIAS NIGER   PM
Black Tern
Guifette noir

Abundant Palaearctic visitor (*C. n. niger*) to the coast, including the lagoons and shoreline, recorded in all months except Jun. Numbers at Lomé increase Aug–Sep, e.g. in 1989, 16 on 17 Aug, 70 (of which 2 still in breeding dress) on 18 Aug, 100 on 14 Sep and 500 on 26 Sep. Max. count: 1000, of which about 100 were in breeding plumage, Lomé, 14 Apr 1988. Flocks form night roosts along foreshore near Lomé harbour.

Birds ringed in the Netherlands (3) and Morocco (1) (Urban *et al.* 1986) recovered on the coast.

| 205. | CHLIDONIAS LEUCOPTERUS | PM |

White-winged Black Tern
Guifette leucoptère

Uncommon Palaearctic passage migrant to inland lakes such as Ayengré, Domaine Gravillou and Tantigou, Sep–Nov and Mar–May, and to the coast, Sep–Nov. Max. inland count – 10, of which one in full summer plumage, Domaine Gravillou, Apr; highest coastal count – 40 to 50, Anécho, Sep (PMC).

| 206. | ANOUS MINUTUS | V |

Black Noddy
Noddi noir

Vagrant (*A. m. atlanticus*). One Lomé, 26 May 1989.

| 207. | ANOUS STOLIDUS | V |

Brown Noddy
Noddi brun

Vagrant (*A. s. stolidus*). One found injured at the water's edge Lomé, 29 Jan 1971 (Robinson 1972); bird later died. An unidentified Noddy (probably *stolidus*) Lomé, 31 Jan 1988.

RYNCHOPIDAE

| 208. | RYNCHOPS FLAVIROSTRIS | V, AfM |

African Skimmer
Bec-en-ciseaux d'Afrique

Vagrant to coast and inland rivers. One collected Mango, date unknown (Reichenow 1902a). Singles beside the Oti R. at 09°27'N, Apr 1987, Feb 1988 and Feb 1990, Lomé, Aug 1987 (Walsh *et al.* 1990), and Anécho, Sep 1992 (PMC). Listed as a candidate species for treatment as threatened in Appendix G of Collar & Stuart (1985).

PTEROCLIDAE

| 209. | PTEROCLES EXUSTUS | AfM/NB? |

Chestnut-bellied Sandgrouse
Ganga à ventre brun

Not uncommon dry season migrant (*P. e. exustus*) from the Sahel to northern savannas, Dec–Apr, usually in flocks of 10–20 but occasionally as many as 150, e.g. Namoundjoga, Jan 1990. Southernmost record: many in the Keran Park, 12 Dec

1978 (Cheke & Walsh 1980). Regular at Tantigou, where parties come to drink in evenings.

No records for Ghana (Grimes (1987) but a vagrant is marked on the Ghana/Burkina Faso border on the map in Urban *et al.* (1986). Thonnerieux *et al.* (1989) mentioned 7 records from near Ouagadougou in Burkina Faso, Jan–Apr, and suggested they were visitors from the Sahel.

210.   PTEROCLES QUADRICINCTUS   AfM/B, R?B

Four-banded Sandgrouse
Ganga quadribande

Common dry season visitor to northern savannas, Oct–Jul, sometimes in well-wooded savanna as far south as Landa-Pozanda. Possibly resident in far north where breeds. Usually encountered in pairs or small parties, but flocks of up to 30 Naboulgou, Nov–Feb.

Breeding. C/3 Korbongou, near Namoundjoga, 8 Apr 1990. Female behaving as if nesting Tantigou, Apr.

COLUMBIDAE

Treroninae

211.   TRERON CALVA   R(B)

African Green Pigeon
Pigeon vert à front nu

Common resident (*T. calva sharpei*) of forest, where often occurs in small flocks of 10–50, either feeding high in the canopy or in pre-roost flights. It is the predominant fruit pigeon south of Faille d'Aledjo, but is also common in riparian habitats with good tree cover as far north as Naboulgou and along the coast.

Breeding. Male with enlarged testes collected Kara, Apr, specimen in BMNH. Carrying nesting material Fazao, Apr.

212.   TRERON WAALIA   RB

Bruce's Green Pigeon
Pigeon vert waalia

Common resident of savannas, principally in the arid north but also overlaps with *T. calva* at forest edges in the south, e.g. Fazao, Idifiou, and recorded along the Sio R. near Lomé, Feb and Dec.

Breeding. Bird incubating Kpaya, Jun.

Columbinae

213.   TURTUR BREHMERI   R(B)

Blue-headed Wood Dove
Tourtelette demoiselle

Rare resident (*T. b. infelix*) of forest. Presence in Togo overlooked by Urban *et al.* (1986) although collected Misahöhe, Feb (Reichenow 1902a). Sight records: Djodji, Mar and Oct (Cheke *et al.* 1986); Agou, Apr (JBT); Kpalimé, date unknown (TC).

214.   TURTUR TYMPANISTRIA   R(B)

Tambourine Dove
Tourtelette tambourette

Not uncommon resident of forest zone. Presence in Togo overlooked by Urban *et al.* (1986) although collected Ahoué-houé, Apéyémé, Dzogbégan, Misahöhe, Ounabé and Tététou (Reichenow 1894b, 1902a, De Roo 1970, De Roo *et al.* 1969, 1971, 1972). Sight records: Djodji, Idifiou, Klouto, Misahöhe, Tasso and Tinkiro.

215.   TURTUR AFER   RB

Blue-spotted Wood Dove (Red-billed Wood Dove)
Tourtelette améthystine

Locally abundant resident of forest and not uncommon in savannas and farmland throughout, at least as far north as the Keran Park, overlapping with *T. abyssinicus*.
   Breeding. Brooding birds Bismarckburg, Apr (Reichenow 1902a).

216.   TURTUR ABYSSINICUS   R(B)

Black-billed Wood Dove
Tourtelette d'Abyssinie

Abundant resident of northern savannas but also occurs sparingly south to the coast (De Roo *et al.* 1969, 1971, Browne 1980), overlapping with *T. afer* in much of its geographical range.
   Breeding. Bird repeatedly carrying sticks and involved in prolonged interspecific fight (including wing-buffeting) near Kara, Feb.

217.   OENA CAPENSIS   AfM/(B)

Namaqua Dove
Tourtelette à masque de fer

Common dry season intra-African migrant, Oct–Apr, to northern savannas. Occasionally locally abundant, e.g. in the Keran Park, Feb 1988. Regular as far south as Kara. Most southern records: a flock of 20, 10 km north of Anié, 1 Apr 1988; one at Lomé, 17 Jan 1954 (Douaud 1957).

218.   COLUMBA IRIDITORQUES   RB

Western Bronze-naped Pigeon
Pigeon à nuque bronzée

Not uncommon resident of forest. Presence in Togo overlooked by Urban *et al.* (1986) although collected Bismarckburg, date unknown, and described as a new species *Turturoena büttikoferi* (Reichenow 1891a, b), later synonymised with *iriditorques* (see Bannerman 1931). Subsequent specimens collected Ahoué-houé, Jul (De Roo *et al.* 1969), and Ezimé, Nov (De Roo 1970). Many recent records from the Kpalimé area, especially the Misahöhe forest, and also noted Badou and its environs.
   Breeding. Displaying Misahöhe, Feb, and building activity and a bird sitting on a flimsy nest there, Apr (Walsh *et al.* 1990).

219.   COLUMBA GUINEA   RB, AfM/(B)

Speckled Pigeon
Pigeon de Guinée

Abundant resident (*C. g. guinea*) of northern savannas and towns, especially in the

Dapaon and Mango areas. Groups of more than 200 Tantigou, Apr. Also common as far south as the Kara area. Rare further south but collected last century at Bassar and Kirikri (Reichenow 1902a). May be intra-African migrant as numbers increase in dry season.

Breeding. A bird sitting tight on an old nest of a Yellow-billed Stork *Mycteria ibis* Mango, Jan. Sitting bird on sparse stick nest on the girders of the bridge over the Oti river at Mango, Jan.

220.   COLUMBA LIVIA   R(B)

Rock Dove
Pigeon biset

Resident (presumably *C. l. gymnocyclus*) restricted to the Gambaga escarpment, where not uncommon. Recorded at the Ghana border near the Kuluguna cascade, Aug, near Nano, Aug, and at Fosse aux Lions, Apr, Aug and Sep. Usually in pairs or small parties but flock of 75 Fosse aux Lions, Aug 1987 (Walsh *et al.* 1990).

Feral populations (*C. l. 'domestica'*) occur in many towns and cities, e.g. Atakpamé, Blitta, Lomé and Sotouboua; birds kept in dovecotes are widespread, e.g. Dapaon, Kara, Kpalimé.

221.   STREPTOPELIA SEMITORQUATA   RB

Red-eyed Dove
Tourterelle à collier

Abundant resident of well-wooded savanna, riverine forest and forest edge from the Fosse aux Lions Park south to the coast.

Breeding. Incubating in a tree in riverine forest Landa-Pozanda, Dec. Building: Landa-Pozanda, Jan and Nov; Fosse aux Lions, Aug; 7 km north of Nyamassila, Aug.

222.   STREPTOPELIA DECIPIENS   R(B)

African Mourning Dove
Tourterelle pleureuse

Uncommon resident (*S. d. shelleyi*), usually found in well-wooded but arid savannas with *Borassus* palms in the far north such as the Dapaon area. Occasional records further south including Mango (Reichenow 1902a, a pair Jun 1990, one 26 Aug), the Keran Park, Kpani, the Oti R. at the Kara R. outfall, the Kara area, Atakpamé airstrip and Lomé (Browne 1980).

223.   STREPTOPELIA VINACEA   RB

Vinaceous Dove
Tourterelle vineuse

Abundant resident of savannas from Kara northwards, but also occurs sparingly further south, reaching the coast.

Breeding. Nestling Naboulgou, Apr.

224.   STREPTOPELIA TURTUR   PM

European Turtle Dove
Tourterelle des bois

Uncommon Palaearctic migrant (probably *S. t. turtur*), Jan–Apr, but likely to arrive Oct. Most records from arid savanna in the north but singles further south: Kara, Feb; at the confluence of the Amou R. with the Mono, Jan; and noted as rare near the coast at Agoué, date unknown (Millet-Horsin 1923). Largest flock: 50 at Oti-Toutionga, Mar.

225.   STREPTOPELIA HYPOPYRRHA   V

Adamawa Turtle Dove
Tourterelle à poitrine rose

Status uncertain, probably vagrant. The only record is of a bird which stayed beside the Ove R., near Tasso, Mar–May 1988, behaving as if defending a territory (Cheke & Walsh 1989). No other records between Nigeria and Senegal, where recently discovered: bird trapped and photographed at Niokolo-Koba, Senegal, Jan 1991 (F. Baillon per R. Beecroft) and heard there, Feb 1991 (R. Beecroft). Listed as a candidate species for treatment as threatened in Appendix G of Collar & Stuart (1985).

226.   STREPTOPELIA SENEGALENSIS   RB

Laughing Dove
Tourterelle maillée

Abundant resident (*S. s. senegalensis*) of savanna throughout including along the coast, but rare in forested habitats.
   Breeding. Extended. Single well-grown fledgling in nest in straw roof Dapaon, Feb (in both 1988 and 1989) and Aug. Nestling Kara, Aug. C/1 (nest in Neem tree *Azadirachta indica*), Dapaon, Jan; C/1 (nest in *Balanites* tree) Tantigou, Apr. Incubating birds: Kara (in *Gmelina* tree), Apr; Dapaon, Jan, Apr, Jun, Aug and Oct. Building: Kara, Jun and Sep; Ketao, Jul; Sirka, Jul; Dapaon, Aug. Copulation: Dapaon, Jan and Nov. Displaying birds: Dapaon, Aug; Lomé, Mar and Sep.

PSITTACIDAE

Psittacinae

227.   PSITTACUS ERITHACUS   R(B)

Grey Parrot
Perroquet gris

Very rare resident (*P. e. erithacus*), possibly now extinct in Togo. Previously rare north of the lagoon near Lomé, but becoming less so further north (Millet-Horsin 1923). The only subsequent record is of a bird flying over Mo, 11 May 1979 (Cheke & Walsh 1980). Many are seen for sale but these probably originate in neighbouring countries or from as far afield as Zaïre. In 1993 Togo agreed not to issue any more export permits and the CITES (The Washington Convention on International Trade in Endangered Species of Wild Fauna and Flora) Secretariat requested all parties to cease imports from Côte d'Ivoire, which is not a party to the CITES agreement (IUCN 1994).
   Brunel (1958) failed to find the species during a 20 month stay in southern Benin and thought its absence was due to lack of suitably large trees, which are its usual nesting sites. Bouet (1914) had previously remarked on its rarity in Benin.

228.   POICEPHALUS ROBUSTUS   R(B)

Brown-necked Parrot
Perroquet robuste

Status uncertain. Only known from specimen (*P. r. fuscicollis*) collected by R. Büttner at Bismarckburg, date unknown (Reichenow 1892, 1902a). J. von Zech collected a male west of Mpoti, 16 Jan 1899, which could be a site in Togo at 08°14'N, 00°46'E. It is more likely, however, to be a site in Ghana with a similar name at 06°49'N, 00°08'W, as von Zech also collected 2 males and a female from Kratschi (= Kété Kratschi at 07°46'N, 00°03'W). None of these specimens, which are in the MNB, were noted by Grimes (1987).

229.   POICEPHALUS SENEGALUS   R(B)
Senegal Parrot
Perroquet youyou

Common resident (*P. s. versteri*) of well-wooded savanna and forest-edge throughout. Usually seen in pairs but sometimes in groups of 6. Most common in the Southern Guinea Savanna belt where baobabs *Adansonia digitata* are present. Only the southern race *versteri* has been collected, including specimens from as far north as Borgou (De Roo *et al.* 1972), Mango (Reichenow 1902a), Namoundjoga (De Roo *et al.* 1971) and Nanergou (De Roo *et al.* 1969). The occurrence of the more northerly distributed *senegalus*, distinguishable by its orange rather than scarlet abdomen, awaits confirmation.
Breeding. Courtship feeding Ketao, Feb 1990.

Loriinae

230.   AGAPORNIS PULLARIA   R(B)
Red-headed Lovebird
Inséparable à tête rouge

Rare resident (*A. p. pullaria*) of riverine forest in well-wooded savanna. Only 3 records: one in gallery forest along the Akama R., 10 km south of Akaba, Jun 1979; one along Ware R. at 08°34'N, 00°53'E, Jul 1979 (Cheke & Walsh 1980); a flock of 8, 10 km north of Naboulgou, Feb 1987. The specimens mentioned by Reichenow (1902a) were from localities in Ghana.

231.   PSITTACULA KRAMERI   R(B)
Rose-ringed Parrakeet
Perruche à collier

Common resident (*P. k. krameri*) of savanna throughout. Flocks of 25–30 birds occasional, e.g. Kanté, Oct, Landa-Pozanda, Jun.

MUSOPHAGIDAE

Corythaeolinae

232.   CORYTHAEOLA CRISTATA   RB
Great Blue Turaco
Touraco géant

Rare resident of forest, where collected Misahöhe, Nov (Reichenow 1902a), densely-wooded savanna and gallery forest. Main strongholds are the Fazao mountains and the Adelé area, where collected Bismarckburg, Mar (Reichenow 1902a) and where

Douaud (1956b) saw a dozen at Kalabo. Also occurs in riverine forest beside the Mono R., e.g. Kpéssi, Landa-Mono and Nangbeto. Almost certainly declining in concert with de-forestation and increased disturbance. Recent records are usually only singles or pairs, but 5 near Fazao, Jun 1980 (Cheke 1982), 3 at Kpéssi, Aug 1989, and 3 at Nangbeto, Jun 1990 (JBT).

Breeding. C/1 found by E. Baumann (Anon 1894a), date and place unknown but probably Misahöhe, where he collected a male, 2 Nov 1893 (Reichenow 1897).

Tauracinae

233.   TAURACO PERSA   R(B)

Green Turaco
Touraco vert

Common resident (*T. p. persa*) of gallery forest in well-wooded savanna and forest from the Aledjo forest southwards.

234.   MUSOPHAGA VIOLACEA   R(B)

Violet Turaco
Touraco violet

Common resident of gallery forest beside the wider rivers. Occurs from as far north as Namoundjoga (De Roo *et al.* 1971) south to the Chutes d'Adjarala of the Mono R. in the east, and to Alokoégbé in the west.

Criniferinae

235.   CRINIFER PISCATOR   RB

Western Grey Plantain-eater
Touraco gris

Common and widespread resident throughout the savanna zones.

Breeding. C/2 Kpayando, Mar 1987. Nestlings being fed regurgitated food near Kpayando, Apr 1988. Bird disturbed off nest (contents unknown) 5 km south of Kara, Apr.

CUCULIDAE

Cuculinae

236.   OXYLOPHUS JACOBINUS   AfM/(B)

Jacobin Cuckoo
Coucou jacobin

Uncommon seasonal migrant (*O. j. pica*) to far north, Apr–Sep, with one anomalous record of 2 adults at Tantigou, 6 Dec 1987. The few records in the south suggest passage birds only with gradual movement northwards as the year progresses: Badou, Feb; Idifiou, Mar; Kpessidé, Mar; Bassar, Jun–Jul, but also there, Dec (PMC).

237.   OXYLOPHUS LEVAILLANTII   AfM/(B), R?(B)
African Striped Cuckoo
Coucou de Levaillant

Common intra-African migrant to savannas and forest edges throughout. A few
may be resident, but records suggest arrivals in the south late Dec (recorded
Misahöhe, 28 Dec (De Roo *et al.* 1972)) with passage birds present there until Apr.
Migrants reach the Kara valley in the first week of Feb, where a few may remain
until end Nov. Some continue to the far north.
Breeding. A pair copulating Misahöhe, 31 Jan.

238.   CLAMATOR GLANDARIUS   PM, R?(B)
Great Spotted Cuckoo
Coucou geai

Rare Palaearctic migrant. G. Thierry collected 3 specimens from Mango (2
undated, the 3rd., Jul), which are in the MNB (Reichenow 1902a). One seen Lomé,
date unknown (Browne 1980), and another Mango, date unknown (TC). Douaud
(1957) wrote that the species was resident in southern Togo but gave no details.
A female in the MNHN was collected in Benin by Waterlot at Porto-Novo,
2 Jan 1912.

239.   PACHYCOCCYX AUDEBERTI   R(B)
Thick-billed Cuckoo
Coucou d'Audebert

Rare resident (*P. audeberti brazzae*) of forest and well-wooded savanna. Collected
Bismarckburg and Mango, dates unknown (Reichenow 1902a). One calling
Okpahoué, Mar 1990, and one at Misahöhe, 28 Apr 1990. Listed as a candidate species
for treatment as threatened in Appendix G of Collar & Stuart (1985).

240.   CUCULUS SOLITARIUS   R(B), AfM/(B)
Red-chested Cuckoo
Coucou solitaire

Not uncommon resident (*C. s. solitarius*) in forest and seasonal migrant to thick
gallery forest as far north as Naboulgou, Apr–Sep. Although occasionally seen,
most records rely on the bird's distinctive call and so information on movements
unreliable if the species is silent in the non-breeding season.

241.   CUCULUS CLAMOSUS   R(B), AfM/NB
Black Cuckoo
Coucou criard

Rare resident of forest (*C. c. gabonensis*) and wet season migrant to savanna
(*C. c. clamosus*). Records of calling birds, presumed *gabonensis*, are: Bénali, Jul
1989; Misahöhe, Apr and Jun 1990 (JBT); Pagala, Jul 1953 (Douaud 1956b).
C. c. clamosus observed Tasso, May 1988. Both races collected Agomé Tongwe,
Ghana, close to Togo border, Jul (Reichenow 1897, 1902a).

242.   CUCULUS CANORUS   PM

Common Cuckoo (European Cuckoo)
Coucou gris

Rare Palaearctic passage migrant (*C. c. canorus*), Oct–Dec; collected Mango, date
unknown (Reichenow 1902a). According to Douaud (1957) arrives in small numbers
in the Baobab-dominated coastal plain, Nov, and leaves within the same month, but
one straggler there, 7 Dec 1953. One ringed in the Netherlands was recovered near
Akoumapé, Oct (Seel 1977; Fry *et al.* 1988).

243.   CUCULUS GULARIS   AfM/B

African Cuckoo
Coucou africain

Common intra-African migrant throughout, Jan–Sep. Earliest record 28 Jan, Kara.
   Breeding. A fledgling fed caterpillars by each of a group of 3 Long-tailed Shrikes
(*Corvinella corvina*) at Kara, Jul. Recently fledged bird Lomé, Jul (JBT).

244.   CERCOCOCCYX MECHOWI   R(B)

Dusky Long-tailed Cuckoo
Coucou de Mechow

Rare resident of forest, only 3 records: a male and a female collected at Bismarckburg,
Apr (Reichenow 1891a); a female collected at Misahöhe, Nov (Reichenow 1897); a
bird calling near Badou, 25 Mar 1990.

245.   CHRYSOCOCCYX CUPREUS   R(B), Afm/(B)

African Emerald Cuckoo
Coucou foliotocol

Not uncommon resident (*C. c. cupreus*) of thick forest and forest edges and rare migrant
to northern savannas. Most recent records from the Misahöhe forest, where heard
Jan Apr, but also noted Amou-Oblo, Badou, Balla (JBT) and Idifiou. Only one record
in the north: a bird calling in rich gallery forest at Naboulgou, Aug 1989. This is
consistent with the wet season movements northwards that occur in Nigeria (Elgood
*et al.*1994). Millet-Horsin (1923) wrote that the species was mostly hunted out but
recorded it from Glidgi and Zébé.

246.   CHRYSOCOCCYX FLAVIGULARIS   R(B)

Yellow-throated Cuckoo
Coucou à gorge jaune

Very rare forest resident (*C. f. flavigularis*) known only from specimens collected by
E. Baumann (Reichenow 1897, 1902a): a male from Misahöhe, May; a female from
Podji, May; a male from Liati, Nov. Liati was west-northwest of Misahöhe on the
road to Kpandu (Reichenow 1900–1904; Moberley 1931) and was probably the present
day Liati Datem at 6°58'N, 0°29'E in Ghana, and not Lyato which is in Togo. The
specimens were assigned to the nominate race as they have pale bellies and under tail
coverts, clearly differing from the description by Dickerman (1994) of *C. f. parkesi*,
and illustrated in Fry *et al.* (1988).
   Reichenow (1897, 1902a) listed a bird from Kpakple (? = Pakli Kopé), said to
be south of Kpélé, Apr, but the specimen, a female in the MNB, is an Emerald Cuckoo
C. cupreus.

247.   CHRYSOCOCCYX KLAAS   R(B), Afm/(B)

Klaas's Cuckoo
Coucou de Klaas

Common resident throughout southern half of country north to Aledjo, where collected in Dec (De Roo *et al.* 1972). Also seasonally common Kara area, Jan–Oct, and as far north as Naboulgou, Mar–Aug.
   Breeding. Recently fledged juvenile Landa-Pozanda, Jun. Courtship feeding Landa-Pozanda (DP) and Misahöhe, Apr.

248.   CHRYSOCOCCYX CAPRIUS   R(B), Afm/(B)

Diederik Cuckoo
Coucou didric

Common resident (*C. c. ?chrysochlorus*) in the southern half of the country, especially in forest clearings but also in more open habitats, e.g. beside the Sio R. near Lomé, where present all year (JBT). Noted as most frequent at Lomé, Feb–Jun (Browne 1980). Probably calls throughout the year where resident since heard at Badou, Jan–Apr, Jul and Oct. Also common visitor (*C. c. ?caprius* and *C. c. ?chrysochlorus*), Apr–Aug, in woodland in savannas as far north as Mango. The anomalous records of 2 juveniles at Naboulgou, Feb, and one calling Ketao, Oct, suggests that a few may also be resident in rich galleries in the north. Alternatively, some birds may arrive in the north earlier than supposed but remain silent. Clarification would be provided by confirmation of the suggestion (Clancey 1990a) that there are two subspecies present in West Africa: transequatorial long distance migrants with long wings (*caprius*), and short-winged *chrysochlorus* which are sedentary or only short-range migrants. The wing of an unsexed bird collected by E. Baumann, Misahöhe, 1 Nov 1894, measured 118 mm, suggestive of *caprius* on a late return migration.
   Breeding. Courtship feeding, repeated 3 times, lower Sio R., near Lomé, Sep.

Phaenicophaeninae

249.   CEUTHMOCHARES AEREUS   R(B)

Yellowbill
Malcoha à bec jaune

Common resident (*C. a. flavirostris*) of forest and thick vegetation of forest edges. Recorded in riverine forest as far north as Bafilo.

Centropodinae

250.   CENTROPUS LEUCOGASTER   R(B)

Black-throated Coucal
Coucal à ventre blanc

Rare resident of forest (*C. l. leucogaster*), known only from sightings at Badou, Djodji and Kouniohou (Cheke *et al.* 1986), but probably overlooked owing to skulking habits. The record quoted by Reichenow (1902a) refers to a Ghanaian locality.

251.   CENTROPUS GRILLII   AfM/(B)

Black Coucal
Coucal de Grill

Uncommon intra-African migrant, usually found in rank vegetation beside wetlands. Records suggest that it is only in the south from Nov to Jul: Tabligbo, Nov (Cheke *et al.* 1986); Sio R. near Lomé, Feb (JBT), and 12 there, in non-breeding plumage, 20 Apr 1990, of which 10 still present 1 May, including one in almost complete breeding dress; Lomé, Apr (Browne 1980); lower Mono R., Jun (JBT); Kévé, Jul (JBT). Present in the north only in the wet season, Jul–Aug, when birds are in breeding dress: Domaine Gravillou, Jul–Aug; Kara, Jul (Cheke *et al.* 1986); Fosse-aux-Lions, Jul–Aug; Tantigou, Jul; Tatale, Aug (PMC). Most northern record is of one collected Namoundjoga, Jul (De Roo *et al.* 1971). G. Thierry collected a specimen at Mango, date unknown, which was described by Reichenow (1899) as *Centropus thierryi*.
   Breeding. Territorial behaviour Kara, Jul.

252.   CENTROPUS SENEGALENSIS   RB

Senegal Coucal
Coucal de Sénégal

Very common resident (*C. s. senegalensis*) throughout, occurs in all habitats except thick forest. Possibly absent from swampland in the south, where replaced by *C. monachus*.
   Breeding. Nestlings Misahöhe, May (Reichenow 1902a). At least one fledgling reared from nest in Mango tree (*Mangifera indica*) at Kara, Jul. Adult with dependent fledgling Badou, Oct. Adult carrying food Imoussa, Jul.

253.   CENTROPUS MONACHUS   RB

Blue-headed Coucal
Coucal moine

Rare resident (*C. m. fischeri*) frequenting edges of swamps in the south, where said to have been common by Millet-Horsin (1921c, 1923); also recorded, Klouto (Dekeyser 1951). The only recent records are from the Dadja dam, Jul, and Badou, Jul (JBT), but probably overlooked owing to similarity to *C. senegalensis*.
   Breeding. A nest with 4 young Anécho, 5 Jul (Millet-Horsin 1921c).

TYTONIDAE

254.   TYTO ALBA   R(B)

Barn Owl
Chouette effraie

Not uncommon resident (*T. a. affinis*) throughout savanna areas, often associated with human habitation. Recorded Mango (Reichenow 1902a), Sokodé (skin in MNB collected by Kersting), Togokomé (De Roo *et al.* 1969), Atakpamé (De Roo 1970), Fazao (Minster Agriculture Limited 1984), Mo (Cheke *et al.* 1986), Notsé (H&S), Anié, Bafilo, Kara and Landa-Pozanda.

STRIGIDAE

255.   OTUS SCOPS   R(B), PM

Common Scops Owl
Hibou petit-duc

Uncommon resident (*O. s. senegalensis*) throughout savanna areas, and Palaearctic migrant (*O. s. scops*). Specimens of *senegalensis* collected Mango, Jul (Reichenow 1902a) and 2 more there, date unknown (MNB), Porto Séguro, Jun and Jul (De Roo *et al.* 1969), Tchonou, Sep, Adina, Dec (De Roo 1970), Niamtougou, Jul, Togoville, Sep (De Roo *et al.* 1971) and Ebéva, Nov (De Roo *et al.* 1972). Only recent record: heard at Kara, Jul 1989. *O. s. scops* obtained Edifou, Dec, and Evou, Feb (De Roo 1970) and Borgou, Dec (De Roo *et al.* 1972). On the basis of voice differences, Morel & Chappuis (1992) have argued that *scops* and *senegalensis* deserve specific rank.

256.   OTUS LEUCOTIS   R(B)

White-faced Scops Owl
Petit-Duc à face blanche

Not uncommon resident (*O. l. leucotis*) in savanna areas. Collected Mango and Sokodé (Reichenow 1902a), Témedja and Nanergou (De Roo *et al.* 1969), Kamina and Atakpamé (De Roo 1970), and Togoville (De Roo *et al.* 1971). Sight records from the Kara area, Lomé (JBT) and Danyi monastery (JBT). Heard 16 km northwest of Mango (H&S).

257.   BUBO AFRICANUS   RB

Spotted Eagle Owl
Grand-Duc africain

Not uncommon resident (*B. a. cinerascens*) of well-wooded savanna, and probably forest also; occurs throughout. Collected last century at Bassar, Bismarckburg and Sokodé (Reichenow 1902a) and more recently at Atakpamé (De Roo 1970), Borgou and Apéyémé (De Roo *et al.* 1972). Sight records from Atakpamé, Evou Apegamé, Fazao (Minster Agriculture Limited 1984), Kara, Landa-Pozanda, Naboulgou (Cheke & Walsh 1980), Pagala (JBT) and Péwa.
   Breeding. Downy young Sokodé, Apr (Reichenow 1902a).

258.   BUBO LACTEUS   R(B)

Verreaux's Eagle Owl
Grand-Duc de Verreaux

Rare resident, only 2 records: a female collected by Kersting in gallery forest near Kirikri, Feb (Reichenow 1902a); one in riverine forest beside the Sio river, near Koviakopé, 22 Jan 1987 (Walsh *et al.* 1990).

259.   SCOTOPELIA PELI   R(B)

Pel's Fishing Owl
Chouette-pêcheuse de Pel

Very rare resident, probably extinct in Togo. Never seen by the authors despite their extensive helicopter flights throughout Togolese river systems during 1979–90.
   Collected in gallery forest near Kirikri by Kersting, Feb (Reichenow 1902a); the only known record for Togo and overlooked by Fry *et al.* (1988).

260.   GLAUCIDIUM PERLATUM   R(B)

Pearl-spotted Owlet
Chevêchette perlée

Common resident (*G. p. perlatum*) of savanna. Recorded from Dadja in the south, north to Tantigou, Nanergou (De Roo *et al.* 1969) and Namoundjoga (De Roo *et al.* 1971). Characteristic calls heard during hours of darkness in Kara area, all months. Occasionally seen by day.

261.   STRIX WOODFORDII   R(B)

African Wood Owl
Chouette africaine

Not uncommon resident (*S. w. nuchalis*) of forest and gallery forest. Collected Ahoué-houé (De Roo *et al.* 1969), Odjolo and Ounabé (De Roo 1970), Apéyémé, Ebéva and Misahöhe (De Roo *et al.* 1972). Heard Tchifoma (Douaud 1956b). Recent sight records from Fazao (Minster Agriculture Limited 1984), Kpalimé, Misahöhe and Kati.

CAPRIMULGIDAE

Caprimulginae

262.   CAPRIMULGUS CLIMACURUS   R(B), AfM/(B)

Long-tailed Nightjar
Engoulevent à longue queue

Common resident and intra-African migrant, found in all savanna habitats and at forest edges. There are records for all months of the year, but the migrations and the status of the two sub-species, which are both likely to occur, are unclear. All birds identified to sub-species have been ascribed to the northern race *C. c. climacurus* (De Roo *et al.* 1969, 1971, 1972; De Roo 1970), including birds collected in the south (Adeta, Nov; Apéyémé, Dec; Ebéva, Oct–Nov; Edifou, Dec; Evou, Feb; Fazao, Aug; Tchonou, Aug) and the far north (Namoundjoga, Jul; Nanergou, Aug). Thus it is not known whether the southern race *sclateri* occurs or not, but it is possible that birds seen at or near Lomé, Jul, Sep (JBT), and date unknown (Browne 1980), are of this race.

Breeding. Churring birds: Kara area, Feb–Apr; Tantigou, Apr and Jul. A juvenile bird Landa-Pozanda, Aug.

263.   CAPRIMULGUS NIGRISCAPULARIS   R(B)

Black-shouldered Nightjar
Engoulevent à épaulettes noires

Rare resident of forest or forest edges, only 2 records: one collected Ezimé, 28 Nov 1968 (De Roo 1970) and another collected at Klabé Azafie, 1 Apr 1988 (Walsh *et al.* 1990, specimen in BMNH).

264.   CAPRIMULGUS INORNATUS   AfM(B), Afm?/(B)

Plain Nightjar
Engoulevent terne

Not uncommon intra-African migrant, found in savanna and at edges of forest. Probably present in the south only in the dry season, moving north to breed in the wet season, but status unclear. Recorded in the far north at Namoundjoga, Jul (De Roo *et al.* 1971), in the Kara area, Oct–Nov and Apr–Jun, and further south at Evou, Feb–Mar (De Roo 1970), and Tinkiro, Mar.

265.   CAPRIMULGUS TRISTIGMA   R(B)

Freckled Nightjar
Engoulevent pointillé

Locally not uncommon resident (*C. t. sharpei*) of rocky outcrops in savanna areas. At least 3 pairs regular at an inselberg at Péwa, where calling birds heard in all months except Jun, Oct and Dec. Collected at Aledjo, near Péwa, Aug (De Roo *et al.* 1969). Singles Kpaya, Aug, and Dapaon, Jan.

266.   CAPRIMULGUS AEGYPTIUS   V

Egyptian Nightjar
Engoulevent du Sahara

Vagrant. 4, probably *C. a. aegyptius* judging by their greyness, Landa-Pozanda, Jun 1983 (Cheke & Walsh 1984); another there, 17 May 1988.

267.   MACRODIPTERYX LONGIPENNIS   AfM/B

Standard-winged Nightjar
Engoulevent à balanciers

Common intra-African migrant, mainly found in savanna, but occasionally at forest edges; no records south of 7°30'N. Returns southwards, late Sep to Dec, and probably breeds throughout the savanna zone in the latter part of the dry season, before migrating north. Present Kara area, Oct–May, with peak passage in Nov. Males with developing standards noted there Oct–Nov, with almost complete standards early Jan, and with full standards Feb–May.

Breeding. C/1 Bismarckburg, Mar (Reichenow 1891a). Displaying pair Keran Park, Feb. Activity at 'display arenas', similar to descriptions by Colston & Curry-Lindahl (1986), Landa-Pozanda, most intense in Mar. Recently fledged birds Landa-Pozanda, Apr.

268.   MACRODIPTERYX VEXILLARIA   V, AfM

Pennant-winged Nightjar
Engoulevent porte-étendard

Vagrant. A female, in the MRAC and collected Aledjo, 20 Jul 1969, was wrongly identified as *M. longipennis* (De Roo *et al.* 1971, M. Louette, pers. comm.). A male (with pennants) photographed, Landa-Pozanda, 12 and 22 Jul 1989.

It is noteworthy that there is one Jul record for the W National Park in southwest Niger (Koster & Grettenberger 1983), and it may prove to be a regular, albeit uncommon, trans-equatorial migrant during the rains to Togo, Benin, Niger and Nigeria (Elgood 1982, Elgood *et al.* 1994).

APODIDAE

Apodinae

269.   RHAPHIDURA SABINI   R(B)

Sabine's Spinetail
Martinet de Sabine

Uncommon forest resident; all records are from the Plateaux Region in the wet season.
A pair at Djodji, May 1988 (Walsh *et al.* 1990) and 15 there, Jul 1989. A single at
Kpété Béna, Jul 1988, and a pair near Adossa, Jul 1989.

270.   TELACANTHURA MELANOPYGIA   R(B)

Black Spinetail
Martinet de Chapin

Rare forest resident. Only known from sight record at Pagala, date unknown (TC).

271.   TELACANTHURA USSHERI   R(B)

Mottled Spinetail
Martinet d'Ussher

Not uncommon resident (*T. u. ussheri*) of Guinea Savanna, seen singly or in pairs
wherever *Borassus* palms or Baobabs (*Adansonia digitata*) abound. Maximum
count of 8, circling large Baobab tree in Keran Park, Sep. Not recorded south of
Ayengré.

272.   NEAFRAPUS CASSINI   R(B)

Cassin's Spinetail
Martinet de Cassin

Vagrant, only 2 records: a pair flying over forest at Djodji, 20 Jul 1983; one there,
21 Mar 1985.

273.   CYPSIURUS PARVUS   RB

African Palm Swift
Martinet des palmes

Abundant resident throughout wherever palms, especially *Borassus,* occur. Probably
C. p. parvus in the northern savannas and *C. p. brachypterus* elsewhere, but only the
latter confirmed by specimens (De Roo *et al.* 1969; De Roo 1970).
   Breeding. A broken egg found beneath exotic palm at Kara, Mar; several birds
were visiting the palm. Birds either feeding young or mates in nests in a *Borassus*
palm at Djamdé, Aug.

[APUS BARBATUS

African Black Swift
Martinet du Cap

Very dark swifts, flying along rocky hillsides, Bafilo, Jun 1978 and Aug 1981, and
above Evou Apégame, Mar 1985, may have been *A. barbatus*.]

274.   APUS PALLIDUS   PM

Pallid Swift
Martinet pâle

Uncommon Palaearctic migrant (*A. p. brehmorum* or *A. p. pallidus*), probably only
occurring on passage. Mackworth-Praed & Grant (1970) cite Togo as a locality for
brehmorum but the source of this information has not been traced.

One at Oti Toutionga, 19 Nov 1987, is the only autumn record. All other sightings,
Feb–May, when usually seen in company of other swifts such as migrant *A. apus* or
T. melba or local *A. affinis*. Usually occurs singly, in pairs or threesomes but more than
200 were with *T. melba* and *T. aequatorialis* in a heavy passage in the Atakpamé area,
Mar 1987 (Walsh *et al.* 1990); also flocks of 25 at Kpalimé, Feb (Walsh *et al.* 1990),
and 15 near Mango, Apr.

275.   APUS APUS   PM

European Swift
Martinet noir

Common Palaearctic migrant (*A. a. apus*). Records near Atakpamé, Kpalimé, Tététou
and Lomé, Jan–Feb, suggest a few may winter in the south, but most birds are seen on
passage, when they may be abundant, Mar–May, e.g. 200 Cinkansé, May (Cheke &
Walsh 1984), 1000 Kara, Mar, 200 Klouto, Apr, and 500 Sokodé, Apr. Latest spring
birds: 6 Sara-Kawa, 4 Jun. Few autumn records, all mid Aug to mid Sep.

276.   APUS CAFFER   AfM/(B)

White-rumped Swift
Martinet cafre

Not uncommon intra-African migrant; no evidence of resident populations such as
occur in parts of Ghana and Nigeria (Grimes 1987, Elgood 1982). All records to date
occur north of Glei. Largest flock of 20, Péwa, Jun, and Keran Park, Jul. Birds move
north before the main rains, late Mar to May, and return after them, Sep–Oct. Earliest
sighting: 2 at Kpayando, 6 Mar. Latest: 2 at Péwa, 4 Nov. No records Dec–Feb.
Populations in Togo may be trans-equatorial migrants.

277.   APUS AFFINIS   RB

Little Swift
Martinet des maisons

Abundant resident (*A. a. aerobates*) throughout, especially in towns. Less common
in the Plateaux Region, where only recorded Djodji, Koniouhou and Wobé.
Breeding. Extended. Eggs Kara, Apr–Oct. Nest construction Kara, Feb and Jul.
Active colonies on houses and in garages, or in old nests of Lesser Striped Swallows
Hirundo abyssinica under bridges and in culverts, noted Amoussokopé, Oct, Anécho,
Nov, Atakpamé, Jan–Feb, Cinkansé, Jan, Kara, Mar–Oct, Kpalimé, Feb and Oct,
Mo, May–Jul, Notsé, Feb, Apr and Jun, Tététou, Mar, and Titira, Mar and Jul.

278.   TACHYMARPTIS AEQUATORIALIS   AfM/NB

Mottled Swift
Martinet marbré

Rare, occasionally numerous, sporadic visitor; all records Feb–Mar, except 21 at
Landa Pozanda, 5 May 1990. Status uncertain, but it is possible that some may be

resident along the mountainous zone bordering Togo and Ghana, e.g. 5 at Yikpa-Dikpé, Mar. Birds identified as *lowei* by the extent of white on their underparts noted on several occasions, Mar–May, but the possibility of the involvement of *furensis* should not be discounted. When numerous, they are usually in company of other swifts, especially *T. melba,* e.g. 50 at Atakpamé, Mar, 20 Kpalimé, Feb (Walsh *et al.* 1990), 80 Péwa, Mar, and 21 Landa-Pozanda, Mar. The birds are likely to be from the populations which probably breed in the Mampong Quarry, Shai Hills, Ghana (Grimes 1987), but intra-African migration on a wider scale may be involved.

279.   TACHYMARPTIS MELBA   PM/?AfM

Alpine Swift
Martinet alpin

Not uncommon passage migrant, Jan–Jul, occasionally abundant especially in mountainous areas. The first records for West Africa were Douaud's observations in mountains near Atakpamé, Apr 1953 and Apr 1956 (Douaud 1957). Numerous records since (Cheke 1980, Cheke & Walsh 1984, Cheke *et al.* 1986, Minster Agriculture Limited 1984, Walsh *et al.* 1990) have established Togo as an important wintering area for the species. The birds are often seen in the company of other swifts, ahead of storm fronts. Spectacular passages may include in excess of 1000 birds, e.g. between 0630 and 0845 at Aledjo, 16 Mar 1986, between 0930 and 0945 at Atakpamé, 11 Mar 1987, and at Fazao, 7 Mar 1988 (Walsh *et al.* 1990). As yet there are no autumn records. Earliest sighting 30 Jan (in both 1986 and 1988), latest 1 Jul.

Origin and subspecies of birds uncertain. Cheke & Walsh (1984) (not Walsh & Grimes (1981) as stated by Fry *et al.* 1988) commented that the paleness of birds seen at close quarters suggested *T. m. tuneti*, and this is likely as *tuneti* breeds in Algeria, Libya and east to the Middle East and southern Iran (Goodman & Watson 1983). However, the recovery in Ghana of a Swiss-ringed *T. m. melba* (Grimes 1987) confirms that European birds reach West Africa. The populations which probably breed in Mali (Fry *et al.* 1988) may also stray to Togo.

TROGONIDAE

280.   APALODERMA NARINA   R(B)

Narina's Trogon
Couroucou narina

Uncommon forest resident (*A. n. constantia*), straying as far north as the gallery forest along the Koumongou R. at Naboulgou, in the Keran Park. Collected Bismarckburg, Apr (Reichenow 1891a), Misahöhe, Dec (Reichenow 1902a) and Aug (De Roo *et al.* 1971), where recently recorded, Mar (JBT) and Apr. Also recorded Naboulgou, Mar and Nov, and one at Landa-Pozanda, Nov.

ALCEDINIDAE

Daceloninae

281.   HALCYON LEUCOCEPHALA   AfM/B

Grey-headed Kingfisher
Martin-chasseur à tête grise

Common dry season visitor (*H. l. leucocephala*), Nov–Jun, to Southern Guinea

Savanna woodland, riverine forest and forest edge; most records Feb–Apr. Few records in the north, Jan–Apr, and only one north of Mango: one at 10°29'N in the Oti valley, 31 Mar.

Breeding. Nest-hole in sandy bank near Landa-Pozanda, 2 Apr 1988 (adults greatly agitated because of the nearness of a Night Adder *Causus rhombeatus*); adult entering hole with food (? a grasshopper), 16 Apr. A pair displaying Landa-Pozanda, 3 Mar 1990. A pair prospecting a hole in a river bank near Oti-Toutionga, 3 Apr. Courtship feeding (food item a 20 cm long snake) beside the Sin-Sin R. at 07°36'N, 00°42'E, 7 Mar.

282.   HALCYON MALIMBICA   R(B)

Blue-breasted Kingfisher
Martin-chasseur à poitrine bleue

Common resident (*H. m. forbesi* and *torquata*) of forest and thick riverine woodland as far north as Fosse aux Lions. Also occurs around L. Togo.

Millet-Horsin (1921d) described *H. torquatus pontyi* (considered synonymous with *torquata*) from the lagoons of Togo and Dahomey (= Benin). De Roo (1970) and De Roo *et al.* (1969, 1971, 1972) also attributed their specimens to *torquata* but Dekeyser (1951) identified his as *forbesi*, albeit tentatively. The latter race occurs in neighbouring Ghana and Nigeria, whereas *torquata* is restricted to Senegambia and West Mali according to Fry *et al.* (1988, 1992).

Breeding. A pair displaying Djodji, Jul (Cheke & Walsh 1984).

283.   HALCYON SENEGALENSIS   R(B), AfM/(B)

Woodland Kingfisher
Martin-chasseur du Sénégal

Common resident (*H. s. senegalensis*) of forest and southern riverine forest, and wet season visitor to all savannas, May–Nov.

Breeding. One excavating nest-hole in tree at Fosse aux Lions, Aug. Open-wing display near Kouniohou, Jul.

284.   HALCYON CHELICUTI   AfM/(B)

Striped Kingfisher
Martin-chasseur strié

Not uncommon intra-African migrant (*H. c. chelicuti*), preferring Southern Guinea Savanna woodland. Probably occurs in northern savannas only during the wet season, Jun–Aug, and in all areas south of c. 8°N, Aug–Mar. Supportive evidence of migration provided by following data (sites are listed from south to north, each followed by dates): Lomé, Nov (Cheke *et al.* 1986); 20 km north of Lomé, Mar (Cheke *et al.* 1986); Misahöhe, Sep (Reichenow 1902a); Nangbeto, Aug (JBT); Ezimé, Nov (De Roo 1970); Evou, Mar (De Roo 1970); Tinkiro, Mar; Pagala, Mar; Bismarckburg, Apr (Reichenow 1902a), Jul (Douaud 1956b) and Aug (JBT); Blitta, Dec (Bouet 1961); Fazao, Aug (De Roo *et al.* 1971); Mo valley, Jun (Cheke *et al.* 1986); Kara, Jul; Ketao, Jul–Aug; Niamtougou, Jul (De Roo *et al.* 1971); Hago, Aug (Reichenow 1902a); Paio, Aug (De Roo *et al.* 1969); Titira, Aug. Two records of calling birds near Mango, Nov (H&S), are anomalous, but these may have been Greater Honeyguides (*Indicator indicator*). These have similar calls to *H. chelicuti* and occur in the Mango area but were not recorded by H & S.

Breeding. A pair holding territory Ketao, Jul–Aug 1989.

Alcedininae

285.   CEYX PICTA   RB, AfM/B

African Pygmy Kingfisher
Martin-pêcheur pygmée

Not uncommon resident (*C. p. picta*) and intra-African migrant. Douaud (1957) wrote
that birds only appeared in the Lomé area each dry season. Most sightings in northern
savannas, Mar–Aug, but records from Landa-Pozanda, Nov, and Mango, Dec
(De Roo *et al.* 1972), suggest some may be resident. No records north of Mango,
where recorded Aug and Dec.
   Breeding. Dependent young Lomé, Feb (JBT). A pair excavating in a spoil heap
beside a small stream near Djamdé, Jul. A fledgling uttering begging 'chip' calls near
Landa-Pozanda, Nov.

286.   CORYTHORNIS LEUCOGASTER   R(B)

White-bellied Kingfisher
Martin-pêcheur à vent blanc

Rare resident (*C. l. bowdleri*) of dense forest. Only known from 2 specimens collected
at Ahoué-houé, Jul 1968 (De Roo *et al.* 1969).

287.   CORYTHORNIS CRISTATA   R(B)

Malachite Kingfisher
Martin-pêcheur huppé

Common resident (*C. c. galerita* and *C. c. cyanostigma*) near swamps, lakes, rivers and
lakes throughout, except forest. Specimens collected Porto Séguro, Paio, (De Roo *et
al.* 1969), Niamtougou (De Roo *et al.* 1971), Borgou and Mango (De Roo *et al.* 1972)
were ascribed to the nominate race *C. c. cristata*. However, this is now considered to be
restricted to Africa south of the Zambezi R. (Clancey 1990b) and West African
populations are represented by 2 forms: *galerita* from Senegal to Ghana (Dickerman
1989) and *cyanostigma* from Nigeria eastwards (Clancey 1990b). Specimens from
Kirikri (collected by Kersting) and Mango (2 obtained by G. Thierry) were identified
as *C. cyanostigma* by Reichenow (1902a). The Kirikri specimen and one of the Mango
birds have wing lengths of 52 mm, and are dark rufous below, consistent with *galerita*,
but the other Mango bird has a wing of 57 mm showing that *cyanostigma* reaches
further west than previously thought. A bird, which killed itself by flying into a window
at Kara, Jun 1989, was *galerita* and confirmed the continuing presence in Togo of the
western race. The bird's belly from chest to vent was a rich dark rufous and its wing
length was 53 mm, culmen (from nostril to tip) 25, bill 30, tail 26 and tarsus 10.

288.   ALCEDO QUADRIBRACHYS   R(B), Afm?

Shining-blue Kingfisher
Martin-pêcheur azuré

Uncommon resident (*A. q. quadribrachys*) found along rivers with dense cover such as
the Gban-Houa, e.g. at Brouffou and Djodji (Cheke *et al.* 1986), and the Amoutchou
R. in the Idifiou area. Northern records from the Mo R., 29 Jul 1986, and Landa-
Pozanda, 15 Jul 1979 (Cheke & Walsh 1980), when the banks of the Kara R. were still
well-wooded, suggest northward migration during the rains. Collected Bismarckburg,
Apr, and Kirikri, Dec (Reichenow 1902a).

Cerylinae

289. MEGACERYLE MAXIMA   R(B)

African Giant Kingfisher
Alcyon géant

Not uncommon resident (*M. m. maxima*) in riverine forests in savanna areas, recorded from Alamassou northwards. Occasionally found beside lakes and dams: Aléhéride, Sep; Domaine Gravillou, Apr; Nangbeto, Jun 1990 (JBT); Sara-Kawa, Aug. Also occurs in the well-wooded Fazao highlands along the Kpaza and Koué rivers and in forest: Djodji, Mar and Oct; Idifiou, Mar. The forest birds may be *M. m. gigantea*.

290. CERYLE RUDIS   RB

Pied Kingfisher
Alcyon pie

Locally common resident, found beside large rivers, dams and lakes throughout, except forest. Occasionally roosts communally: at least 16 birds involved in roost at Lomé Lagoon, Oct (Robinson 1974); another of 6 birds at Tantigou, Apr.
  Breeding. Many droppings at entrances of nest holes Lomé lagoon, Nov–Jan (Robinson 1974). Courtship feeding, copulation, hole excavation and birds taking fish into holes, Jul; also entering holes, Apr (when excavating as well), May and Sep (Robinson 1974).

MEROPIDAE

[MEROPS MUELLERI

Blue-headed Bee-eater
Guêpier à tête bleue

Snow (1978) indicated a specimen was collected on the Togolese coast, which is included in the range maps of Fry (1984) and Fry *et al.* (1988), but details of the specimen have not been traced. It is known that a specimen (*M. m. mentalis*) was collected by Aubinn in Ghana in "Fantee country" (Grimes 1987) and it is possible that this specimen was incorrectly mapped by Snow (1978), who did not include any specimens from Ghana in his map.]

291. MEROPS GULARIS   RB

Black Bee-eater
Guêpier noir

Rare resident (*M. g. gularis*) of forest edge, recorded only from Idifiou and Amou-Oblo.
  Breeding. A pair probably bred at Idifiou during 1988 (Walsh *et al.* 1990). The pair was seen 6 Feb, 25 Feb and 13 May but on the latter date was accompanied by 2 free-flying young birds. One had a red throat but was brownish black on the head and nape, the other lacked the red throat. One juvenile begged from the adults but was not fed.

292. MEROPS PUSILLUS   R(B), Afm?/(B)

Little Bee-eater
Guêpier nain

Common resident (*M. p. pusillus*) throughout, except forest, but most frequently encountered in savanna north of Sokodé. Abundance of records, Jan–Apr, suggests influx in dry season.

Breeding. A pair with 3 juveniles (still lacking yellow chins) at Domaine Gravillou, Jul.

293.   MEROPS HIRUNDINEUS   R?/(B), AfM?/(B)

Swallow-tailed Bee-eater
Guêpier à queue d'aronde

Status uncertain, probably resident. Uncommon (*M. h. chrysolaimus*) north of 8°N in mature woodland in savanna, Jan–Aug and once in Nov.

Breeding. 3 juveniles, lacking the yellow throat, with an adult pair at Péwa, 27 Jul 1986. A group of up to 6 birds resident near Ketao, 15 Jul to 16 Aug 1989, juvenile present with adults, 11 Aug.

294.   MEROPS BULLOCKI   RB

Red-throated Bee-eater
Guêpier à gorge rouge

Common resident (*M. b. bullocki*) in suitable habitat in savanna from the Mo R. northwards.

Breeding. At least 3 active colonies in the bank of the Koumongou R., within the Keran Park, Feb 1987. One of these, near the "Mare aux Lions", was again active in Mar 1990 with 150 nest holes. A colony (with 80 holes and 6 birds present) in a bank of the Oti R. at 10°29'N, 00°31'E, Mar; another active colony (birds returning with grasshoppers) further downstream at 10°15'N, 00°21'E, Apr (Walsh *et al.* 1987).

295.   MEROPS ALBICOLLIS   AfM/NB

White-throated Bee-eater
Guêpier à gorge blanche

Common dry season visitor, especially to forest, forest edge and gallery forest in the south, Nov–Jun. Occasionally abundant, e.g. 100 Tinkiro, 9 Feb 1988. Flocks of 10–100 birds, on passage northwards, late Feb to Jun. Returning migrants appear in northern savannas during early Nov.

296.   MEROPS PERSICUS   AfM/NB

Blue-cheeked Bee-eater
Guêpier de Perse

Rare intra-African migrant, known only from remark by Douaud (1957) that *M. superciliosus chrysocercus* (= *M. persicus chrysocercus*) is a migrant to Togo, probably from the Sahel. No further records.

297.   MEROPS APIASTER   PM

European Bee-eater
Guêpier d'Europe

Uncommon Palaearctic passage migrant throughout, Sep–Oct and Mar–Apr. Records outside these months suggest that some possibly over-winter: one collected by Baumann at Misahöhe, Dec (Reichenow 1902a); several at Fazao, Jan 1989. Migrant flocks usually comprise 5–35 birds, but one of 109 at Bafilo, 25 Sep 1987.

298.   MEROPS MALIMBICUS   AfM/NB

Rosy Bee-eater
Guêpier gris-rose

Uncommon intra-African migrant, presumably from breeding grounds in Nigeria, to southern quarter of Togo. Recorded Lomé, Jan–Apr (Browne 1980), Agouć, and beside the Mono R., site and date unknown (Millet-Horsin 1923). Other records: 6 near Pasa, Mar; 4 at Amoussokopé, Jan; 11 near Nyivé, Feb (Walsh *et al.* 1990). Listed as a candidate species for treatment as threatened in Appendix G of Collar & Stuart (1985).

299.   MEROPS NUBICUS   Afm/B, R?(B)

Carmine Bee-eater
Guêpier écarlate

Common migrant (*M. n. nubicus*) in the dry season, mainly Oct–Apr, breeding in the north and occurring as far south as Sokodé. As there are records in all months, except Jul, some may be resident. Away from breeding colonies, flocks of 10–50 birds are usual, but occasionally are larger, e.g. 150 at Landa-Pozanda, 26 Feb.
   Breeding. Breeds along the Oti and Kara rivers (Walsh *et al.* 1987). Oti R. colonies: one at 10°29'N, 00°31'E (50–100 birds at site containing 630 holes, Mar–Apr); one at 10°18'N, 00°27'E (40 birds entering holes at site with 250 holes, Apr); one at 10°15'N, 00°21'30"E (40 birds at site with 500 holes, Apr). Kara R. colonies: one at 10°01'30"N, 00°25'30"E (50 birds at site with 350–400 holes, 4 fresh eggs found below colony, Apr); one at 09°58'30"N, 00°25'45"E (350 holes, Apr); one at 09°57'N, 00°29'45"E (490 holes, Apr).

CORACIIDAE

300.   CORACIAS NAEVIA   Afm/(B), R(B)

Rufous-crowned Roller
Rollier varié

Common intra-African migrant (*C. n. naevia*) with small resident populations in the north. Recorded throughout the savanna zones south to Kpélé, but prefers open savanna north of the Oti R. Influx of migrants in dry season, Dec–Mar, with birds returning north, Apr–Jul.
Breeding. Aerial displays Landa-Pozanda, Mar.

301.   CORACIAS CYANOGASTER   RB

Blue-bellied Roller
Rollier à ventre bleu

Not uncommon resident, preferring Guinea Savanna woodland from Fosse aux Lions south to within 30 km of Lomé. Most common between Atakpamé and Kpalimé.
   Breeding. Pair visiting nest in a dead tree near Djamdé, May; one adult brought a lizard (Cheke & Walsh 1980). A pair performing acrobatic aerial displays Fazao, Jul.

302.   CORACIAS ABYSSINICA   AfM/NB, R(B)

Abyssinian Roller
Rollier d'Abyssinie

Common intra-African migrant, Nov–Jun, occurring as far south as Atakpamé. Also, a small resident population from Mango northwards.

[CORACIAS GARRULUS

European Roller
Rollier d'Europe

The distribution map in Fry *et al.* (1988) includes Togo but no records have been traced.]

303. EURYSTOMUS GULARIS   R(B)

Blue-throated Roller
Rolle à gorge bleue

Not uncommon resident (*E. g. gularis*) of forest zones, e.g. Badou, Idifiou and Misahöhe, and of gallery forest in the south, e.g. along the Amou and Sio rivers.
Breeding. Courtship feeding Misahöhe, Apr.

304. EURYSTOMUS GLAUCURUS   R(B), Afm(B)

Broad-billed Roller
Rolle violet

Common resident (*E. g. afer*) and intra-African migrant. Between Dec and Mar occurs in well-wooded savanna and forest edge from 8°N to the coast, e.g. Anécho, Jan (JBT). Northward movement begins Mar; birds are common in northern savannas, Apr–Oct, and reach as far as Tantigou and Namoundjoga.

PHOENICULIDAE

305. PHOENICULUS PURPUREUS   R(B)

Green Wood-Hoopoe
Irrisor moqueur

Common resident (*P. p. guineensis*) throughout including forest, e.g. Misahöhe, but most frequently encountered in northern savannas.
Breeding. A pair prospecting tree hole near Naboulgou, Apr. Two juveniles with 3 adults at Tantigou, Apr. One of a pair carrying food near Landa-Pozanda, Feb.

306. PHOENICULUS ATERRIMUS   R(B)

Black Wood-Hoopoe
Irrisor noir

Not uncommon resident (*P. a. aterrimus*). Collected Bismarckburg, Mar, and Misahöhe, Feb (Reichenow 1902a). Recent records (all from northern savannas) of singles or pairs: Binako, Sep; Fosse aux Lions, Aug; Landa-Pozanda, Jan, Mar, Apr and Jul; Naboulgou, Feb, Apr and Aug; Mango, Feb, Aug and Oct; also Bassar, Jul, Oct and Dec (PMC).

UPUPIDAE

307. UPUPA EPOPS   AfM/(B), PM

Hoopoe
Huppe fasciée

Uncommon intra-African migrant (*U. e. senegalensis*), collected Bismarckburg, Mar,

Kirikri, date unknown, and Mango, date unknown (Reichenow 1902a). Birds with characteristics of the Palaearctic *U. e. epops* seen in northern savanna, e.g. at Cinkansé, Landa-Pozanda, Mango, Naboulgou and Niamtougou, 14 Feb–5 Mar. Recorded from the Keran Park, race unspecified, late Mar (Minster Agriculture Limited 1984).

BUCEROTIDAE

308.   BUCORVUS ABYSSINICUS   R(B)

Abyssinian Ground Hornbill
Calao terrestre d'Abyssinie

Rare resident, now almost restricted to the Fazao-Malfacassa and Keran reserves. Records from Fazao-Malfacassa include a pair near Bagan (Cheke & Walsh 1984), 5 on 8 Aug 1989, and a pair beside the Woro R. at 8°35'N, 1 Sep 1988; those from Keran Park, late Mar (Minster Agriculture Limited 1984), May (A&W) and late Aug (PM). Also 3 at Mandouri, 11 Jul 1989. Collected Bismarckburg, Jan, Sokodé, Apr, and Kirikri, Apr (Reichenow 1902a).

309.   TOCKUS ALBOCRISTATUS   R(B)

White-crested Hornbill
Calao à huppe blanche

Not uncommon forest resident (*T. a. macrourus*). Collected Klouto, Jun (Dekeyser 1951), and Misahöhe, Aug (De Roo *et al.* 1971). Regularly seen Misahöhe, and near Atakpamé at Ayomé, Idifiou and Okpahoué.
    Breeding. One specimen from Klouto, Jun, was still in juvenile plumage (Dekeyser 1951). 2 birds in territorial dispute with interlocked bills at Misahöhe, Feb. An almost flightless bird near Akloa, Jul, was probably moulting just after breeding.

310.   TOCKUS HARTLAUBI   R(B)

Black Dwarf Hornbill
Calao pygmée à bec noir

Uncommon forest resident (*T. h. hartlaubi*). Singles (sex unknown) sighted Misahöhe, Jan 1988 (Walsh *et al.* 1990), and Apr 1990 (JBT), and at 7°N beside the Gonobé R., 25 Apr 1989 and 20 Nov 1989. A male 10 km ESE of Koniouhou, Mar 1990.

311.   TOCKUS ERYTHRORHYNCHUS   R(B)

Red-billed Hornbill
Petit calao à bec rouge

Not uncommon resident (*T. e. erythrorhynchus*) of dry bush, usually found in Sudan Savanna, e.g. Borgou, Cinkansé, Dapaon, and Mandouri but also occurs in Guinea Savanna as far south as Kara, Oct.

312.   TOCKUS FASCIATUS   RB

African Pied Hornbill
Calao longibande

Common forest resident (*T. f. semifasciatus*), but also found in savanna wherever there is thick cover with tall trees or gallery forest; occurs as far north as Kara but also along the coastal plain. Commoner than *C. fistulator* in open country.

Breeding. Young squawking within tree-hole at Idifiou, Feb, were brought what appeared to be fruit by an adult. Bird brought mantis to nest hole in tree at Misahöhe, Feb. Carrying food Kévé, Mar, and Badou, Mar (Walsh *et al.* 1990).

313.   TOCKUS NASUTUS   Afm/B, R?B

African Grey Hornbill
Petit calao à bec noir

Abundant intra-African migrant (*T. n. nasutus*), inhabiting savannas throughout. Recorded in every month and some populations may be resident, e.g. at Kara and Naboulgou, but many move north, May–Jun, returning southwards, Oct. Visible migration in both directions with flocks of 10–70 birds.
Breeding. Carrying stick near Kara, Mar. Carrying food Atakpamé, Jan, and Gaougblé, Mar. Displaying Naboulgou, Feb.

314.   CERATOGYMNA FISTULATOR   R(B)

Piping Hornbill
Calao siffleur

Common resident (*C. f. sharpii* and *C. f. fistulator*) of forest. Particularly fond of gallery forest, especially beside the Kpaza and Koué rivers in the Fazao mountains. Recorded from Bafilo southwards as far as Kati and 20 km south of Tététou. Often seen along the Amou, Ogou, Pasa and Sio rivers. Although some *C. f. fistulator* occur, e.g. Pagala and Sotouboua, 19 Jun 1984, Cheke (1982) pointed out that some Togolese populations have characteristics of *C. f. sharpii*. This is usually thought to occur only east of the Niger R., where it is said to replace the more western *C. f. fistulator*. However, Brunel (1958) recorded both forms in southern Benin and, as Grimes (1987) discussed, *sharpii* has been recorded in Ghana by Lowe (1937) and Macdonald & Taylor (1977).

315.   CERATOGYMNA SUBCYLINDRICUS   R(B)

Black-and-white-casqued Hornbill
Calao à joues grises

Rare forest resident (presumably *C. s. subcylindricus*), known only from the following 4 sightings: one in gallery forest beside the Mono R. at 08°25', 01°14'E, 15 Oct 1987 (Walsh *et al.* 1990); 3 at the confluence of the Koloware and Mono rivers, 15 Jul 1987; a pair in the Koué R. valley, 1 Sep 1987; a pair beside the Mono R. at 07°59'N, 4 Jul 1989. Allport (1991) has proposed that the species should be added to the near-threatened category.

316.   CERATOGYMNA CYLINDRICUS   R(B)

Brown-cheeked Hornbill
Calao à joues brunes

Rare resident (probably *C. c. cylindricus*) known only from sighting of a pair at the confluence of the Na and Mono rivers, 17 May 1990.

317.   CERATOGYMNA ATRATA   RB

Black-casqued Wattled Hornbill
Grand calao à casque noir

E. Baumann collected a female nestling at Bueta (exact location of this site unknown), 21 Apr 1894 (Reichenow 1897, 1902a). No subsequent records.

Breeding. Nestling close to fledging, but with tail feathers still in pin, collected Bueta, Apr (Reichenow 1902a).

318.   CERATOGYMNA ELATA   R(B)

Yellow-casqued Wattled Hornbill
Grand calao à casque jaune

Rare forest resident. A young male collected Bismarckburg, date unknown (Reichenow 1891a). One in gallery forest beside the Mono R. at 07°18'N, 01°27'E, 20 Jan 1987 (Walsh *et al.* 1990), another in the Koué valley at 08°21'N, 00°45'E, 2 Sep 1988. Listed as a candidate species for treatment as threatened in Appendix G of Collar & Stuart (1985).

CAPITONIDAE

319.   GYMNOBUCCO PELI   R(B)

Bristle-nosed Barbet
Barbican à narines emplumées

Uncommon forest resident. Collected Ahoué-houé and Tomegbé, Jul (De Roo *et al.* 1969). Singles Kpimé-Tomegbé, Apr, and beside the Sin-Sin R. at 07°37'N, 00°42'E, Mar. Pairs at Amou-Oblo, Jul, Djodji, Mar, and Wobé, Mar.
   Breeding. Entering nest-holes in dead tree in mixed colony with *G. calvus* at Wobé, Mar.

320.   GYMNOBUCCO CALVUS   RB

Naked-faced Barbet
Barbican chauve

Common and locally abundant resident (*G. c. calvus*) throughout forest zone, usually gregarious.
   Breeding. Dependent young on branch of colony tree and many nestlings peering from holes near Deguingué, Mar. Nestlings being fed berries Djodji, Mar. Parents visiting nest-holes containing noisy young (one seen with gape flange and downy head) Misahöhe, Apr. Entering nest-holes: Badou, Mar; Tomegbé, Jul; Wobé, Mar, where in mixed colony with *G. peli*.

321.   POGONIULUS SCOLOPACEUS   RB

Speckled Tinkerbird
Barbion grivelé

Common resident (*P. s. scolopaceus*) of forest, e.g. Ahoué-Houé, Djodji, Idifiou and Misahöhe, and forest edge.
   Breeding. A bird, presumably feeding young, seen every 3 or 4 minutes entering and leaving a nest hole at Ewa, Mar (Walsh *et al.* 1990).

322.   POGONIULUS ATROFLAVUS   R(B)

Red-rumped Tinkerbird
Barbion à croupion rouge

Uncommon resident of forest and gallery forest. One in riverine forest, near Nyamassila, 18 Jul 1989. Calls heard in Jul at Adossa, Ayagba and Djodji.

323.   POGONIULUS SUBSULPHUREUS   R(B)

Yellow-throated Tinkerbird
Barbion à gorge jaune

Rare resident (*P. s. flavimentum* or *chrysopygius*) of forest zones. One calling at Ayagba, 27 Jul 1989, is the only known record although both Mackworth-Praed & Grant (1970) and Fry *et al.* (1988) state that *flavimentum* occurs from Togo eastwards and *chrysopygius* from Ghana to the west. The map in Snow (1978) does not show any specimens in Togo.

324.   POGONIULUS BILINEATUS   R(B)

Yellow-rumped Tinkerbird
Barbion à croupion jaune

Common resident (*P. b. leucolaima*) of forest (Djodji, Misahöhe) and northern forested areas such as Faille d' Aledjo where numerous.

325.   POGONIULUS CHRYSOCONUS   R(B)

Yellow-fronted Tinkerbird
Barbion à front jaune

Common resident (*P. c. chrysoconus*) of woodland savanna throughout, but most numerous north of the Bafilo ridge.
  Breeding. A pair excavating a nest-hole in a tree at Kpayando, Mar.

326.   BUCCANODON DUCHAILLUI   R(B)

Yellow-spotted Barbet
Barbican à taches jaunes

Rare resident of forest. One calling Badou-Dzindzi on the Ghana/Togo border, 26 Mar 1990, is the only record. This represents the easternmost locality for the populations on the western side of the Togo-Benin or "Dahomey" Gap.

327.   TRICHOLAEMA HIRSUTA   R(B)

Hairy-breasted Barbet
Barbican hérissé

Not uncommon resident (*T. h. hirsuta*) of forest zones, often recorded in the Badou and Misahöhe areas.
  Breeding. 2 separate cases of birds excavating holes at Djodji, Oct.

328.   LYBIUS VIEILLOTI   R(B)

Vieillot's Barbet
Barbican de Vieillot

Common resident (*L. v. rubescens*) of savanna zones throughout. Usually seen in pairs or detected by characteristic duetting calls, noted Mar–Aug.
  Breeding. 2 immature birds with adult near Nangbeto, Aug (JBT).

329.   LYBIUS BIDENTATUS   R(B)

Double-toothed Barbet
Barbican bidenté

Common resident (*L. b. bidentatus*) of forest edges and clearings in forest zone, especially in the Plateaux region, e.g. Badou, and well-wooded savanna as far north as Agbandé and Bassar (Reichenow 1902a). Also recorded Lomé (Browne 1980).

330.   LYBIUS DUBIUS   R(B)

Bearded Barbet
Barbican à poitrine rouge

Common resident throughout savanna zones. Becomes more scarce south of Sokodé but reaches as far south as 7°30'N (De Roo *et al.* 1969; JBT).
Breeding. Allopreening and display Kara, Mar, and allopreening, Aug.

331.   TRACHYPHONUS PURPURATUS   R(B)

Yellow-billed Barbet
Barbican pourpre

Not uncommon resident (*T. p. goffini* and *T. p. togoensis*) of forest and forest edge, e.g. at Agbossomou Kopé, Ayagba, Badou, Balla, Djodji and Koniouhou. Reichenow (1891a) described *togoensis* from a specimen collected by R. Büttner at Bismarckburg, Aug, and later illustrated the taxon and recorded a specimen obtained by E. Baumann at Agomé Tongwe, Ghana, Jul (Reichenow 1897). A specimen from Ounabé, Oct, was also *togoensis* (De Roo 1970). However, *goffini* also occurs and probably breeds at Djodji, close to the Ghana border (Cheke *et al.* 1986 and see below). Both *goffini* and *togoensis* have been seen in the Kpalimé area, Apr.
Breeding. 3 birds (*goffini*) regularly entering and leaving a nest-hole near Djodji, Mar (Cheke *et al.* 1986), another (*goffini*) entering a hole in a *Borassus* palm at Ayagba, Jul. Duetting calls, Mar and Jul.

INDICATORIDAE

332.   PRODOTISCUS INSIGNIS   R(B)

Cassin's Honeybird
Indicateur pygmée

Rare resident of forest (*P. i. flavodorsalis*). Collected Misahöhe, Feb and Jul, and Koussountou, May (Reichenow 1897). One sighted Misahöhe, 31 Jan and 2 Feb 1988 (Walsh *et al.* 1990).

333.   PRODOTISCUS REGULUS   R(B)

Wahlberg's Honeybird
Indicateur de Wahlberg

Rare resident. Known only from specimen collected Kolokopé, Aug (De Roo *et al.* 1971, Snow & Louette 1981).

334.   INDICATOR MACULATUS   R(B)

Spotted Honeyguide
Indicateur tacheté

Uncommon resident (*I. m. maculatus*) of forest zones. Collected Fazao, Aug (De Roo *et al.* 1971), Ebéva, Oct, and Dzobégan, Dec (De Roo *et al.* 1972). One calling Wobé, 23 Mar 1990.

335.   INDICATOR INDICATOR   R(B)

Greater Honeyguide
Grand indicateur

Not uncommon resident of Guinea Savanna, often recorded in the Kara area and the Keran Park. Also occurs in Sudan Savanna, e.g. Mandouri, and as far south as Nyivé.

Breeding. An immature bird near Kara, May. Birds persistently calling close to active colony of Red-throated Bee-eaters *M. bullocki*, which is its favoured host (Fry *et al.* 1992), near Mare aux Lions, Feb.

336.   INDICATOR MINOR   R(B)

Lesser Honeyguide
Petit indicateur

Not uncommon resident (*I. m. senegalensis*) of wooded savanna from the coast (one killed Zébé, Millet-Horsin 1923) throughout. Collected Nanergou (De Roo *et al.* 1969).

Breeding. A bird inspecting a woodpecker hole at Landa-Pozanda, Mar.

337.   INDICATOR EXILIS   R(B)

Least Honeyguide
Indicateur minule

Uncommon forest resident (*I. e. exilis*). A female collected Misahöhe, Feb (Reichenow 1897); 2 seen Idifiou, Feb, and one at Misahöhe, Feb (Walsh *et al.* 1990).

Breeding. Pair copulating Idifiou, Feb. Bird in apparent display flight near Misahöhe, Feb (Walsh *et al.* 1990).

[INDICATOR WILLCOCKSI

Willcocks's Honeyguide
Indicateur de Willcocks

Probably occurs as rare, presumed resident (*I. w. willcocksi*). A female collected Agomé Tongwe, Ghana but close to the Togo border, Jul, ascribed by Reichenow (1897) to *I. exilis* is *I. willcocksi*. This was apparently realised by Friedmann (1955) who listed Togoland amongst the known distribution of *I. e. willcocksi* (now given specific rank), presumably on the authority of Stresemann whom he acknowledged for providing information on specimens at the MNB.]

PICIDAE

Jynginae

338.   JYNX TORQUILLA   PM

Northern Wryneck
Torcol fourmilier

Rare Palaearctic migrant (*J. t. torquilla*). Collected Bismarckburg, Feb (Reichenow 1891a). Singles at Péwa, Mar 1987 (Walsh *et al.* 1990), and Fazao, Jan 1989.

Picinae

339.   CAMPETHERA PUNCTULIGERA   R(B)

Fine-spotted Woodpecker
Pic punctué

Not uncommon resident (*C. p. punctuligera*) of well-wooded savanna throughout, including the coast at Lomé (Browne 1980). Collected Mango (Reichenow 1902a), and Fazao, Aug (De Roo *et al.* 1971).

340.   CAMPETHERA MACULOSA   R(B)

Little Green Woodpecker
Pic barré

Rare resident of forest, known only from sight record at Misahöhe, Dec 1989 (JBT). No previous records east of Akropong in Akwapim (05°58'N, 00°06'W) in Ghana. Listed as a candidate species for treatment as threatened in Appendix G of Collar & Stuart (1985).

341.   CAMPETHERA CAILLIAUTII   R(B)

Green-backed Woodpecker
Pic à dos vert

Uncommon resident (*C. c. permista*) of forest and gallery forest. Collected Misahöhe, May, Jul and Nov, Kirikri, Feb (Reichenow 1902a), and Klouto, Jun (Dekeyser 1951). Recent sightings at Misahöhe, Nov 1989 and Apr 1990 (JBT).

The male, collected at Misahöhe, May, and in MNB, is the type used by Neumann (1904) to describe *Dendromus permista togoensis*. Kersting, who collected the Kirikri bird, specified on the label that the bird had been obtained in gallery forest.

342.   CAMPETHERA NIVOSA   R(B)

Buff-spotted Woodpecker
Pic tacheté

Uncommon resident (*C. n. nivosa*) of forest zone and gallery forest. Collected Bismarckburg, Apr, Kirikri, Feb, Misahöhe, Jul, and Podji, May (Reichenow 1902a). Kersting, who collected the Kirikri bird, specified on the label that the bird had been obtained in gallery forest. Recent sightings: Djodji, Mar (Cheke *et al.* 1986); Todomé, May 1988; Wobé, Mar 1990.

343.   DENDROPICOS GABONENSIS   R(B)

Gabon Woodpecker
Pic du Gabon

Not uncommon resident of forest zone. Noted Djodji, Oct (Cheke *et al.* 1986), Déguingué, Mar, Idifiou, Mar, Badou, Mar, Mt Agou, Apr, and Misahöhe, Feb–Apr, Aug and Nov.

344.   DENDROPICOS FUSCESCENS   R(B)

Cardinal Woodpecker
Pic cardinal

Not uncommon resident (*D. f. lafresnayi*) of well-wooded savanna and forest edge. Collected Bismarckburg, Feb, Podji, May (Reichenow 1902a), and Binaparba, Aug

(De Roo *et al.* 1969); 2 seen Yegué, Jul (Douaud 1956b). Recent records from the Kara area, Tinkiro and Cinkansé.

345.   DENDROPICOS PYRRHOGASTER   R(B)

Fire-bellied Woodpecker
Pic à ventre de feu

Common resident of forest zone. Collected Misahöhe, Feb (Reichenow 1902a), where also seen, Jan, Mar (Cheke *et al.* 1986), Apr, Nov and Dec (JBT). Other localities include Badou, Idifiou and Pagala.

Breeding. Courtship feeding (male feeding female with large beetle grub) Misahöhe, Apr.

346.   DENDROPICOS GOERTAE   RB

Grey Woodpecker
Pic gris

Common resident (*D. g. goertae*) of savannas throughout from Lomé to northern borders. Collected Notsé, Jul, and Mango, Aug (De Roo *et al.* 1969), and Namoundjoga, Aug (De Roo *et al.* 1971). Many records from the Bafilo ridge northwards.

Breeding. Female peering out of nest-hole in tree at Landa-Pozanda, 7 and 23 Jan 1988; seen entering with food and leaving without it, 4 Feb (Walsh *et al.* 1990). Male repeatedly seen carrying food at Kpessidé, Jan 1988. A female in a hole in a dead oil palm tree at Landa-Pozanda, and male seen entering with food, 29 Jan 1989. Male entering nest hole near Binako, Feb 1994 (PMC).

347.   PICOIDES OBSOLETUS   R(B)

Brown-backed Woodpecker
Petit pic à dos brun

Uncommon resident of northern savanna woodland (*P. o. obsoletus*). Collected Mango, Aug (De Roo *et al.* 1969). Other records: male at Mo, Jun 1984; females near Landa-Pozanda, Mar and Jun 1986.

PASSERINES

EURYLAIMIDAE

348. SMITHORNIS RUFOLATERALIS   RB

Red-sided Broadbill
Eurylaime à flancs roux

Rare resident of forest (*S. r. rufolateralis*). Collected Bismarckburg, Mar and Apr,
and Misahöhe, Jul (Reichenow 1891a, 1902a). No subsequent records.
  Breeding. R. Büttner collected a nest at Bismarckburg, Apr, together with a male
which seemingly had been incubating (Reichenow 1891a). The nest was described as
oval and completely closed save for a side entrance. It was made mainly of deciduous
leaves and reed-like grass, held together with thread-forming creepers.

349. SMITHORNIS CAPENSIS   R(B)

African Broadbill
Eurylaime du Cap

Rare forest resident (*S. c. delacouri*), only one record: one sighted in gallery forest
fringing the Menou R. at Agbenohoué, 26 Jul 1989.

PITTIDAE

350. PITTA ANGOLENSIS   R(B)

African Pitta
Brève d'Angola

Rare resident (*P. a. pulih*) of dense forest. A female collected Misahöhe, 29 May 1895
(Reichenow 1897), and a pickled specimen from the same site, deposited at the MNB
on 30 Jun 1904 by Smend, are the only confirmed records. A woman from Bassar
recalled seeing one near Mo, date unknown, in the 1940s (PMC).

ALAUDIDAE

351. MIRAFRA CANTILLANS   AfM/NB

Singing Bush-Lark
Alouette chanteuse

Rare dry season visitor (*M. c. chadensis*) to Sudan Savanna. Singles at Tantigou,
Feb–Mar, and Mandouri, Apr (Walsh *et al.* 1990). A pair on rocky ground with
extensive stone slabs, Korbongou near Namoundjoga, 8 Apr 1990, and one near
Domaine Gravillou, 22 Apr 1990. No records from Ghana (Grimes 1987) but occurs as
far south as Zaria in Nigeria (Elgood 1982). Breeds during the wet season in the Sahel,
where Senegalese populations have recently been studied (Mullié & Keith 1991).

352. MIRAFRA RUFOCINNAMOMEA   R(B)

Flappet Lark
Alouette bourdonnante

Common resident (*M. r. buckleyi*). Most records Mar–Aug, when conspicuous display flights regular. Prefers well-wooded Northern Guinea Savanna but also occurs in Sudan Savanna, e.g. Tantigou, and may occur throughout. Southern records: Kouniohou, Jul; Pagala, Aug (JBT). Collected Nanergou, Aug (De Roo *et al.* 1969), and Borgou, Dec (De Roo *et al.* 1972).

Breeding. Display flights: Mango area, Apr and Jul–Aug; Kara area, Jun–Aug; Bouzalo, Jun; Péwa, Jul; Tantigou, Jul.

353.   MIRAFRA RUFA   V

Rusty Bush-Lark
Alouette rousse

Vagrant. One (*M. r. nigriticola*) seen well and photographed near Tantigou, 10 Apr 1988 (Walsh *et al.* 1990). No records of this Sahelian species from Côte d'Ivoire (Thiollay 1985b) or Ghana (Grimes 1987) and only a dubious record of a bird seen at Lagos Harbour, Nigeria (Elgood 1982).

354.   PINAROCORYS ERYTHROPYGIA   AfM/(B)

Rufous-rumped Lark
Alouette à queue rousse

Uncommon intra-African migrant to Sudan Savanna and Northern Guinea Savanna woodland. A dry season visitor which probably arrives Sep–Oct but so far only recorded Feb to mid Apr (latest date 10 Apr, Naboulgou). A migratory flock of 30, perched together in a tall tree in riverine woodland at Naboulgou, 1615–1630h on 6 Apr 1990, was later joined by more birds as the sky darkened with an approaching storm. Collected Bismarckburg, Feb (Reichenow 1891a), and Mango, date unknown (Reichenow 1902a).

355.   GALERIDA MODESTA   R(B)

Sun Lark
Cochevis modeste

Common resident (*G. m. modesta*) of Northern Guinea Savanna and Sudan Savanna, usually associated with rocky ground. Collected Aledjo and Niamtougou (De Roo *et al.* 1969, 1971, 1972).

Breeding. Probably breeds along the Bafilo Ridge in the Aledjo and Péwa areas. A juvenile together with 4 adults near Péwa, Mar. Up to 3 pairs defending territories Péwa, Jul. Song flight Sirka, Oct.

356.   GALERIDA CRISTATA   R(B)

Crested Lark
Cochevis huppé

Not uncommon local resident (*G. c. senegallensis*) of open ground in northern savanna from near Mango in the Keran Park northwards. Collected Mango by G. Thierry, date unknown (Reichenow 1902a).

Breeding. A juvenile bird recently fledged Domaine Gravillou, Feb (Walsh *et al.* 1990).

357.   EREMOPTERIX LEUCOTIS   AfM/(B)

Chestnut-backed Sparrow-Lark
Alouette-moineau à oreillons blancs

Common, locally abundant, e.g. Keran Park, dry season visitor from the Sahel to northern savannas. Occasionally reaches as far south as Landa-Pozanda, Feb, and Sara-Kawa, Jan–Mar. Only recorded Nov–Apr; most birds depart Mar. Latest record, 6 at Domaine Gravillou, 22 Apr.

HIRUNDINIDAE

Hirundininae

358.   PSALIDOPROCNE NITENS   R(B)

Square-tailed Saw-wing
Hirondelle à queue courte

Rare resident (*P. n. nitens*), known only from sightings by Douaud (1956b): a pair near Pagala and one at Tchifoma, 22 Jul 1953. The latter was harassing a group of *H. abyssinica*.

359.   PSALIDOPROCNE OBSCURA   RB

Fanti Saw-wing
Hirondelle fanti

Locally common resident of well-wooded Southern Guinea Savanna and forest clearings south of 9°25'N. One coastal record: collected Porto Séguro, Jul (De Roo *et al.* 1969). Usually solitary but occasionally up to 4 birds together, e.g. Wobé, Mar, and 20 at Danyi Plateau, Feb (JBT). Douaud (1956b) noted several near Katchanké, Jul.

Breeding. A single dependent young (short-tailed and an inexpert flier) with adults at Tchimmbéré, 29 Aug 1989.

360.   RIPARIA PALUDICOLA   R?(B), AfM?

Brown-throated Sand Martin
Hirondelle paludicole

Rare, only 5 records: 2 at 9°28'N, 0°59'E, 6 May 1979; 2 at Landa-Pozanda, 7 Jul 1979; at least one near Mango, 25 Jul 1979 (Cheke & Walsh 1980); others in Bassar-Kabou area, 25 Aug and 29 Sep 1991 (PMC). Status uncertain but probably resident (*R. p. paludibula*) in northern savanna.

361.   RIPARIA RIPARIA   PM

Common Sand Martin
Hirondelle de rivage

Uncommon Palaearctic migrant (*R. r. riparia*) recorded in low numbers throughout, early Oct to end Apr. Usually over reservoirs or along rivers and often in company of *H. rustica* or *D. urbica*. Maximum counts: 15 at Djodji, Feb and Mar (Cheke *et al.* 1986); 12 along Sio R., Dec (Douaud 1957).

362.   RIPARIA CINCTA   AfM/NB

Banded Martin
Hirondelle à collier

Scarce dry season visitor (*R. c. cincta*). Known only from statement of Douaud (1957) that it was common on the plains around L. Togo, Oct–May, and absent during the rainy season.

363.   HIRUNDO SEMIRUFA   AfM/B

Red-breasted Swallow
Hirondelle à ventre roux

Not uncommon intra-African migrant (*H. s. gordoni*) recorded in low numbers in all habitats, Feb–Sep. Maximum count: 10 near Lomé, Feb.

Breeding. 2 pairs attending nests in culvert near Fosse aux Lions, Sep (Walsh *et al.* 1990). Collecting mud for nests Klouto and Misahöhe, Apr.

364.   HIRUNDO SENEGALENSIS   AfM/(B)

Mosque Swallow
Hirondelle des mosquées

Uncommon intra-African migrant (*H. s. senegalensis* and ?*H. s. saturatior*) to savanna habitats throughout, including coast (Robinson 1972), mid-Feb to Aug. G. Thierry collected 2 *senegalensis* at Mango, date unknown (Reichenow 1902a).

365.   HIRUNDO ABYSSINICA   Afm/B

Lesser Striped Swallow
Hirondelle striée

Common intra-African migrant (*H. a. puella*), Jan–Aug. Travels from more southern latitudes to breed at onset of rains. No records Sep–Dec. Earliest date 13 Jan 1989 (2 at Fazao), latest date 13 Aug 1989 (3 at Naboulgou). Occurs throughout, except thick forest, but prefers well-wooded savanna. Nests, usually placed under bridges or in culverts, often taken over by *Apus affinis*. Mocking Cliff-Chat *Myrmecocichla cinnamomeiventris* observed pecking at a nest of the swallow, presumably attempting to take over the nest, which was placed on a rocky outcrop near Péwa, 25 Jun 1989.

Breeding. Feeding young in nests: Titira, Jul. Entering nests: Tététou, Mar; 5 km south of Kara and Landa-Pozanda, Apr; Mo, May (6 pairs); Notsé, Apr–Jun (6 pairs in mixed colony with *H. preussi*); Péwa, Jun; Titira, Jun–Jul (20 pairs and 6 recently-fledged juveniles, 3 Jul 1980, in mixed colony with *H. preussi*). Nest-building: Fazao, Apr; Kpayando, Jul. A pair defending a nest against *M. cinnamomeiventris* near Péwa, Jun.

366.   HIRUNDO DAURICA   R(B), AfM/(B)

Red-rumped Swallow
Hirondelle rousseline

Common resident (*H. d. domicella*) in savanna habitats throughout but especially in the far north, augmented in the wet season by an influx of intra-African migrants, May–Aug. Usually in pairs or small groups of up to 50, but flocks of 100 at Mango, May, and 150 near Landa-Pozanda, Jun.

H. d. disjuncta (= *kumboensis*) collected Aledjo, Jul, where sympatric with *domicella* (De Roo *et al.* 1969, 1971), and Namoundjoga, Jul (De Roo *et al.* 1971).

Breeding. Collecting mud for nests: 2 pairs near Domaine Gravillou, Jul; a pair at Dapaon, Sep. 3 adults in vicinity of 2 damaged nests in concrete culvert under road, 9 km NW of Dapaon, Nov (H&S).

367.   HIRUNDO PREUSSI   AfM/B

Preuss's Cliff Swallow
Hirondelle de Preuss

Common intra-African migrant to all savanna areas, but more abundant in north.

Movements unclear but probably retreats south in dry season (no records Aug–Dec) and returns Jan, when seen Badou area, Dapaon, Kara and Notsé. Flocks of 50–100 regular between Kandé and Mango, Feb–May.

Breeding. Nests in a colony are closely packed, retort-shaped, and usually placed under bridges (Cheke 1982b); widespread. 62 fresh nests, 3 at least with well-grown and hungry juveniles, under a bridge at Tététou, Mar–Apr 1987 (Walsh *et al.* 1990); bridge completed in 1981. Nesting activity also noted Notsé, Feb–Apr; young being fed there, Jun. Other active sites: Titira, Jun (Cheke 1982b); Domaine Gravillou, Jan and May–Jul. Douaud (1955) noted nesting along Mono R., Jan.

368.   HIRUNDO FULIGULA   RB

Rock Martin
Hirondelle isabelline

Locally not uncommon resident (*H. f. bansoensis*) of rocky, hilly areas in the savanna, e.g. the Aledjo and Bafilo ridges and Mt Djamdé. At least 10 pairs present on the Gambaga escarpment near Nano, Aug 1989. Collected Bismarckburg (Reichenow 1891a).

Breeding. Probably double brooded. A pair feeding 3 small young in a nest at Péwa, Oct 1986 (Walsh *et al.* 1990). Nest building: a pair at Péwa, Jul 1989; a pair at the Faille d'Aledjo rocks, through which the main road has been excavated, Aug–Sep 1984 (Cheke *et al.* 1986). An adult emerged from a nest there, Jul 1989 and Oct 1987 (Walsh *et al.* 1990). 3 fresh nests under road bridge at Binako, Jul 1986, one of which occupied by adult (Walsh *et al.* 1990), and a pair attending a nest there, Jun 1989.

369.   HIRUNDO SMITHII   RB

Wire-tailed Swallow
Hirondelle à longs brins

Common resident (*H. s. smithii*) occurring in low numbers in riverine habitats and at dammed lakes in Guinea Savanna from about 6°50'N north to Mango. Maximum count: 12 roosting together (15 cm apart) on a rocky ledge at Landa Pozanda, 1 Jul 1983.

Breeding. Extended and may have two breeding seasons per annum. Data from Landa-Pozanda show that the species is double-brooded, as it is in India (Whistler 1949). Breeding data for Landa-Pozanda, by year, as follows: 1981, 3Y in nest and another with young, Oct (Cheke 1982b); 1984, bred successfully, Sep; 1987, nests with C/3 and 3Y, 25 Jan, – the 3Y were reared successfully from their nest in which there was a C/3, 11 Apr, and a dead half-grown chick, 26 Apr, a third nest with 3Y also present, 26 Apr; 1988, 2Y, 15–22 Mar, in nest which had C/1 on 2 Apr; 1990, C/2, 15 Mar, 2Y in same nest, 31 Mar. Other data: 3 nestlings and a fourth fledgling at Mo, May (Cheke & Walsh 1980); nesting activity Kpaya, Feb and Aug 1986 and again in Feb 1987; nest-building, Sara-Kawa, Feb, Kpayando, Mar, Titira, Oct.

370.   HIRUNDO NIGRITA   R(B)

White-throated Blue Swallow
Hirondelle noire

Rare resident of forest and gallery forest, only one certain record: one Djodji, 15 Oct 1985. Brunel (1958) collected a pair beside the Mono R. in Benin where the river forms the border with Togo. The site may have been Ounkémé-Monoto, as it was stated as being in the Parawé (= Aplahoué) region. E. Baumann also collected one at Akroso in Nov (Reichenow 1897; 1902a), but this is in Ghana.

371.   HIRUNDO LEUCOSOMA   AfM?/(B)

Pied-winged Swallow
Hirondelle à ailes tachetés

Uncommon visitor, presumed to be intra-African migrant but status uncertain. All records fall within Feb–Apr or Jul–Sep. Records for Feb–Apr are: at least 5 at Mare aux Lions in the Keran Park, Feb 1987; one collected Bismarckburg, Mar (Reichenow 1891a; 1902a); singles at Bafilo and Kara, Mar 1987; 6 at Péwa, Mar 1988; one Kpayando, 17 Apr 1988. Wet season records are: one collected Gridji (= Glidji near Anécho), Jul (Reichenow 1897; 1902a); one collected Nuatja (= Notsé), Jul, and another at Binaparba, Aug (De Roo *et al.* 1969); 6 at Kpayando, Jul; 2 near Bafilo, Aug (Cheke *et al.* 1986); one near Mango, Aug; 3 at Naboulgou, Sep.

Breeding. No records. Breeds during the wet season in Ghana (Grimes 1987).

372.   HIRUNDO AETHIOPICA   AfM/NB, ?R(B)

Ethiopian Swallow
Hirondelle d'Ethiopie

Rare dry season visitor (*H. a aethiopica*), Nov–Apr, but status uncertain owing to paucity of records: adult and 3 immatures collected Kolékopé (= Kolokopé), Mar 1970 (Louette 1975); 30 Fazao, 22 Nov 1981 (Cheke 1982b); 5 on the coast near the Benin border, 30 Dec 1989 and 2 at Tabligbo, on the same day; several north of Anécho, Apr 1989 (JBT). Togolese birds may be migrants from Ghana and/or Benin and Nigeria. Some populations are resident and breed during the wet season in parts of Ghana but numbers increase there during the rains (Grimes 1987). Recorded breeding in Benin at Pobé, Aug (Brunel 1958). Also breeds during the wet season in Nigeria, but populations in the southeast of that country are only present Feb–Nov (Elgood *et al.* 1994).

373.   HIRUNDO LUCIDA   RB, AfM?/(B)

Red-chested Swallow
Hirondelle à gorge rousse

Common resident (*H. l. lucida*) throughout, especially in towns and villages, but most abundant in northern savannas. May be migratory after wet season breeding as few records, Sep–Dec, and most flocks (20–50 or more birds) are seen Jan–Apr.

Breeding. Almost certainly has 2 broods a year and possibly 2 breeding seasons. This supposition supported by local information and the following nesting activities at a site at Blitta: occupied nest, Mar 1987, where young were said to have been reared the previous Dec (Walsh *et al.* 1990); no activity Jan–Feb; nest being entered by one of 3 adults present, Apr 1988; 2 young (about 10 days old) being fed, 20 Jun 1989; 2 nests being attended, with one bird incubating or brooding, 27 Jul 1989; nest with 3 young about to fledge and another with one half-grown young, 20 Aug 1989; 4 nests with attendant adults, 23 Jun 1990. Dependent young Fazao, Jul (Cheke 1982b). Fledgling Kara, Aug. Recently fledged juveniles Naboulgou, May, and prospecting a nest site there, Apr.

374.   HIRUNDO RUSTICA   PM

Barn Swallow
Hirondelle de cheminée

Common Palaearctic migrant (*H. r. rustica*) with passage and wintering birds recorded throughout, late Aug to mid May, but majority of over-wintering birds found in the south especially in the hills and along the coast. Peak of autumn passage, Oct to end Nov (Douaud 1957). Concentrations of presumed migrants mostly in the highlands

Plate 1.   Sudan savanna on rocky pavement near Namoundjoga, 8 April 1990.
(R. A. Cheke)

Plate 2.   Sudan savanna near Mandouri, 9 April 1988. (R. A. Cheke)

Plate 3. Aerial view of the Gambaga escarpment and cultivated land near Nano, 8 August 1989. (R. A. Cheke)

Plate 4. The Gambaga escarpment at Fosse aux Lions, 7 April 1990. (R. A. Cheke)

Plate 5.　Cultivated land at Sawaga, 9 April 1988. (R. A. Cheke)

Plate 6.　The Oti valley in flood, September 1988. (J. F. Walsh)

Plate 7.   Northern Guinea Savanna in the Keran Park at the height of the wet season, 30 August 1984. (R. A. Cheke)

Plate 8.   An elephant *Loxodonta africana* in Northern Guinea Savanna near Naboulgou, Keran Park, at the height of the dry season, 15 February 1987. (R. A. Cheke)

Plate 9.   The Sirka forest reserve near Kara, 26 May 1979; yam plantations are in the foreground. (R. A. Cheke)

Plate 10.   Flooded iron pan near Ketao, 18 August 1989; nesting ground of African Wattled Lapwing *Vanellus senegallus*. (R. A. Cheke)

Plate 11. Aerial view of the Kara R. valley and cultivated areas east of Kara, 27 June 1979. (R. A. Cheke)

Plate 12. Aerial view of intensively cultivated land with scattered trees and *Borassus* palms near Kara, 10 May 1979. (R. A. Cheke)

Plate 13. The Bafilo ridge viewed from the south, 30 October 1981. (R. A. Cheke)

Plate 14. A crag at Péwa, 25 March 1988; the habitat of Freckled Nightjar *Caprimulgus tristigma* and Mocking Cliff-Chat *Myrmecocichla cinnamomeiventris*. (R. A. Cheke)

Plate 15. Woodland near Péwa with *Euphorbia* spp. in the foreground, 8 February 1987. (R. A. Cheke)

Plate 16. Aerial view of the Aledjo forest, 14 July 1989. (R. A. Cheke)

Plate 17. Guinea savanna woodland and storm near Alehéridé, 31 May 1980.
(R. A. Cheke)

Plate 18. Aerial view of the Anié forest reserve near Fazao, 26 April 1989.
(J. F. Walsh)

Plate 19. Aerial view of the Kpaza R. valley with the Fazao mountains in the background, 27 June 1989. (R. A. Cheke)

Plate 20. Aerial view of mountain ridges near Fazao with their characteristic grassland and low density tree cover, and the thick gallery forest in the valleys, 13 July 1979. (R. A. Cheke)

Plate 21. Gallery forest and Koué R. in the Fazao-Malfakassa faunal reserve, 13 June 1980. (R. A. Cheke)

Plate 22. Guinea savanna woodland in the Fazao-Malfakassa faunal reserve, 13 July 1980. (R. A. Cheke)

Plate 23. The Boulo waterfall on the western escarpment of the Fazao mountains, northwest of Fazao, 24 September 1981. (R. A. Cheke)

Plate 24. The overgrown site of Bismarckburg, near Katchanké, 20 March 1990.
(J. F. Walsh)

Plate 25. Forest at Misahöhe, May 1989. (J. F. Walsh)

Plate 26. Forest beside the Asawkawkaw R. along the border of Togo and Ghana, 26 May 1980. (R. A. Cheke)

Plate 27. Deforestation in progress near Déguingué, 20 March 1990. (R. A. Cheke)

Plate 28. Deforestation and burning near Amou-Oblo, 22 March 1990. (R. A. Cheke)

Plate 29. The forest on Mt. Tamania with the Amoutchou R. near Idifiou in the foreground, October 1985. (R. A. Cheke)

Plate 30. The Plateau de Danyi, 13 March 1985. (R. A. Cheke)

Plate 31. Hills along the border with Ghana near Yikpa-Dikpé, and close to known sites of Long-billed Pipit *Anthus similis* in Ghana. (J. F. Walsh)

Plate 32. Deforested hillsides near
           Badou, 26 April 1989.
           (J. F. Walsh)

Plate 33. Cultivations on deforested
           slopes near Badou, 26 July
           1989. (R. A. Cheke)

Plate 34. Partially degraded forest near Badou, 26 July 1989. (R. A. Cheke)

Plate 35. Aerial view of gallery forest near Kpéssi on the Mono R. in the wet season, 12 July 1979. (R. A. Cheke)

Plate 36. Aerial view of gallery forest near Tététou along the Mono R. in the dry season, 1 December 1981. (R. A. Cheke)

Plate 37. The foreshore at Lomé with coconut palms and mixed flock of waders, 24 March 1985. (R. A. Cheke)

Plate 38. The harbour at Lomé with flock of waders, 31 March 1985. (R. A. Cheke)

Plate 39. L. Togo, Anécho, 8 March 1985. (R. A. Cheke)

Plate 40. Nestling Yellow-billed Storks *Mycteria ibis*, Mango, January 1988. (J. F. Walsh)

Plate 41. Smaller Banded Snake Eagle *Circaetus cinerascens*, Domaine Gravillou, 4 March 1990. (R. A. Cheke)

Plate 42. Male Plain Nightjar *Caprimulgus inornatus* near Tinkiro, 20 March 1990. (R. A. Cheke)

Plate 43. Long-tailed Nightjar *Caprimulgus climacurus* near Landa-Pozanda, 22 July 1989. (R. A. Cheke)

Plate 44. Male Standard-winged Nightjar *Macrodipteryx longipennis* near Landa-Pozanda, 10 March 1990. (R. A. Cheke)

Plate 45. Female Standard-winged Nightjar *Macrodipteryx longipennis* near Landa-Pozanda, 8 March 1990. (R. A. Cheke)

Plate 46. Jacana *Actophilornis africana*, Domaine Gravillou, 2 July 1989. (R. A. Cheke)

Plate 47. Crowned Cranes *Balearica pavonina* in the Oti R. valley, near Mango, 2 February 1987. (J. F. Walsh)

Plate 48. Great Snipe *Gallinago media*, Domaine Gravillou, 7 April 1990. (R. A. Cheke)

Plate 49. Denham's Bustard *Neotis denhami* near Mango in the Keran Park, 18 March 1990. (R. A. Cheke)

Plate 50. Black Coucal *Centropus grillii*, Domaine Gravillou, 1 July 1989.
(R. A. Cheke)

Plate 51. Carmine Bee-eater *Merops nubicus*, Domaine Gravillou, 7 April 1990.
(R. A. Cheke)

Plate 52. Red-throated Pipit *Anthus cervinus*, Domaine Gravillou, 7 April 1990. (R. A. Cheke)

Plate 53. Yellow-crowned Bishop *Euplectes afer*, Domaine Gravillou, August 1989. (J. F. Walsh)

and sometimes in forested areas, e.g. more than 1000 over Plateau de Danyi, 13 Mar 1985, which consisted of a flock of 500 at Dzobégan, and 5 other flocks of 100+ (Cheke *et al.* 1986). Other records of flocks of 100 or more are: Anié, Mar; Badou, Apr; Dadja, Mar; Djodji, Mar and Oct; Idifiou, Oct; Ounabé, Apr; Okpahoué, Feb.

Birds ringed in France (3) and Switzerland (1) recovered in southern Togo (Anon 1956; Douaud 1957).

375.   DELICHON URBICA   PM

Common House Martin
Hirondelle de fenêtre

Common Palaearctic visitor and passage migrant (*D. u. urbica*), mid Oct to mid May. Wintering populations prefer Southern Guinea Savanna, the mountains of the Plateaux Region and forested zones, e.g. Badou, and occur in small groups and flocks of up to 200–300, e.g. at Ayengré, where birds are regularly seen, Dec–Feb, and often drink at the lake. Occasional records of flocks of up to 50 in Northern Guinea Savanna, Dec–Jan. Passage migrants in both the autumn and spring may be encountered anywhere with flocks of up to 1000, e.g. Ayengré, 29 Mar 1988, but usually in groups of 50–100. Autumn arrivals first noted 16 Oct (2 at Djodji). The return passage northwards, mostly in late Mar, is sometimes spectacular with birds often accompanied by Swifts (*A. apus* and *T. melba*) and Swallows (*H. rustica*). Latest date 27 May (3 at Kpessidé).

The importance of Togo for wintering House Martins was established by Douaud (1956a), who saw many in the savannas in the centre of the country between Kambolé and Atakpamé during Dec 1955. He noted the birds' association with bush fires, where they were described as locally abundant, and that they sometimes flew 100 m high, thereby eluding observers. In his later paper, he also mentioned flocks of 2–3 hundred in mountainous valleys, 7 Apr 1956 (Douaud 1956b).

MOTACILLIDAE

376.   MOTACILLA FLAVA   PM

Yellow Wagtail
Bergeronnette printanière

Common and locally abundant Palaearctic migrant occurring throughout all savanna zones, Sep–May. Especially common along the coast (Douaud 1957); more than 100 along Sio R. near Lomé, 20 Feb 1990. Most birds are *M. f. flava* (Douaud 1957), confirmed by subsequent observations and specimens from Ebéva, Oct, and Lomé, Dec (De Roo *et al.* 1972). Other races have been reported at the coast (Douaud 1957): 3 yellow-headed birds, Feb and Apr, were assigned to *M. f. flavissima* but, as assumed by Cramp (1988), they were probably *M. f. lutea*; *M. f. thunbergi*, Jan and Feb; 4 probable *thunbergi*, but *cinereocapilla* was not ruled out, 1 May. One *thunbergi* amongst 22 birds at Lomé, 1 Nov 1985 and 4 there, 15 Apr 1988.

A bird ringed in Sweden recovered near Kpalimé, Jan, and an Italian ringed bird recovered Lomé, Oct.

377.   MOTACILLA ALBA   PM

White Wagtail
Bergeronnette grise

Rare Palaearctic migrant (*M. a. ?alba*). One at Oti Toutionga, 10 Jan 1987 (Walsh *et al.* 1990) and another at Bassar, Sep 1991 (PMC).

378.   MOTACILLA AGUIMP   RB
African Pied Wagtail
Bergeronnette pie

Locally abundant resident (*M. a. vidua*) in forest areas, towns and along riversides throughout the Plateaux region. Also occurs commonly in towns and beside rivers in savanna zones from Kara south to the coast. Rare north of Kara but collected Mango, date unknown (Reichenow 1902a).

Breeding. Almost certainly nested on the roof of the Kara Hotel, Kara, where carrying food, Jun 1983 (Cheke & Walsh 1984) and Jul 1980 (Cheke 1982b). Also carrying food Pele Ele, Mar. Copulation at Kpalimé, Feb. Many juveniles present at Badou, Jul (Cheke & Walsh 1984).

379.   ANTHUS CAMPESTRIS   PM
Tawny Pipit
Pipit rousseline

Rare Palaearctic migrant (*A. c. campestris*) to northern savannas. One at Mango, 22 Feb 1986, and 2 at Sara-Kawa, 14 Feb 1988 (Walsh *et al.* 1990).

[ANTHUS SIMILIS
Long-billed Pipit
Pipit à long bec

No confirmed records of this species in Togo, but it occurs in Ghana, where it frequents grassy, rocky hills devoid of trees. Taylor & Macdonald (1979) saw it only 10 km west of the border and it has subsequently been seen at 3 sites within 1 km of Togo (JFW unpub.). It probably occurs in Togo, and likely sites include hills on the Danyi Plateau, e.g. near Yikpa-Dikpé.]

380.   ANTHUS LEUCOPHRYS   R(B)
Plain-backed Pipit
Pipit à dos roux

Not uncommon resident (*A. l. zenkeri*) of savannas throughout, including the coast; usually singles or pairs. A pair near Tinkiro, Feb, had characters of *A. l. gouldii*.

381.   ANTHUS TRIVIALIS   PM
Tree Pipit
Pipit des arbres

Common Palaearctic migrant (*A. t. trivialis*), Oct–Apr, mostly to northern savannas. Occasional in forest clearings in the south, e.g. Amou-Oblo, Feb, Djodji, Mar, Evou, Feb (De Roo 1970) and Kpalimé, Mar.

382.   ANTHUS CERVINUS   PM
Red-throated Pipit
Pipit à gorge rousse

Uncommon Palaearctic migrant to savanna habitats, Nov–Apr. Has been recorded in coastal areas, Jan–Apr (Browne 1980), near Kpalimé, Mar, and 2 at Ayengré, Mar, but mostly recorded north of the Bafilo ridge. Regular Domaine Gravillou, where maximum 10, Dec (Walsh *et al.* 1990).

383.   MACRONYX CROCEUS   RB

Yellow-throated Longclaw
Sentinelle à gorge jaune

Common resident of grassland in savanna areas throughout, usually seen in
pairs.
   Breeding. Nest with 3 blind but well-quilled young Landa-Pozanda, 17 Aug 1986
(Walsh *et al.* 1990). Carrying nesting material Kara, Jul (Walsh *et al.* 1990). Display
flights Kara, Aug (Walsh *et al.* 1990), and Sara-Kawa, Aug.

CAMPEPHAGIDAE

384.   CAMPEPHAGA PHOENICEA   Afm/(B), AfM?/(B)

Red-shouldered Cuckoo-Shrike
Echenilleur à épaulettes rouges

Not uncommon wet season migrant, mid Mar to Sep, to well-wooded savanna and
gallery forest, north to Barkoissi; most retreat to forest for dry season but a few
occasionally remain in north, e.g. Kara, Dec. Usually seen in pairs or singly. One at
Lomé, Sep (JBT). A male with yellow shoulder patches, presumably a rare morph
(Keith *et al.* 1992 refer to some birds having entirely orange or orange-yellow patches)
Déguingué, 20 Mar 1990.

385.   CAMPEPHAGA QUISCALINA   R(B)

Purple-throated Cuckoo-Shrike
Echenilleur pourpré

Uncommon forest resident (*C. q. quiscalina*). Collected Bismarckburg by
R. Büttner, Mar (Reichenow 1891a), and Ahoué-houé, 17 Jul 1968 (De Roo
et al. 1969). Sight records: Badou, 25 Mar 1990 and Jun 1990 (JBT); Misahöhe,
29 Apr 1990.

386.   CORACINA PECTORALIS   R(B)

White-breasted Cuckoo-Shrike
Echenilleur à gorge blanche

Not uncommon resident preferring well-wooded Guinea Savanna. Regular in
gallery forest near Landa-Pozanda. Also recorded Aledjo (De Roo *et al.* 1969), Fazao
(De Roo *et al.* 1971; HL), Keran Park (Minster Agriculture Limited 1984), Kirikri
(Reichenow 1902a), Mo (Cheke 1982b), Paio (De Roo *et al.* 1969) and Sokodé
(Reichenow 1902a).
   Breeding. 2 males in territorial disputes and chasing female Landa-Pozanda, Oct
(Cheke 1982b).

387.   CORACINA AZUREA   R(B)

Blue Cuckoo-Shrike
Echenilleur bleu

Rare forest resident. Only confirmed record is a male collected Klouto, 3 Jun 1950
(Dekeyser 1951).

PYCNONOTIDAE

[ANDROPADUS MONTANUS

Cameroon Montane Greenbul
Bulbul concolore

Dekeyser (1951) listed a specimen, collected by A. Villiers at Klouto, 4 Jun 1950, as *A. montanus* (IFAN Museum no. 50.7.348). This was thought to be a misidentification by Collar & Stuart (1985) and by Grimes (1987). Support for these views comes from the published measurements of the wing (86 mm) and the bill (15 mm), which are both outside the ranges of 73–84 and 16.5–18.5, respectively, quoted for *montanus* by Keith *et al.* (1992). In addition, B. Treca (pers. comm.) has examined the skin and has confirmed that it is not *A. montanus* (already questioned by an anonymous writer on the label), but could not be sure of its identity. The nearest confirmed records of *A. montanus* are in south-east Nigeria on the Obudo Plateau and Mt. Gangirwal (Keith *et al.* 1992).]

388.   ANDROPADUS VIRENS   R(B)

Little Greenbul
Bulbul verdâtre

Common and widespread resident (*A. v. erythropterus*) of forest and forest edges. Collected Adina, Agadji, Ahoué-houé, Apéyémé, Atakpamé, Azafi, Ebéva, Ezimé, Evou, Kamina, Koutoukpa, Idifiou, Misahöhe, Odjolo, Ounabé, Tchonou and Tététou (Reichenow 1897; De Roo 1970; De Roo *et al.* 1969, 1971, 1972). Other records from Ayagba, Bismarckburg (Douaud 1956b), Idifiou, near Lomé (Millet-Horsin 1923) and Misahöhe (Cheke *et al.* 1986; JBT).

389.   ANDROPADUS GRACILIS   R(B)

Little Grey Greenbul
Bulbul gracile

Not uncommon resident (*A. g. extremus*) of forest and forest edge. Collected Ounabé (De Roo 1970) and Misahöhe (De Roo *et al.* 1972). One at Idifiou, 23 Mar 1990.

390.   ANDROPADUS ANSORGEI

Ansorge's Greenbul
Bulbul d'Ansorge

Rare forest resident (*A. a. ansorgei*). One Idifiou, 28 Feb 1987. Probably overlooked as said to be commoner than *A. gracilis* at Cape Coast in Ghana (Grimes 1987).

391.   ANDROPADUS CURVIROSTRIS   R(B)

Plain Greenbul
Bulbul curvirostre

Not uncommon forest resident (*A. c. curvirostris*). Specimens collected at Avétonou, Dec, Ebéva, Oct and Nov, Koutoukpa, Dec, Misahöhe, Aug, Odjolo, Feb, and Ounabé, Oct and Nov (De Roo 1970; De Roo *et al.* 1971, 1972). Sight records Balla and Klouto, Apr 1990.

392.   ANDROPADUS GRACILIROSTRIS   R(B)

Slender-billed Greenbul
Bulbul à bec grêle

Not uncommon resident (*A. g. gracilirostris*) of forest and forest clearings.
Collected Koussountou (Reichenow 1897) and Misahöhe (Reichenow 1894c;
De Roo *et al.* 1971, 1972). Recent sight records from Agbenohoué, Misahöhe,
Okpahoué and Wobé.

393.   ANDROPADUS LATIROSTRIS   R(B)

Yellow-whiskered Greenbul
Bulbul à moustaches jaunes

Common resident of forest (*A. l. congener*) and forest edges. Specimens from
Klouto (Dekeyser 1951), Ahoué-houé, Apéyémé, Dzobégan, Ebéva, Misahöhe,
Ounabé and Tomegbé (De Roo 1970; De Roo *et al.* 1969, 1971, 1972). Recent
records (1989–90) from Agbossomou Kopé, Badou, Balla, Djodji and Misahöhe.
Type of *congener* collected Agomé Tongwe, Ghana, near the border with Togo
(Reichenow 1897, 1902a).

394.   CALYPTOCICHLA SERINA   R(B)

Golden Greenbul
Bulbul doré

Rare forest resident, only one record: one near Badou, 25 Mar 1990.

395.   BAEOPOGON INDICATOR   R(B)

Honeyguide Greenbul
Bulbul à queue blanche

Not uncommon resident (*B. i. leucurus*) of mature forest and forest edge. Collected
Apéyémé (De Roo *et al.* 1972) and Misahöhe (Reichenow 1897; De Roo *et al.*
1971). Also collected Agomé Tongwe, Ghana, close to the border with Togo
(Reichenow 1897; specimen used as type for *Phyllastrephus indicator togoensis*
described by Reichenow 1917). Sight records: 3 at Agbossomou Kopé, Mar;
Idifiou, Mar; Katchanké, Jul (Douaud 1956b); Misahöhe, Feb, Apr and Oct
(Cheke *et al.* 1986); Yegué, Mar.

396.   CHLOROCICHLA SIMPLEX   R(B)

Simple Greenbul
Bulbul modeste

Common resident of forest, forest edges and thickets in forest zones and well
wooded savanna in the south. Collected by E. Baumann at Kuma Ga (Reichenow
1897), but this site has not been located: it may refer to Kouma but it could also be
a village in present-day Ghana. Other specimens from Adina, Ebéva, Evou,
Koutoukpa, Porto Séguro, Tététou and Togoville (De Roo 1970; De Roo *et al.*
1969, 1971, 1972). Millet-Horsin (1923) considered the species common in savanna
thickets around L. Togo and in fig trees, the fruits of which it ate in addition to
insects. Other records from Adosso, Agbo Kopé, Anonoe, Djodji (Cheke *et al.*
1986), Misahöhe (JBT) and Wobé.

397.   CHLOROCICHLA FLAVICOLLIS   R(B)

Yellow-throated Leaf-love
Bulbul à gorge claire

Common and widespread resident (*C. f. flavicollis*) of Guinea Savanna, often found
in small parties in thickets beside rivers. Also noted Misahöhe and at Lomé on the
coast (Browne 1980). Collected Aledjo, Aug (De Roo *et al.* 1969), Binaparba, Aug
(De Roo *et al.* 1969), Bismarckburg, May (Reichenow 1892), and Nanergou, Aug
(De Roo *et al.* 1969).

398.   THESCELOCICHLA LEUCOPLEURA   R(B)

Swamp Palm Bulbul
Bulbul des raphias

Not uncommon resident, preferring riversides, thickets and swamps in the forest zone
and well wooded savanna. Recorded Agbossomou Kopé, Badou, Bethel, Djodji (Cheke
et al. 1986), Fazao and Kati. Gregarious and noisy: usually encountered in groups of
4–10.

399.   PYRRHURUS SCANDENS   R(B)

Leaf-love
Bulbul à queue rousse

Not uncommon resident (*P. s. scandens*) of forest, including the forest reserve at Aledjo;
no records further north.
   Breeding. Building Aledjo, Mar (Walsh *et al.* 1990).

400.   PHYLLASTREPHUS BAUMANNI   R(B)

Baumann's Greenbul
Bulbul de Baumann

Uncommon forest resident, but status uncertain as probably overlooked. Reichenow
(1895) described the species as *Phyllostrephus baumanni* from a male collected by Ernst
Baumann at Misahöhe, 13 Feb 1895 (Reichenow 1897). The only other records are of
specimens obtained at Ahoué-houé, Jul (De Roo *et al.* 1969), Misahöhe, Dec (De Roo
et al. 1972) and Ounabé, Oct–Nov (De Roo 1970). Allport (1991) has proposed that
the species should be added to the near-threatened category.

401.   PHYLLASTREPHUS ICTERINUS   R(B)

Icterine Greenbul
Bulbul ictérin

Uncommon forest resident, only one record: one sighted Déguingué, 20 Mar 1990.

402.   PHYLLASTREPHUS ALBIGULARIS   R(B)

White-throated Greenbul
Bulbul à gorge blanche

Uncommon forest resident (*P. a. albigularis*). Collected by R. Büttner at Bismarckburg,
Apr (Reichenow 1891a), and Misahöhe, Dec (De Roo *et al.* 1972); one bird seen
Misahöhe, 23 Mar 1990.

403.   BLEDA CANICAPILLA   R(B)

Grey-headed Bristlebill
Bulbul fourmilier

Not uncommon resident (*B. c. canicapilla*) of forest. Collected Abala (? = Abalakopé
or Balla) (Reichenow 1897), Bismarckburg (Reichenow 1893), Misahöhe (De Roo
et al. 1971, 1972) and Odjolo (De Roo 1970). Recent sightings (all singles): Misahöhe,
Dec (JBT) and Mar–Apr, and Kpalimé, date unknown (TC).

404.   CRINIGER BARBATUS   R(B)

Western Bearded Greenbul
Bulbul crinon occidental

Rare forest resident (*C. b. barbatus*), known only from a male collected by E. Baumann
at Misahöhe, 21 Nov 1893 (Reichenow 1897). Baumann also collected another male
at Konfokrum, 20 Nov 1894, but this locality is probably in Ghana where there are 2
Komfokroms (one at 7°31'N, 01°14'W, the other at 7°57'N, 01°15'W).

405.   CRINIGER CALURUS   R(B)

Red-tailed Greenbul
Bulbul à barbe blanche

Not uncommon forest resident (*C. c. verreauxi*). Females collected Misahöhe, 12 Dec
1894 (Reichenow 1897), and Tohoun, 23 May 1950 (Dekeyser 1951). Recent records:
Agbenohoué, 26 Jul 1989; Agbossomou Kopé, 20 Mar 1990; Balla, Apr 1990 (JBT);
Dzobégan, 12 May 1988.

406.   PYCNONOTUS BARBATUS   RB

Common Bulbul
Bulbul commun

Abundant resident (*P. b. inornatus*), found throughout except in dense forest.
Dekeyser (1951) identified 3 specimens from Klouto and one from Aledjo,
collected Jun 1950, as *P. b. arsinoë* which occurs in Chad, Egypt and Sudan (Keith
et al. 1992). However, all 94 of the series collected by De Roo's collaborators were
ascribed to *inornatus* (De Roo 1970; De Roo *et al.* 1969, 1971, 1972). Often imitates
calls of Paradise-Flycatchers *Terpsiphone viridis* (Douaud 1956b).

Breeding. Dependent young: Lomé, Aug–Sep (JBT). Displaying birds: Lomé,
Jan (Walsh *et al.* 1990). Nest-building: Aledjo, Apr; Badou, Feb (Walsh *et al.* 1990);
Fosse aux Lions, Jul; (with leaf) Kara, Mar; (with grass stem) Kpayando, Mar;
(with cobwebs) Landa-Pozanda, Mar; Misahöhe, Apr (Walsh *et al.* 1990). Carrying
food: Kewa, Jun; Sokodé, Jul.

TURDIDAE

407.   STIPHRORNIS ERYTHROTHORAX   R(B)

Forest Robin
Rougegorge de forêt

Status uncertain but probably uncommon resident of forest. Collected Bismarckburg,
date unknown (Reichenow 1891a), and Misahöhe, 27 Feb 1895 (Reichenow 1897).

408.   LUSCINIA MEGARHYNCHOS   PM

Nightingale
Rossignol philomèle

Common Palaearctic migrant (*L. m. megarhynchos*), overwintering in southern forest-savanna mosaic, forest edge, and thickets in savanna from L. Togo north to Anié, Oct–Apr. Passage birds noted as late as early Jun. Reichenow (1897, 1902a) documented specimens from Misahöhe, Feb, Podji, Dec, and Porto Séguro, Mar. The Belgian collections in the MRAC include specimens from Adina, Nov, Ebéva, Nov, Edifou, Dec, Evou, Feb–Mar, Kodegbé, Nov, Koutoukpa, Dec, Odjolo, Feb, and Ounabé, Oct–Nov (De Roo 1970; De Roo *et al.* 1972). Douaud (1957) described Nightingales as abundant during the dry season with 3 or 4 birds singing in the same coppice, only 10 m apart from each other. Also recorded Lomé, Feb–Mar (Browne 1980), Idifiou, Mar, and Djamdé, 5 Jun 1983 (Cheke & Walsh 1984).

409.   LUSCINIA SVECICA   PM

Bluethroat
Gorgebleue à miroir

Rare Palaearctic migrant (subspecies unknown). One in a *Mimosa pigra* thicket at Tantigou, 12 Jan 1990.

410.   COSSYPHA CYANOCAMPTER   R(B)

Blue-shouldered Robin-Chat
Cossyphe à ailes bleues

Rare forest resident (*C. c. cyanocampter*), known only from specimen collected at Misahöhe, 9 Aug 1969 (De Roo *et al.* 1971).

411.   COSSYPHA NIVEICAPILLA   R(B)

Snowy-crowned Robin-Chat
Petit Cossyphe à tête blanche

Common resident (*C. n. niveicapilla*) of thickets, gallery forest and forest throughout. Collected: Bismarckburg and Misahöhe (Reichenow 1902a); Aledjo, Binaparba, Namoundjoga, Paio, Porto Séguro and Togoville (De Roo *et al.* 1969, 1971). Recent records from Fazao (Minster Agricultural Limited 1984), Kara, Keran Park (HL), Kpayando, Landa-Pozanda (Cheke & Walsh 1980), Lomé (Browne 1980), Naboulgou and Péwa.

412.   COSSYPHA ALBICAPILLA   R(B)

White-crowned Robin-Chat
Grand Cossyphe à tête blanche

Not uncommon resident (*C. a. giffardi*) of thick vegetation beside rivers in northern savanna. May also occur near the coast, where noted as rare by Millet-Horsin (1923), but his birds were more likely to have been *C. niveicapilla*. Collected Mango, date unknown (Reichenow 1902a). Recent records from Dapaon (H&S), Kara, Kandé (Cheke & Walsh 1980), Landa-Pozanda and Naboulgou.

413.   ALETHE DIADEMATA   R(B)

Fire-crested Alethe
Alèthe à huppe rousse

Not uncommon forest resident (*A. d. diademata*). Collected (2 females) at Bismarckburg, Apr (Reichenow 1891a), and Misahöhe, Aug (De Roo *et al.* 1971). Recent records of calling birds at Agbo Kopé, 26 Jul 1989, Badou, 25 Mar 1990, and Kamétonou, 23 Nov 1995.

414.   NEOCOSSYPHUS POENSIS   R(B)

White-tailed Ant-Thrush
Grive fourmilière à queue blanche

Rare forest resident, only one record: a bird seen on the ground in dense forest in the Fazao mountains beside the Koué R., 27 Jun 1989.

415.   NEOCOSSYPHUS FINSCHII   R(B)

Finsch's Flycatcher-Thrush
Grive fourmilière de Finsch

Rare forest resident, only one record: a bird at Koniouhou, 19 Jul 1989.

416.   CERCOTRICHAS GALACTOTES   RB

Rufous Scrub-Robin
Agrobate roux

Rare resident of northern savannas (*C. g. minor*), only 2 records: one in thickets beside the Oti R. at Mango, 21 Aug 1984 and reported from Togo by Keith *et al.* (1992). Recorded even further south than Mango, near Bétérou (09°12'N, 02°16'E), in Benin (Claffey 1995).
   Breeding. Egg-laying reported in Togo, May, place unknown (Keith *et al.* 1992).

417.   PHOENICURUS PHOENICURUS   PM

Common Redstart
Rougequeue à front blanc

Uncommon Palaearctic migrant (*P. p. phoenicurus*), Dec–Apr, from Sokodé northwards. Collected Sokodé, date unknown (Reichenow 1902a), and Mango, 15 Dec 1969 (De Roo *et al.* 1972). Subsequent sight records of single males: 45 km south of Dapaon, 22 Feb 1986; Kara, 15 Jan – 24 Feb 1987; Landa-Pozanda, 13 Feb 1988; Sara-Kawa, 14 Feb 1988; Tantigou, 8–9 Apr 1990. A female Naboulgou, 27 Jan 1989.

418.   SAXICOLA RUBETRA   PM

Whinchat
Traquet tarier

Common Palaearctic migrant to open savanna habitats including cultivated land throughout, Sep–May. Earliest record: 2 at Piya, 21 Sep 1988; latest: 8 May (Douaud 1957). An adult male ringed Gabès, Tunisia, recovered You, 5 km south of Blitta, 4 Dec 1956 (Douaud 1957).

419.   OENANTHE OENANTHE   PM

Northern Wheatear
Traquet motteux

Uncommon Palaearctic migrant (*O. o. oenanthe*), Oct–Mar, recorded on the coast and in the north. Only 6 records: a female at Lomé airport, 3–5 Oct 1956 (Douaud 1957); a male near Sara-Kawa, 14 Feb and 19 Mar 1988; a female on Dapaon airstrip, 28 Feb 1988; 2 at Fosse aux Lions, 26 Nov 1988; a female near Koumongou in the Keran Park, 18 Mar 1990 and one at Mango, date unknown (TC).

420.   OENANTHE BOTTAE   R(B), Afm?/(B)

Red-breasted Wheatear
Traquet à poitrine rousse

Rare resident (*O. b. heuglini*) of, or possibly dry season migrant to, Northern Guinea Savanna and Sudan Savanna. 3 on grass-covered hills near Défalé, 7 Dec 1981 (Cheke 1982b) and singles in northern part of the Keran Park, 21 Feb 1988, and at Mandouri, 9 Apr 1988.

421.   CERCOMELA FAMILIARIS   R(B)

Familiar Chat
Traquet de roche à queue rousse

Uncommon resident (*C. f. falkensteini*) on rocky outcrops in savanna from the Bafilo Ridge northwards. Locally common in the Aledjo area where 3 males collected, 9 Jun 1950 (Dekeyser 1951), 11 specimens collected, Jul–Aug, and one, Dec (De Roo *et al.* 1969, 1971, 1972). Also seen in that vicinity, Feb–Mar and Jun–Aug (Cheke 1982b; Cheke & Walsh 1984). Only other known site is the Défalé pass: one on 3 Jul 1983 (Cheke & Walsh 1984); 4 there 3 Apr 1988.

422.   MYRMECOCICHLA ALBIFRONS   R(B)

White-fronted Black Chat
Traquet noir à front blanc

Not uncommon resident (*M. a. frontalis*) of well-wooded Northern Guinea Savanna. Collected Bismarckburg (Reichenow 1891a, 1893) and Binaparba (De Roo *et al.* 1969). Sightings from near Mo and Naboulgou (Cheke *et al.* 1986), Défalé and Ketao.
   Breeding. One of a pair carrying food near Naboulgou, 7 Apr 1990. Possibly bred Ketao, where 2 juveniles seen with adult, 28 Jul 1989. These 2 records are consistent with the bird breeding during the dry season, after fires have burnt the grass (Keith *et al.* 1992).

423.   MYRMECOCICHLA CINNAMOMEIVENTRIS   R(B)

Mocking Cliff-Chat
Traquet de roche à ventre roux

Locally not uncommon resident (*M. c. coronata* and *M. c. ?cavernicola*) restricted to rocky outcrops, inselbergs and hilly areas in northern savanna from the Bafilo ridge northwards. Populations of *M. c. coronata* (identified by presence of white-crowned males) occur alongside black-crowned males (thought to be *M. c. cavernicola*) but the latter, partly because of their sympatry, may be a separate species (Keith *et al.* 1992). Both occur in similar habitat but *cavernicola* is rare.

G. Thierry collected the type of *coronata* at Dapaon (sometimes known as Dapong, and written as Tapong in the description), 11 Aug 1901 (Reichenow 1902a,b). Others have been collected at Aledjo (9 skins) and Namoundjoga (4 skins) (Dekeyser 1951, De Roo *et al.* 1969, 1971) and it is regularly seen at Péwa (where they probably breed) and noted at Défalé, Djamdé (Cheke & Walsh 1984) and on the Gambaga escarpment near Nano. There are only 3 records of black-crowned birds: 2 males with a male *coronata* and 3 unidentified females at Péwa, 18 Jul 1980, (Cheke 1982b); one Défalé, Aug 1989; one Sara-Kawa, Sep 1988.

Breeding. A female (?*coronata*) was observed attacking the base of the nest of a Lesser Striped Swallow *Hirundo abyssinica* (a species whose nest they usurp) near Péwa, 25 Jun 1989. Courtship display by male *coronata* and singing birds near Péwa, 21 Mar 1988. Singing also noted Péwa, but at a different site, Aug (Cheke 1982b).

424.   MONTICOLA SAXATILIS   PM

Mountain Rock-Thrush
Merle de roche

Rare Palaearctic migrant, only 3 records: one collected Mango, date unknown (Reichenow 1902a); a female at Péwa, 1 Mar 1987 (Walsh *et al.* 1990) and one Mango, date unknown (TC).

425.   TURDUS PELIOS   RB

African Thrush
Grive grisâtre

Common resident (*T. p. saturatus*) throughout. Usually seen singly or in pairs.

Breeding. 2 separate nests in Mango trees (*Mangifera indica*) with 2 Y each at Kara, Jul 1989. One nest was exposed by a gardener and attacked by a group of 6 Long-tailed Shrikes (*Corvinella corvina*) which killed one fledgling, the other escaping to be reared by its parents. The other nest still contained 2 Y on 4 Aug. Eggs were described by Reichenow (1897), but their origin was unclear. They were possibly removed from the female collected at Misahöhe, May. Nest-building in a *Borassus* palm at Kara, Jun (Cheke & Walsh 1980). Adult repeatedly seen carrying food (presumably to nestlings) Kara, Jun 1980 and 1983 (Cheke & Walsh 1984).

SYLVIIDAE

426.   MELOCICHLA MENTALIS   R(B)

Moustached Scrub-Warbler
Fauvette à moustaches

Locally common resident (*S. m. mentalis*), preferring rank vegetation beside rivers, streams, marshes and other wet areas. Although occurs near the coast, e.g. Zébé (Millet-Horsin 1923), more common in Guinea Savanna north of 7°N. Recorded from the Atakpamé region, e.g. Nangbeto, and clearings in forest near Badou, e.g. Akloa, north to Mango, where collected by G. Thierry (Reichenow 1902a). Others collected Bismarckburg, Hagu (? = Hago) and Misahöhe (Reichenow 1902a), Adina, Ahoué-houé, Borgou, Dzobégan, Evou, Kamina and Tchonou (De Roo 1970, De Roo *et al.* 1969, 1972).

Breeding. Carrying food Kara, Oct. Nest building: bird taking dead grass stems into reeds beside the Kara R. at Kara, Jun (Cheke 1982b); bird carrying rigid thin stalks

(10–12 cm long) into a *Raphia* palm at Kpaya (not Péwa as stated by Walsh *et al.* 1990), Aug. Sings during the wet season, e.g. Anié and Kpayando, Jun, Katchenké, Jul (Douaud 1956b), Djamdé and Landa-Pozanda, Jul (Cheke & Walsh 1984).

427.   ACROCEPHALUS SCHOENOBAENUS   PM

Sedge Warbler
Phragmite des joncs

Common Palaearctic migrant to swamps, riversides and lakes bordered with vegetation in savanna areas throughout, Nov–Apr (Walsh *et al.* 1990). Usually only 1–4 encountered but at least 30 at Tantigou, Jan. Most records from the northern savanna but also noted Ayengré, Lomé, Sika-Kondji and Tokpli. Latest date: Tantigou, 27 Apr.

428.   ACROCEPHALUS SCIRPACEUS   PM

Eurasian Reed-Warbler
Rousserolle effarvatte

Not uncommon Palaearctic migrant (*A. s. scirpaceus*), Oct–Mar, to a variety of habitats in savanna areas, including watersides, forest edge, farmland, in elephant grass (*Typha* sp.), *Cassia* bushes and *Andropogon* grass (Douaud 1957). Collected Borgou, Dec (De Roo *et al.* 1972), Témedja, Oct, and Odjolo, Feb (De Roo 1970).
    A bird ringed Switzerland recovered Kpalimé, Feb (Douaud 1957), and one ringed Germany recovered Dzedrame, near Klouto, Nov (Reiser 1973).

429.   ACROCEPHALUS ARUNDINACEUS   PM

Great Reed-Warbler
Rousserolle turdoïde

Not uncommon, widespread Palaearctic migrant (*A. a. arundinaceus*), Sep–May, to swampland and grass verges of rivers and lakes. Douaud (1957) heard singing birds from 20 Nov to 27 Mar; some of these were found in dry areas away from water, e.g. cassava fields, others were in habitat beside the Sio R. Collected in the Atakpamé region, Sep and Mar (De Roo 1970), Ebéva, Oct, and Borgou, Dec (De Roo *et al.* 1972). Sight records Lomé, date unknown (Browne 1980), Feb (Robinson 1972), Apr and 1 May.
    In Ghana, birds arriving in the north, Sep–Oct, remain there to moult and then continue south to stay from mid Dec to Mar or Apr in humid zones near or at the coast, with some possibly travelling as far as Zaïre (Hedenström *et al.* 1993).

430.   ACROCEPHALUS RUFESCENS   RB

Greater Swamp-Warbler
Rousserolle des cannes

Locally common resident (*A. r. ?rufescens* or else *senegalensis*, described by Colston & Morel 1985), known only from the Lomé area. Occurs in reedbeds along the coast (Walsh *et al.* 1990) and in swampy areas bordering the Sio R.
    Breeding. Both adults of a pair seen incubating or brooding alternatively on a nest beside the Sio R. at Lomé, 7 Sep 1989 (JBT). The nest contained at least 2 young on 15 Sep, when 2 other nests, contents unknown, were located. Apparent territorial behaviour by 3 or more pairs at the same site, 28 Apr and 1 May 1990.

[ACROCEPHALUS MELANOPOGON

Moustached Warbler
Lusciniole à moustaches

Vagrant (presumably *A. m. melanopogon*). One trapped and photographed near Lomé, sometime between 1962 and 1965 (JRD). This previously unpublished record needs substantiation as all African records away from north Africa, apart from a sighting in southern Libya, have been questioned (Cramp 1992).]

431.   HIPPOLAIS PALLIDA   PM

Olivaceous Warbler
Hypolaïs pâle

Uncommon Palaearctic migrant (*H. p. opaca*) to Sudan Savanna and Northern Guinea Savanna, Nov–Apr. Collected Borgou, 9 Dec (De Roo *et al.* 1972). Earliest record: 2 at Tantigou, 25 Nov; latest record: 2 at Domaine Gravillou, 8 Apr (Walsh *et al.* 1990). Other sightings (all singles): Domaine Gravillou, 8 Jan; Naboulgou, 18 Mar; Tantigou, 12 Jan.

432.   HIPPOLAIS POLYGLOTTA   PM

Melodious Warbler
Hypolaïs polyglotte

Common, widespread Palaearctic migrant, late Oct to May, to savanna and forest edge, e.g. Badou, Deguingué, Djodji, and Idifiou, including the coast (Browne 1980). Sings throughout its stay (Douaud 1957). Collected Misahöhe, Feb and Apr (Reichenow 1902a), Atakpamé, Edifou, Evou, Ezimé, Kamina and Koutoukpa, Nov–Mar (De Roo 1970). Earliest record 31 Oct (Douaud 1957); latest 11 May.

433.   HIPPOLAIS ICTERINA   PM

Icterine Warbler
Hypolaïs ictérine

Rare Palaearctic migrant. Seen Lomé, Mar and Nov (Browne 1980), and Badou, 26 Jan 1987.

434.   CISTICOLA ERYTHROPS   R(B)

Red-faced Cisticola
Cisticole à face rousse

Common, widespread resident (*C. e. erythrops*) of rank grass beside rivers and wetlands. Collected Bismarckburg (Reichenow 1902a), Ahoué-houé, Paio and Port Séguro (De Roo *et al.* 1969), Adina, Atakpamé, Edifou, Evou, Ezimé and Kodegbé (De Roo 1970), Aledjo and Namoundjoga (De Roo *et al.* 1971, 1972).
   Breeding. Carrying food Kara, Aug. Singing Landa-Pozanda, May, and Yégué, Jul (Douaud 1956b).

435.   CISTICOLA CANTANS   RB

Singing Cisticola
Cisticole chanteuse

Common, widespread resident (*C. c. swanzii*) of savanna and forest edges. Collected Misahöhe (Reichenow 1902a), Ahoué-houé, Binaparba, Nanergou, Notsé, Paio and Tchonou (De Roo *et al.* 1969), and Témedja (De Roo 1970).

Breeding. Nest building Kara, Aug (Walsh *et al.* 1990). Carrying food and scolding, as if with dependent young, Péwa, Jun. Carrying food: lower Sio R. near Lomé, May; near Nangbeto, Jun; Kara, Jul (Cheke & Walsh 1980); Ketao, Aug.

436. CISTICOLA LATERALIS   R(B)

Whistling Cisticola
Cisticole siffleuse

Not uncommon resident (*C. l. lateralis*) of Southern Guinea Savanna, encountered in well-wooded bush, often at edges of cultivated land or forest edges. Collected Bismarckburg and Misahöhe (Reichenow 1902a), Azafi (De Roo *et al.* 1969), Adina, Atakpamé, Edifou, Kamina, Kodegbé and Koutoukpa (De Roo 1970), Fazao and Kolokopé (De Roo *et al.*1971).
  Breeding. Singing birds: Aledjo, Jul–Aug; Bafilo, Aug; Pagala, Jul (Douaud 1956b).

437. CISTICOLA ABERRANS   R(B)

Lazy Cisticola
Cisticole des rochers

Locally not uncommon resident (*C. a. petrophila*) restricted to rocky outcrops in Northern Guinea Savanna. Collected Aledjo (Dekeyser 1951, De Roo *et al.* 1969, 1971), where seen regularly since, and at other sites nearby on the Bafilo ridge. Also recorded Defalé and Djamdé (Cheke & Walsh 1980, 1984; Cheke 1982b).
  Breeding. Display and song Defalé, Apr. Singing birds recorded at all known localities, Apr–Aug.

438. CISTICOLA RUFICEPS   R(B)

Red-pate Cisticola
Cisticole à tête rousse

Uncommon resident (*C. r. guinea*) of well-wooded parts of Northern Guinea Savanna. Collected Binarparba (De Roo *et al.* 1969) and Niamtougou (De Roo *et al.* 1971). Recent records from Aledjo, Kara, Ketao, Landa-Pozanda and Tantigou.
  Breeding. Nest-building Ketao, Aug. Display flight Tantigou, Jul.

439. CISTICOLA GALACTOTES   RB

Winding Cisticola
Cisticole roussâtre

Common resident (*C. g. amphilecta*) in all savanna areas, but usually found near water. Collected Niamtougou (De Roo *et al.* 1971).
  Breeding. Parent feeding dependent young (only 1–2 days out of the nest) Lomé, Apr (Walsh *et al.* 1990). Carrying food Kara, Jun (Cheke & Walsh 1980). A pair repeatedly flying with food to a nest, lower Sio R. near Lomé, Sep. Song Kara, Jun–Aug.

440. CISTICOLA NATALENSIS   R(B)

Croaking Cisticola
Cisticole striée

Common resident (*C. n. strangei*) of grassland throughout savanna areas. Collected Abala (? = Abalokopé or Balla) (Reichenow 1902a), Aledjo, Binaparba, Nanergou, Notsé and Tchonou (De Roo *et al.* 1969), Atakpamé, Evou and Kamina (De Roo

1970), Fazao and Kolokopé (De Roo *et al.* 1971). Millet-Horsin (1923) shot one in a marsh near Zébé and Douaud (1956b) also reported the species from the lagoons of the south, the only place (apart from the mountains) where he found them common.

Breeding. Display flight and song Katchenké, Jul (Douaud 1956b), and Domaine Gravillou, Jul. Singing birds: Kara area, Jun–Jul.

441. CISTICOLA BRACHYPTERUS   RB
Shortwing Cisticola
Cisticole à ailes courtes

Common resident (*C. b. brachypterus*) of Guinea and Sudan Savanna throughout. Collected Aledjo, Binaparba, Dapaon, Ebéva, Evou, Kamina, Kolokopé, Mango, Namoundjoga, Nanergou, Niamtougou, Notsé, Paio, Sokodé, Tchonou, Témedja and Tététou (De Roo 1970; De Roo *et al.* 1969, 1971, 1972).

Breeding. Bird with faecal pellet (flushed, presumably from a nest) Kpayando, Aug (Cheke *et al.* 1986). Singing birds: Kara, Jun–Jul (Cheke & Walsh 1984), Katchenké, Jul (Douaud 1956b).

442. CISTICOLA RUFUS   R(B)
Rufous Cisticola
Cisticole rousse

Not uncommon resident in savanna areas in the north, but also collected Misahöhe (Reichenow 1897, 1902a). All recent records either in Northern Guinea Savanna, e.g. Kara area (Walsh *et al.* 1990) and Mango, or Sudan Savanna, e.g. Tantigou. An exceptional sighting was a flock of 16 in low scrub, beside a dry rice stubble field, Kara, 29 Jan 1989.

443. CISTICOLA JUNCIDIS   R(B)
Zitting Cisticola
Cisticole des joncs

Common resident (presumably *C. j. uropygialis* but no specimens) throughout savanna zone and in coastal areas. Prefers open grassland, degraded areas or farmland, often in dry habitats.

Breeding. Song flight Kara, Jun and Oct, and Tantigou, Apr. Intense territorial behaviour Lomé shore, Apr and Sep.

444. CISTICOLA EXIMIUS   R(B)
Black-backed Cisticola
Cisticole à dos noir

Uncommon resident (*C. e. occidens*) of open grassland areas within the Guinea Savanna zone. Collected Mango, Aug (De Roo *et al.* 1969).

Breeding. Song flight and display Kara, Jul (Cheke & Walsh 1980), and Domaine Gravillou, Jun.

445. PRINIA SUBFLAVA   RB
Tawny-flanked Prinia
Prinia commune

Abundant resident (*P. s. melanorhyncha*) of degraded forest and savanna throughout. In Ghana *P. s. subflava* occurs in the north of the country and *melanorhyncha* in the south (Grimes 1987). Although the nominate race *subflava* may also occur in Togo, all specimens (c. 25) listed by De Roo (1970) and De Roo *et al.* (1969, 1971, 1972), which were collected at sites ranging from the coast to as far north as Borgou, were ascribed to *melanorhyncha*.

Breeding. C/3 Kara, Jul (SAS). Carrying food Kara, Jul (Cheke & Walsh 1980). Song Atakpamé, Jun.

446.   PRINIA ERYTHROPTERA   R(B)

Red-winged Prinia
Fauvette à ailes rousses

Common resident (*P. e. erythroptera*) of savanna and forest edge throughout, preferring degraded areas, thickets and woodland. Collected Bismarckburg and Misahöhe (Reichenow 1891a, 1897), Klouto (Dekeyser 1951), Binaparba and Notsé (De Roo *et al.* 1969), Evou, Kamina and Témedja (De Roo 1970).

Breeding. Song Fazao and Landa-Pozanda, Jul.

447.   APALIS FLAVIDA   AfM?/(B), R?(B)

Yellow-breasted Apalis
Apalis à gorge jaune

Uncommon. Status uncertain but possibly intra-African migrant as few dry season records and no information from the south. Apart from one bird, 3 Jan, records of singles or pairs at Landa-Pozanda all occur from 3 Mar to 4 Nov, suggesting migration from the south (see discussion by Thonnerieux *et al.* 1989). Only 2 records elsewhere: a bird collected Binaparba, Aug (De Roo *et al.* 1969), and one at the Faille d'Aledjo, Jun. These fit the migration pattern suggested by Thonnerieux *et al.* (1989) but Holyoak & Seddon (1990) saw 4 at 9°54'N in Benin at the end of Nov.

448.   APALIS SHARPII   R(B)

Sharpe's Apalis
Apalis de Sharpe

Rare resident of forest, only one record: a female at Agbenohoué, 26 Jul 1989. Listed as a candidate species for treatment as threatened in Appendix G of Collar & Stuart (1985).

449.   CAMAROPTERA BREVICAUDATA   RB

Grey-backed Camaroptera
Camaroptère à tête grise

Common and widespread resident (*C. b. brevicaudata* and *C. b. tincta*) throughout. Occurs at the coast, in forest areas, e.g. Djodji and Misahöhe, and in savanna, reaching the northern border region, e.g. Tantigou. Prefers secondary growth at forest edges, thickets or well-wooded areas in savanna, and found in gardens everywhere. Grimes (1987) ascribed Ghanaian populations to *C. b. tincta*, but specimens collected in a variety of habitats in Togo are *brevicaudata* (Dekeyser 1951; De Roo 1970; De Roo *et al.* 1969, 1971, 1972). *C. b. tincta* has, however, been collected at Kolékopé (Louette 1975) and Porto Séguro (Reichenow 1902a), and both sites are in the south as expected.

Breeding. One dependent young with adult at Badou, Oct. Adult carrying nesting material Moretan, Jul.

450.   CAMAROPTERA SUPERCILIARIS   R(B)

Yellow-browed Camaroptera
Camaroptère à sourcils

Uncommon resident (*C. s. flavigularis*) of forest clearings. Collected Ahoué-houé
(De Roo *et al.* 1969), Atakpamé (De Roo 1970) and Ebéva (De Roo *et al.* 1972). Sight
record from the south end of the Danyi Plateau, Feb 1990 (JBT).

451.   CAMAROPTERA CHLORONOTA   R(B)

Olive-green Camaroptera
Camaroptère à dos vert

Common forest resident (*C. c. chloronota*). Misahöhe is the type locality for
the species, which was described by Reichenow (1895) from a female collected by
E. Baumann, 12 Feb 1895 (Reichenow 1897). Baumann also collected a pair at the
type locality 3 days later (MNB). Subsequently collected Dzobégan and Ebéva
(De Roo *et al.* 1972), Klouto (Dekeyser 1951), Misahöhe (De Roo *et al.* 1971) and
Ounabé (De Roo 1970). All these latter specimens were ascribed to the nominate
race, confirming Togo as the western extremity of its range with *kelsalli* replacing
it in Ghana (Grimes 1987). Sight records from Déguingué, Mar 1990, Misahöhe,
Jan 1988.

[EREMOMELA ICTEROPYGIALIS

Yellow-bellied Eremomela
Erémomèle gris-jaune

A party of 6 *Eremomela* spp. with grey backs seen at Koundjouaré, 9 Apr 1988,
may have been *icteropygialis*, but calls were those of *pusilla*. This species is thought
to be a visitor to northern parts of Ghana at the end of the dry season, Feb–May
(Grimes 1987).]

452.   EREMOMELA PUSILLA   RB

Senegal Eremomela
Erémomèle élégante

Abundant resident (*E. p. pusilla*) of well-wooded savanna throughout. Most common
in Northern Guinea Savanna, but found as far south as the Lomé golf-course, Feb
(JBT). Collected Abudo Karimo (? = Aboudyo Kopé), Bismarckburg and Misahöhe
(Reichenow 1891a, 1902a), Binaparba, Mango and Paio (De Roo *et al.* 1969), Aledjo
and Bafilo (De Roo *et al.* 1971), and Ebéva (De Roo *et al.* 1972).
   Reichenow (1894d) described *E. baumanni* from Misahöhe but Bannerman
(1939), on the advice of E. Stresemann who examined the alcohol-preserved type,
considered the species to be invalid and the specimens to be *E. pusilla*.
   Breeding. An empty nest Landa-Pozanda, Apr.

453.   EREMOMELA BADICEPS   R(B)

Rufous-crowned Eremomela
Erémomèle à tête brune

Not uncommon forest resident (*E. b. ?fantiensis*), often found high in the canopy.
Recorded from Badou, Déguingué and Djodji (Cheke *et al.* 1986). A party of 10
mobbed and drove off a Common Bulbul *Pycnonotus barbatus* at Badou, Aug
1990 (JBT).

454.   SYLVIETTA VIRENS   R(B)

Green Crombec
Crombec verte

Not uncommon resident (*S. v. flaviventris*) of forest, forest edge and well-wooded savanna. Collected Atakpamé and Ounabé (De Roo 1970), and Ebéva (De Roo *et al.* 1972). Sight records from Agbenohoué, Aledjo, near Atakpamé, near Badou (JBT), Dadja, Misahöhe (JBT) and Tinkiro.

Breeding. Bird making repeated visits to same part of a creeper, which suggests nesting, Jun, and a pair at same locality (Aledjo) with singing male, Jul (Cheke *et al.* 1986). Song Pagala, Jul (Douaud 1956b).

455.   SYLVIETTA DENTI   R(B)

Lemon-bellied Crombec
Crombec à gorge tachetée

Rare resident (*S. d. hardyi*) of forest, only one record: one Kpalimé, Nov 1989 (JBT).

456.   SYLVIETTA BRACHYURA   R(B)

Northern Crombec
Crombec

Not uncommon resident (*S. b. brachyura*) of well-wooded Guinea Savanna. Collected Aledjo and 17 km south of Bafilo (De Roo *et al.* 1969), and Kolokopé (De Roo *et al.* 1971, Louette 1975). Other records from Djamdé (Cheke & Walsh 1984), Landa-Pozanda (DP), Mango, Mo (Cheke 1982b) and Péwa.

457.   MACROSPHENUS CONCOLOR   R(B)

Grey Longbill
Fauvette nasique grise

Uncommon forest resident, partial to thickets in forest clearings, but probably overlooked. Collected Ounabé (De Roo 1970). Noted Misahöhe, Feb and Nov (JBT), and 10 km east-southeast of Koniouhou, Mar.

Breeding. Singing birds Misahöhe, Feb.

458.   HYPERGERUS ATRICEPS   R(B)

Oriole Warbler
Moho à tête noire

Locally common resident, preferring clearings in forest or riversides in the savanna with thick gallery forest or dense vegetation. Said by Millet-Horsin (1923) to frequent road side Fig trees (*Ficus* spp.). Occurs from Lomé (Browne 1980) and L. Togo (JBT) at least as far north as Fosse aux Lions. Often heard calling at Naboulgou.

459.   HYLIOTA FLAVIGASTER   R(B)

Yellow-bellied Hyliota
Hyliota à ventre jaune

Rare resident (*H. f. flavigaster*) of forest edge and Southern Guinea Savanna. A pair collected Misahöhe (Reichenow 1897), and a female obtained by Metzger at Haho Balve (? = Haho Baloué), 22 Dec 1907 (MNB). Female observed Tinkiro (Walsh *et al.* 1990).

460.   HYLIOTA VIOLACEA   R(B)
Violet-backed Hyliota
Hyliota à dos violet

Uncommon forest resident (*H. v. nehrkorni*). Males seen Misahöhe, Apr–May and Aug (Walsh *et al.* 1990), and a female at Déguingué, Mar 1990. Mackworth-Praed & Grant (1973) state that *H. v. violacea* occurs in Togo and eastwards but no records of this sub-species west of Cameroon have been traced, other than a recent record in Nigeria (Elgood *et al.* 1994). Listed as a candidate species for treatment as threatened in Appendix G of Collar & Stuart (1985).

461.   HYLIA PRASINA   R(B)
Green Hylia
Hylia verte

Common forest resident (*H. p. superciliaris*), often seen in clearings or in thickets at forest edges. Collected Bismarckburg and Misahöhe (Reichenow 1891a, 1897), Klouto (Dekeyser 1951), Ahoué-houé (De Roo *et al.* 1969), Ounabé (De Roo 1970), Apéyémé, Ebéva and Misahöhe (De Roo *et al.* 1971, 1972). Sightings at Agbenohoué, Amou-Oblo, Badou, Balla, Kpété Béna and Misahöhe.

462.   PHYLLOSCOPUS TROCHILUS   PM
Willow Warbler
Pouillot fitis

Common Palaearctic migrant (*P. t. trochilus* and *P. t. acredula*) mainly to Guinea Savanna woodland and to forest zone but also recorded at the coast, late Oct to Apr. Most birds are *trochilus* but a single *acredula* seen Landa-Pozanda, 7 Feb 1987, and 2 foraging in a *Thevetia* hedge and Neem trees (*Azidirachta indica*) at Badou, 17 Feb 1988. One collected Kolokopé, 15 Mar 1970, was in heavy wing moult and this prevented identification of its race (Louette 1975). It is likely to have been *acredula* as Louette describes it as a grey-brown bird. Specimens of *trochilus* collected Adina, Aledjo, Apéyémé, Dzobégan, Ebéva, Edifou, Evou, Kamina and Koutoukpa, mid Nov to early Mar, (De Roo 1970, De Roo *et al.* 1972). Often sings (Douaud 1957).
   Earliest arrival: 27 Oct (Douaud 1957); latest date: 2 at Domaine Gravillou, 7 Apr 1990.
   Birds ringed Norway (1) and Sweden (1) recovered in southwest Togo (Holgersen 1981; Dowsett *et al.* 1988).

463.   PHYLLOSCOPUS SIBILATRIX   PM
Wood Warbler
Pouillot siffleur

Common Palaearctic migrant, Nov–May. Winters in the forest zone, e.g. Badou, Balla, Kpalimé and Misahöhe. Passage birds at Landa-Pozanda, 14 Nov–12 Dec and 14 Mar–15 Apr, Péwa, 22 Mar, and Klabé Apégamé, 30 Mar. Seen Lomé, as early as 24 Nov (Douaud 1957); latest date – a male collected Misahöhe, 3 May 1894 (Reichenow 1897). Also collected Aledjo, 30 Nov (De Roo *et al.* 1972).

464.   PHYLLOSCOPUS BONELLI   PM
Bonelli's Warbler
Pouillot de Bonelli

Rare Palaearctic migrant (*P. b. bonelli*), only one record: 2 together near Mango,

28 Feb 1988 (Walsh *et al.* 1990). Not listed for Ghana by Grimes (1987) but now known to occur near Navrongo in northern Ghana: up to 9 per day were seen in Nov and Dec (Hedenström *et al.* 1990).

465.   SYLVIA BORIN   PM

Garden Warbler
Fauvette des jardins

Not uncommon, widespread Palaearctic migrant (*S. b. borin*) to forest, forest edge and well-wooded savanna throughout, including coast (Browne 1980), late Oct to Apr. Collected Adina and Ezimé, Nov, and Ounabé, Oct–Nov (De Roo 1970), Aledjo, Dec, Ebéva, Oct–Nov, Misahöhe, Dec and Feb (De Roo *et al.* 1972, Reichenow 1897).

Earliest date – 23 Oct at Ebéva (De Roo *et al.* 1972); latest record – one singing in a *Jatropha curcas* thicket, 7 Apr (Douaud 1957). One at Péwa, 5 Apr 1987, was singing in a thicket where a bird was located in Jan 1990. This is of interest as there is strong evidence of site-fidelity in transit and in wintering grounds (Cramp 1992).

A bird ringed as an adult in Sweden, 25 Jun 1975, recovered Agou, 15 Jan 1978.

466.   SYLVIA COMMUNIS   PM

Greater Whitethroat
Fauvette grisette

Not uncommon Palaearctic migrant (*S. c. communis*) usually to Sudan Savanna in the north, Nov–Apr, but also a female collected Misahöhe, 11 Feb 1895 (Reichenow 1897), and seen Lomé, Mar (Douaud 1957). All recent records from Tantigou, 25 Nov to 9 Apr, with a maximum of 10 on 28 Feb 1988.

MUSCICAPIDAE

467.   MELAENORNIS PALLIDUS   RB

Pale Flycatcher
Gobemouche Pâle

Common resident (*M. p. modestus*) of northern Guinea and Sudan Savanna and not uncommon in Southern Guinea Savanna. Collected Adamé, Misahöhe and Sokodé (Reichenow 1902a), Aledjo, Baoulé, Mango, Paio and 22 km northwest of Sokodé (De Roo *et al.* 1969), Fazao (De Roo *et al.* 1971) and Ebéva (De Roo *et al.* 1972).

Breeding. 2 nestlings (about 2 days old) near Ketao, 28 Jul 1989; on 9 Jul the adult pair had been seen building the nest, which was 3 m up in a Shea butter tree *Butyrospermum paradoxum*.

468.   MELAENORNIS EDOLIOIDES   R(B)

Northern Black Flycatcher
Gobemouche drongo

Locally common resident (*M. e. edolioides*) of well-wooded Guinea Savanna and gallery forests. Collected Bismarckburg, date unknown (Reichenow 1892). Singles or pairs seen Bafilo, Défalé, Fazao, Kandé, Kara, Kpayando, Kpaya, Landa-Pozanda and Naboulgou.

Breeding. Singing and carrying nesting material Landa-Pozanda, Jun. Song Kara, Sep.

469.   MUSCICAPA STRIATA   PM

Spotted Flycatcher
Gobemouche gris

Not uncommon Palaearctic migrant (*M. s. striata* collected (De Roo 1970) but *M. s. balearica* may also occur) to savannas and forest edge throughout, Sep–Apr. Collected Atakpamé, Sep–Mar (De Roo 1970), Bismarckburg, Jan, and Misahöhe, Sep–Nov (Reichenow 1891a, 1897).

Occurs at the coast from Sep until mid Dec, apparently as passage migrant en route for more eastern or southern destinations, but is common there, Oct–Nov, and may stay for a few days, remaining faithful to one site, e.g. a baobab tree (Douaud 1957). When at the coast, some frequent the streets of Lomé (Douaud 1957; JBT).

Earliest date – 3 Sep, Lomé (Douaud 1957); latest – 23 Apr, Landa-Pozanda, but see also ringing recovery below.

A bird of the year ringed Germany, 15 Jul 1981, recovered 10 km east of Namoundjoga, 3 May 1982. This recovery was mapped by Dowsett *et al.* (1988) but omitted from their Table 18.

470.   MUSCICAPA GAMBAGAE   R(B)

Gambaga Flycatcher
Gobemouche de Gambaga

Uncommon resident of Northern Guinea Savanna. Singles or pairs recorded from Aledjo, Mar, Fosse aux Lions, Feb, Ketao, Jul, and Péwa, Jan and Jul (Walsh *et al.* 1990). Probably also occurs along the Gambaga escarpment in Togo, east of the Ghanaian type locality.

471.   MUSCICAPA USSHERI   R(B)

Ussher's Flycatcher
Gobemouche d'Ussher

Rare forest resident, known only from one sighting: Badou, 4 Aug 1990 (JBT). Listed as a candidate species for treatment as threatened in Appendix G of Collar & Stuart (1985).

472.   MUSCICAPA AQUATICA   R(B)

Swamp Alseonax
Gobemouche des marais

Uncommon resident (*M. a. aquatica*), restricted to gallery forest and thick riverside vegetation beside rivers in the Northern Guinea Savanna zone. Only seen along the Oti R. near Mango, where also collected, Dec (De Roo *et al.* 1972), and in the Keran reserve at and near Naboulgou.

Breeding. A recently fledged juvenile Naboulgou, Jul.

473.   MUSCICAPA EPULATA   R(B)

Little Grey Alseonax
Gobemouche cendré

Scarce forest resident, only 2 sightings: Djodji and Wobé, Mar 1990.

474.   MUSCICAPA COMITATA   R(B)

Dusky-blue Flycatcher
Gobemouche ardoisé

Rare resident, only one sight record: Fazao, Apr (Minster Agriculture Limited 1984).

475.   MUSCICAPA CASSINI   R(B)

Cassin's Alseonax
Gobemouche de Cassin

Uncommon forest resident, partial to clearings and riversides. Pairs at Amou-Oblo, Jul, Misahöhe and Tasso, Feb (Walsh *et al.* 1990), and singles at Balla, Apr, and Wobé, Mar.

476.   MUSCICAPA CAERULESCENS   R(B)

Ashy Alseonax
Gobemouche à lunettes blanches

Rare forest resident (*M. c. nigrorum*), but possibly overlooked. Known only from specimens collected Misahöhe, 15 Feb 1895 (Reichenow 1897, but specimen label gives year as 1894), and Tomegbé, 19 Jul 1968 (De Roo *et al.* 1969).

477.   MYIOPARUS PLUMBEUS   R(B)

Grey Tit-Flycatcher
Gobemouche mésange

Scarce resident (*M. p. plumbeus*) of Guinea Savanna woodland. Collected Binaparba, Aug (De Roo *et al.* 1969), and sight records Akloa, Oct (Cheke *et al.* 1986), Mango, Feb, Naboulgou, Feb, and Péwa, Aug (Cheke *et al.* 1986).

478.   FICEDULA HYPOLEUCA   PM

European Pied Flycatcher
Gobemouche noir

Common Palaearctic migrant (*F. h. hypoleuca*), late Sep to mid Apr, mostly on passage in Northern Guinea Savanna, but also winters in Southern Guinea Savanna and forest clearings as far south as Atakpamé and Badou. Occasional near the coast (Douaud 1957). Earliest date – 20 Sep, Tchonou (De Roo 1970); latest – 17 Apr, Anié (Douaud 1957). Bulk of arrivals in late Oct and numbers begin to decline mid Feb; some males are in full breeding plumage before departure, Mar–Apr.

   Collected Bismarckburg, Mar and Apr, Misahöhe, Nov and Feb (Reichenow 1897, 1902a), Edifou, Dec, Evou, Feb, Kamina, Oct, Kodegbé and Ounabé, Nov, and Tchonou, Sep (De Roo 1970), Aledjo and Dzobégan, Dec, and Ebéva, Oct–Nov (De Roo *et al.* 1972).

PLATYSTEIRIDAE

479.   BIAS FLAMMULATUS   R(B)

African Shrike-Flycatcher
Gobemouche écorcheur

Not uncommon, widespread resident (*B. f. flammulatus*) of forest and forest edge. Collected at many sites within the forest zone, mostly in the highlands (Reichenow

1902a, De Roo *et al.* 1972). Recent records from Badou, Misahöhe (Cheke *et al.* 1986) and Tinkiro.

480.   BIAS MUSICUS   R(B)

Black-and-White Shrike-Flycatcher
Gobemouche chanteur

Not uncommon resident (*B. m. musicus*) of gallery forest in Southern Guinea Savanna, forest and forest edge. Collected Ahoué-houé (De Roo *et al.* 1969) and Misahöhe (Reichenow 1891a). Also recorded 10 km east of Adeta, Bénali, Djodji, Katchenké (Douaud 1956b) and Misahöhe (JBT).
   Breeding. Display flights Katchenké, Jul (Douaud 1956b).

481.   BATIS SENEGALENSIS   R(B)

Senegal Batis
Gobemouche soyeux du Sénégal

Locally common resident of undisturbed Guinea Savanna woodland. Collected at numerous sites from savanna habitats at elevations above the forest in the mountains (Dekeyser 1951, Reichenow 1902a) and throughout the savanna belt north to Dapaon. Often seen at sites along the Bafilo ridge and in the Keran Park. Also occurs at the coast, e.g. L. Togo (JBT).

482.   PLATYSTEIRA CYANEA   RB

Brown-throated Wattle-eye
Gobemouche caronculé à collier

Very common, widespread resident (*P. c. cyanea*) of Guinea Savanna throughout, at least as far north as Mango, where collected (Reichenow 1902a). Particularly abundant in the Keran Park. Occasional records from forest clearings, e.g. Djodji.
   Breeding. 2 fledglings being fed by parents at Kara, Sep. Fledgling with parents Lomé, Dec.

483.   PLATYSTEIRA CASTANEA   R(B)

Chestnut Wattle-eye
Gobemouche caronculé châtain

Uncommon forest resident (*P. c. hormophora*). First collected at Bismarckburg and Misahöhe, the type locality of *P. c. hormophora* (Reichenow 1891a, 1897, 1901). Others collected Misahöhe (De Roo *et al.* 1971) and Ebéva (De Roo *et al.* 1972). Other records (all sightings): a pair in a roadside Mango tree (*Mangifera indica*) Misahöhe, Apr and Aug 1987; Agou, 19 Apr 1990 (JBT) and near Kpalimé, Feb 1990 (JBT).

484.   PLATYSTEIRA BLISSETTI   R(B)

Red-cheeked Wattle-eye
Gobemouche caronculé à joues rouges

Rare forest resident (*P. b. blissetti*), only 3 records: a pair collected by E. Baumann at Misahöhe, 13 Feb 1895 (Reichenow 1897 only referred to the male); sightings at Misahöhe, Mar 1990, and at Agou, Apr 1990 (JBT). Listed as a candidate species for treatment as threatened in Appendix G of Collar & Stuart (1985).

MONARCHIDAE

485.   ELMINIA LONGICAUDA   RB
African Blue Flycatcher
Gobemouche bleu

Locally common resident (*E. l. longicauda*) of Northern Guinea Savanna woodland. Collected Bassar, Kirikri, Mango (Reichenow 1902a) and Paio (De Roo *et al.* 1969). All recent records from Kara (Cheke 1982b), Landa Pozanda and Naboulgou.
Breeding. Parent feeding dependent young Landa-Pozanda, 13 Jul 1989.

486.   TERPSIPHONE NITENS   R(B)
Blue-headed Crested Flycatcher
Gobemouche huppé noir

Uncommon resident (*T. n. reichenowi*) of forest and forest edge. A female collected by Baumann at Misahöhe, 2 Dec 1894 (Reichenow 1897). Sight records Fazao, Apr (Minster Agriculture Limited 1984), Mt. Agou, 19 Apr 1990 (JBT) and Yégué, 20 Mar 1990.

487.   TERPSIPHONE RUFIVENTER   R(B)
Black-headed Paradise-Flycatcher
Gobemouche à ventre roux

Common resident (*T. r. nigriceps*) of forested areas, including gallery forest and clearings. Collected by Baumann at Liato (? = Lyato) and Podji (Reichenow 1897). More recent specimens from Misahöhe (De Roo *et al.* 1972), Tététou and Tomégbé (De Roo *et al.* 1971). Also noted Agbenohoué, Akloa, Badou and Djodji (Cheke *et al.* 1986).
Breeding. Carrying nesting material Misahöhe, 31 Jan 1988 (Walsh *et al.* 1990).

488.   TERPSIPHONE VIRIDIS   RB
African Paradise-Flycatcher
Gobemouche de paradis

Common widespread resident (*T. v. ferreti*) of Guinea Savanna, occurring at least as far north as Borgou and Namoundjoga, where collected (De Roo *et al.* 1971). No evidence of migration but likely to move north with the rains as known to be wet season visitor to Ouagadougou, Burkina Faso (Thonnerieux *et al.* 1989). One of the few species which is regularly found in teak (*Tectona grandis*) plantations.
    Collected at many sites (De Roo 1970, De Roo *et al.* 1969, 1971, 1972, Reichenow 1902a). Most males are rufous-phase birds, but white-phased are also common.
Breeding. C/1 Bismarckburg, presumably 4 Apr when adults were collected there (Reichenow 1891a). C/3 Misahöhe, 16 May 1894 (Reichenow 1897). Empty nest (later washed away by heavy rain) Landa-Pozanda, Jul 1989. Adults behaving as if with dependent young Koniouhou, Mar 1990.

TIMALIIDAE

489.   ILLADOPSIS PUVELI   R(B)
Puvel's Akalat
Grive akalat de Puvel

Rare resident of forest (*I. p. ?strenuipes*), but probably overlooked. A specimen from

Atakpamé, 16 Sep 1968, ascribed to *I. rufescens* by De Roo (1970), is now known to be *I. puveli* (M. Louette, pers. comm.). Sight record Misahöhe, 31 Jan 1988. Listed as a candidate species for treatment as threatened in Appendix G of Collar & Stuart (1985).

490.   ILLADOPSIS RUFESCENS   R(B)

Rufous-winged Akalat
Grive akalet du Libéria

Rare resident of thickets at forest edge, only one record: one in a mixed bird party at Agbossomou Kopé, 20 Mar 1990. The specimen from Atakpamé (De Roo 1970) has now been identified as *I. puveli* (M. Louette, pers.comm.). The species is listed as near-threatened (Appendix C of Collar & Stuart 1985), but is not uncommon in Ghana (Grimes 1987).

491.   ILLADOPSIS FULVESCENS   R(B)

Brown Akalat
Grive akalat brune

Not uncommon resident (*I. f. moloneyanus*) of forest thickets and undergrowth, probably overlooked. Collected by E. Baumann at Mt. Agomé (locality untraced, probably Agomé-Palimé south of Misahöhe but possibly in Ghana) and Misahöhe (Reichenow 1897). Other specimens from Adina and Ounabé (De Roo 1970) and Apéyémé, Ebéva and Misahöhe (De Roo *et al.* 1972). Recent sight record Misahöhe, Apr 1990.

492.   TURDOIDES REINWARDTII   R B

Blackcap Babbler
Cratéreop à tête noire

Common resident (*T. r. stictilaema*) of dense riverine scrub in Guinea Savanna from the coast, e.g. Sio R. near Lomé, Lomé (Browne 1980) and Porto Séguro (De Roo *et al.* 1969), to at least as far north as Dapaon. Less conspicuous than *T. plebejus* but also occurs in small family groups, e.g. 10 at Naboulgou, Apr 1990.

Breeding. Dependent young being fed by adult at Kara, 1 Jan 1990. A juvenile in a family group Landa-Pozanda, 24 Feb 1990.

493.   TURDOIDES PLEBEJUS   R(B)

Brown Babbler
Cratérope brune

Common resident (*T. p. platycircus*) of Guinea Savanna and coastal scrub, occurring in noisy parties usually of about 6 birds. Occurs at least as far north as Naboulgou and Mango, where collected (Reichenow 1902a).

Breeding. One pecking the cloaca of another, which had lifted its tail and protruded its vent, Landa-Pozanda, Apr 1988.

494.   PHYLLANTHUS ATRIPENNIS   R(B)

Capuchin Babbler
Cratérope capuchin

Not uncommon resident (*P. a. haynesi*) of forest and dense thickets at forest edge. Collected Bismarckburg (Reichenow 1893) and Misahöhe (De Roo *et al.* 1972). Sight records Dzogbegan, 12 May 1988, 10 km east-southeast of Koniouhou, 23 Mar 1990, and Kpalimé, date unknown (TC).

Picathartinae

[PICATHARTES GYMNOCEPHALUS

Grey-headed Rockfowl
Picatharte chauve de Guinée

Despite the availability of suitable habitat in forested parts of the Atacora chain, there are no confirmed records of this species. It was listed as vulnerable and said to occur in Togo by Collar & Stuart (1985). This report was based on E. Baumann's finding of a nest with two young at Apototsi and collection of a pair there (Baumann 1894b, Reichenow 1897), but the site is in Ghana (Cheke 1986). The skins of the adult pair, a female also collected at Apototsi, and the pullus birds (preserved in spirit) are all in Berlin (MNB).

Robinson (1973) mentioned a wildlife biologist of the Food and Agriculture Organisation reporting *Picathartes gymnocephalus* amongst his list of birds seen in Togo during 1965. This presumably refers to Roure (1967), who listed the species as deserving special protection in Togo, with the implication that its presence had been confirmed but it is unclear whether he used his own data or relied on Reichenow (1897).]

PARIDAE

495.   PARUS LEUCOMELAS   R(B)

White-shouldered Black Tit
Mésange noire à epaulettes blanches

Locally not uncommon resident (*P. l. guineensis*) of well-wooded Guinea Savanna, especially in north. Less common in the south although collected Bismarckburg (Reichenow 1891a, 1893) and Ebéva (De Roo *et al.* 1972). Regular in suitable habitat from Fazao north to Naboulgou, where often observed, and Mango, where collected (Reichenow 1902a).

Breeding. Song Sara-Kawa, 14 Feb 1988.

REMIZIDAE

496.   ANTHOSCOPUS PARVULUS   R(B)

Yellow Penduline Tit
Rémiz à ventre jaune

Rare, presumed resident (subspecies unknown). The only record is of a bird (or birds) seen Lomé, date unknown (Browne 1980).

SALPORNITHIDAE

497.   SALPORNIS SPILONOTUS   R(B)

Spotted Creeper
Grimpereau tacheté

Surprisingly rare resident (*S. s. emini*) of Northern Guinea Savanna, only one record: one near Naboulgou, 22 Apr 1990.

ZOSTEROPIDAE

498.   ZOSTEROPS SENEGALENSIS   R(B)

Yellow White-eye
Oiseau-lunettes jaune

Common resident (*Z. s. senegalensis*) of well-wooded Guinea Savanna from 7°30'N to
at least as far north as 10 km north of Mango. As yet, no records from the coast.

NECTARINIIDAE

499.   ANTHREPTES FRASERI   R(B)

Scarlet-tufted Sunbird
Soui-manga de Fraser

Uncommon forest resident (*A. f. ?idius*), only 2 records: a female at Misahöhe, Apr
1987 (Walsh *et al.* 1990); one at Badou, 27 Jul 1989.

500.   ANTHREPTES LONGUEMAREI   Afm/B, R?(B)

Violet-backed Sunbird
Soui-manga violet

Uncommon intra-African migrant (*A. l. longuemarei*) to Northern Guinea Savanna,
mostly in the dry season, retreating to Southern Guinea Savanna, where may also be
resident. Collected Bismarckburg, Apr (Reichenow 1892), and Sokodé, where obtained
by F. Schröder, 23 Oct 1900 (from label in MNB, no date given by Reichenow 1902a).
Regular at Landa-Pozanda, Jan–Apr, with isolated records in Aug (Walsh *et al.* 1990)
and Nov. A male in the Fazao-Malfacassa reserve near Binako, Feb 1994 (PMC).

The specimen collected Agomé Tongwe, which is in Ghana and close to the Togo
border, 22 May 1894 (Reichenow 1897, Neumann 1906), but quoted as Oct in
Reichenow (1902a), was the type for *A. l. haussarum* (Neumann 1906) but this was
later merged with *longuemarei* by White (1963).

Breeding. A recent nest and pair with juvenile Landa-Pozanda, Mar 1986 (Walsh
et al. 1990). A female building Landa-Pozanda, 26 Feb 1990. This nest was found
empty and on the ground, 3 Mar, and is now in the BMNH. Another was built
nearby by 15 Mar, and a male was in the vicinity of it, 31 Mar.

501.   ANTHREPTES COLLARIS   RB

Collared Sunbird
Soui-manga à collier

Common resident (*A. c. subcollaris*) of coastal scrub, forest, forest clearings and riverine
forest in Guinea Savanna as far north as Tinkiro. In the savanna it feeds on flowers of
Stereospermum sp. and *Berlinia grandiflora*, which flower Feb–Mar.
Breeding. Dependent juveniles: 3 at Glei, 30 Sep 1988; Badou, 25 Mar 1990. Bird
singing from *Thevetia* bushes at Yégué, Jul (Douaud 1956b).

502.   ANTHREPTES PLATURUS   AfM/B

Pygmy Long-tailed Sunbird
Petit soui-manga à longue queue

Not uncommon visitor (*A. p. platura*), Nov–Apr, to Sudan Savanna and Northern
Guinea Savannas, reaching south to Aledjo, where collected, Dec (De Roo *et al.* 1972).

Breeding. Parents feeding nestlings Kara, Feb; male repeatedly carrying food Landa-Pozanda, Apr (Walsh *et al.* 1990).

503.   NECTARINIA SEIMUNDI   R(B)
    Little Green Sunbird
    Petit soui-manga vert

Rare forest resident (*N. s. kruensis*), probably overlooked. Collected Klouto, 1 Jun 1950 (Dekeyser 1951) and Misahöhe, 6 Aug 1969 (De Roo *et al.* 1971).

504.   NECTARINIA OLIVACEA   R(B)
    Olive Sunbird
    Soui-manga olivâtre

Common resident (*N. o. cephaelis* and *N. o. guineensis*) of forest and forest edge. Regularly noted in the Badou, Idifiou and Misahöhe areas. Occasional in gallery forest in savanna, e.g. beside the Sio R. near Tokpli.

Two males collected at Klouto, Jun 1950, were ascribed to *N. o. ragazzi* by Dekeyser (1951) but according to White (1963) and Howard & Moore (1991) this race only occurs in East Africa. Birds from Ahoué-houé, Fazao, Kolokopé, Misahöhe and Tomegbé have been identified as the western race *N. o. guineensis* (De Roo *et al.* 1969, 1971); those from Adina, Agadji, Atakpamé, Ebéva, Misahöhe, Odjolo and Ounabé as the eastern form *N. o. cephaelis* (De Roo 1970, De Roo *et al.* 1972).

Taxonomic note: Clancey (1993) has separated *N. olivacea* into two species, separable by the presence (in *N. olivacea* (Smith)) and absence (in *N. obscura* Jardine) of yellow pectoral tufts in the adult females. On this basis, all the West African forms are *obscura*.

505.   NECTARINIA REICHENBACHII   R(B)
    Reichenbach's Sunbird
    Soui-manga de Reichenbach

Rare presumed resident, status unknown. Millet-Horsin (1923) gave a brief description of a pair of sunbirds, which he identified as "Fernando Po" Sunbirds *Chalcomitra poensis* (= *N. oritis poensis*). However, as the latter is only known from high elevations on the mainland it seems more likely that Millet-Horsin's birds were the not dissimilar *N. reichenbachii*, which is known from the coastal strip of Nigeria (Elgood 1982), Ghana (Grimes 1987), Ivory Coast (Eccles 1985, Demey 1986) and Liberia (Cane & Carter 1988).

506.   NECTARINIA VERTICALIS   R(B)
    Olive-backed Sunbird
    Soui-manga olive à tête bleue

Not uncommon resident (*N. v. verticalis*), principally found in Southern Guinea Savanna but occurs at the coast (Browne 1980) and reaches Landa-Pozanda in the north. Collected Podji (Reichenow 1897), Aledjo (De Roo *et al.* 1969), Evou, Tchonou and Témedja (De Roo 1970), Fazao and Kolokopé (De Roo *et al.* 1971).

507.   NECTARINIA CYANOLAEMA   R(B)
    Blue-throated Brown Sunbird
    Soui-manga à gorge bleue

Rare forest resident (*N. c. octaviae*), only one record: a pair Djodji, 16 Oct 1985 (Cheke *et al.* 1986).

508. NECTARINIA FULIGINOSA   R(B)

Carmelite Sunbird
Soui-manga carmélite

Status unknown. Scarce resident (if still present) of coastal area (*N. f. aurea*). Only information is from observations of Millet-Horsin (1923), who reported the species as rare. Was probably common in neighbouring Benin (and may still be) as there are 9 skins collected by Waterlot between 15 Jan 1910 and 1 Jun 1911 in the MNHN. 3 of these were collected at Porto-Novo, the others are labelled "Dahomey".

509. NECTARINIA SENEGALENSIS   RB, Afm?/(B)

Scarlet-chested Sunbird
Soui-manga à poitrine rouge

Abundant resident (*N. s. senegalensis*) of savanna from the far north south to at least 7°32'N. Most common in the Northern Guinea Savanna zone, where numbers may be augmented by northward movements in the wet season.
Breeding. Dependent young Kara, Sep 1988. A female carrying white feathers, presumably lining material, into a fully built nest in a *Eucalyptus* tree at Djamdé, Aug 1989.

510. NECTARINIA ADELBERTI   R(B)

Buff-throated Sunbird
Soui-manga à gorge rousse

Common resident (*N. a. eboensis*) of forest and forest edge, preferring tall trees. Collected Ahoué-houé (De Roo *et al.* 1969) and Misahöhe (Reichenow 1897), where also recently seen. Other records from the Badou area (Cheke & Walsh 1984, Cheke *et al.* 1986), the Danyi Monastery (JBT), Déguingué, Kpalimé, Kpété Béna, Nyivé and Okpahoué.
   Mackworth-Praed & Grant (1973) included Togo in the range of *N. a. adelberti*, which may also occur, but the specimens in the MNB are *eboensis*. De Roo *et al.* (1969) also ascribed their specimen to *eboensis* and sight records of males seen well were also identified as *eboensis*.

511. NECTARINIA VENUSTA   RB

Yellow-bellied Sunbird
Soui-manga à ventre jaune

Common resident (*N. venusta venusta*) in coastal areas, e.g. in and near Lomé (Browne 1980, De Roo *et al.* 1969, H&S, JBT) and northwards throughout the Guinea Savanna zones to Mango, where seen 5 Feb 1989. Occasional in forest or forest edge, e.g. Idifiou, Misahöhe and Tomegbé.
Breeding. An egg, provenance and date uncertain, described by Reichenow (1897). Nest at Glidji, Jul 1919, described and subsequently illustrated by Millet-Horsin (1921d, 1923); this nest was later colonised by mice.

512. NECTARINIA CHLOROPYGIA   R(B)

Olive-bellied Sunbird
Soui-manga à ventre olive

Not uncommon resident (*N. c. kempi*) occurring in forest, forest edge and gardens from the coast (Browne 1980, De Roo *et al.* 1971, Millet-Horsin 1923) to as far north as Kara (Cheke & Walsh 1980).

513.   NECTARINIA CUPREA   RB, Afm/B

    Copper Sunbird
    Soui-manga cuivré

Common resident (*N. c. cuprea*) in Southern Guinea Savanna and at the coast. Also intra-African migrant to northern savannas, reaching as far north as Mango, Mar–Sep.

Breeding. Nest building and carrying food Naboulgou, Jul (Cheke & Walsh 1980). Nest found by Millet-Horsin (1921d, 1923), locality and date unknown. Unoccupied nest Naboulgou, Aug. Singing birds Kara, Aug. 2 pairs in territorial dispute Kara, Jun.

514.   NECTARINIA COCCINIGASTER   RB

    Splendid Sunbird
    Soui-manga eclatant

Common and widespread resident in coastal areas, residential Lomé, forest edge and savannas throughout, extending north to at least Tantigou. Groups of a dozen or more are attracted to flowering *Berlinia grandiflora* trees, e.g. Landa-Pozanda, Mar, and Mo, May–Jun.

Breeding. Eggs, provenance and date unknown, (Reichenow 1897). Nest, date and locality unknown, described by Millet-Horsin (1921d) and subsequently illustrated (Millet-Horsin 1923). Male visiting nest, probably building, Aledjo, Mar (Walsh *et al.* 1990). Building, Badou, Apr, and near Lomé, Aug. Song, used to establish and maintain territories (Grimes 1974), Klabé Apégamé, Mar, Fazao, Jul, and Katchenké, Jul (Douaud 1956b).

    [NECTARINIA JOHANNAE

    Johanna's Sunbird
    Soui-manga de Jeanne

A female sunbird collected Klouto, 2 Jun 1950, was ascribed to *N. j. fasciata* (Dekeyser 1951). In his list of birds recorded from Togo, Dowsett (1993) was doubtful of this record putting it in the category "occurrence requires proof" and an examination of the specimen (IFAN museum, no. 50.7.414) confirmed these fears (B. Treca, pers. comm.). The specimen is in poor condition and its identity is uncertain, but it is not *N. johannae* as the chin and throat are dark brown not white as in *N. johannae*.]

515.   NECTARINIA SUPERBA   RB

    Superb Sunbird
    Soui-manga superbe

Not uncommon resident (*N. s. ashantiensis*) in the south occurring in forest and gallery forest, e.g. Nyivé, Tététou (De Roo *et al.* 1971) and Tokpli. Usually seen at tops of trees such as *Berlinia grandiflora*, but also noted pecking at the base of banana flowers.

Breeding. Eggs, ascribed to this species, and likely to have been from Misahöhe (no date), described by Reichenow (1897). Female building untidy nest 20 m up in tall tree at Badou, Apr.

516.   NECTARINIA PULCHELLA   AfM/(B), R(B)

    Beautiful Long-tailed Sunbird
    Soui-manga à longue queue

Common visitor (*N. p. pulchella*) to Northern Guinea Savanna, Feb–Aug, reaching as far south as Péwa. Resident in far north, where collected Borgou, Dec (De Roo *et al.* 1972), and sight records in most months.

Breeding. Female carrying white down feather Mango, Oct. Song Mango, Jul. Males in breeding dress, mostly Apr–Aug but occasionally in Jan.

LANIIDAE

517. LANIUS COLLARIS   RB

Fiscal Shrike
Pie-grièche fiscale

Locally common resident (*L. c. smithii*). Especially common in the Lomé region, along the coast to Anécho (Millet-Horsin 1921a) and at Badou.

Breeding. Nest with 2 young Azongo, Jul 1919; nest described and illustrated by Millet-Horsin (1921d, 1923). Incubating Lomé, Feb (JBT). Bird sitting high on nest, probably with small young, and fed by mate near Lomé, Apr.

518. LANIUS SENATOR   PM

Woodchat Shrike
Pie-grièche à tête rousse

Not uncommon Palaearctic migrant to coastal areas and northern savannas, Nov–Jul, (*L. s. senator* and *L. s. badius*). Records split into two groups: birds at or near the coast (Douaud 1957, Robinson 1972, Browne 1980, Cheke *et al.* 1986) and those in northern savannas, from Tantigou south to Landa-Pozanda.

In Ghana *senator* has been collected at the coast and in the north (skins in Smithsonian Institute) and *badius* in the north and in forest clearings (Grimes 1987). This is the opposite way around to the usual expectation (Bannerman 1939), and such a subspecific split, with *badius* predominating in the south and *senator* in the north, probably accounts for the distribution of records in Togo. Both subspecies also occur at the coast as a female collected by Keilhack, Lomé, 20 Apr 1914 (MNB) was *senator* and Douaud (1957) noted 4 *senator* and 28 *badius* there. He also noted *badius* at Anié, but surmised these were passage birds en route north. A male collected by E. Baumann, Misahöhe, 2 Feb 1895, was *badius* whereas a bird obtained in the north by G. Thierry, Gandu (= Gando), 30 Nov 1898, was *senator*; as was a bird at Landa-Pozanda, 5 Mar 1988.

Further support for Bannerman's interpretation comes from specimens from Benin in the MNHN: a pair collected by the Waterlot mission at the coast, Porto Novo, 2 Jan 1912, were *badius*, as was a male obtained by Miègemarque, Bécon (presumably modern Béko at 06°36'N, 02°27'E), 30 Jan 1895 (Oustalet 1898). A second male, probably a first winter bird, collected there the same day is equivocal: there is some white in the primaries suggestive of *senator* but it is only on the outer shafts and not all across the feathers as in undoubted *senator*. Bannerman mentioned some *badius* have the white patch "sometimes faintly indicated" so this specimen and, perhaps, some of Douaud's 4 *senator*, are likely to be *badius*. However, in Nigeria both races have been taken in the north and the south, with *badius* predominating in the south (Elgood *et al.* 1994).

Earliest record: the *senator* collected Gando, 30 Nov (Reichenow 1902a). Douaud heard singing, Jan–Feb, and his earliest arrival date was 20 Dec, and latest date 17 Apr. In the north most birds also leave in Apr: the Jul record (above) refers to Robinson's bird seen on 6 Jul 1971.

519.   CORVINELLA CORVINA   RB

Long-tailed Shrike
Corvinelle

Common widespread resident (*C. c. affinis*) in savanna areas, occurring in conspicuous noisy parties.

Breeding. Breeds cooperatively (Grimes 1980). Dependent young Kara, May, Landa-Pozanda, Jun and Aug. Sitting bird (nest 10 m high in a Flame tree *Delonyx regia*), fed by another at Kara, Jun.

MALACONOTIDAE

520.   NILAUS AFER   R(B)

Northern Brubru
Pie-grièche bru-bru

Very scarce resident (*N. a. afer*) of Guinea Savanna. Collected Bismarckburg (Reichenow 1892) and Mango (Reichenow 1902a). Only three recent records: a pair calling Naboulgou, 13 Aug 1989; one at Pagala, Aug 1990 (JBT); one at Mango, date unknown (TC).

521.   DRYOSCOPUS GAMBENSIS   RB

Puff-back
Pie-grièche cubla de Gambie

Common resident (*D. g. gambensis*) of well-wooded Guinea Savanna, recorded from Namoundjoga, where collected (De Roo *et al.* 1971), and Dapaon in the north, south to Misahöhe (Reichenow 1897) and Tomegbé.

Breeding. A pair with a juvenile Landa-Pozanda, Jul (Cheke & Walsh 1980). Song Péwa, Jun, Yégué, Jul (Douaud 1956b).

522.   DRYOSCOPUS SABINI   R(B)

Sabine's Puff-back
Pie-grièche cubla à gros bec

Uncommon forest resident (*D. s. sabini*), only one record: one in gallery forest beside the Gonobé R., east of Bénali, at 07°34'N, 00°50'E, 25 Apr 1989.

523.   TCHAGRA MINUTA   RB

Blackcap Bush-Shrike
Petit téléphone

Not uncommon resident (*T. m. minuta*) of dense vegetation, often beside rivers, in Guinea Savanna and thickets at forest edge. Recorded from Mango south to Misahöhe.

Breeding. A male collected at a nest near Misahöhe, 18 May 1894 (Reichenow 1897).

524.   TCHAGRA SENEGALA   RB

Black-headed Bush-Shrike
Téléphone tchagra

Very common resident (*T. s. senegala*) of the coastal strip and savannas throughout, but principally in Northern Guinea Savanna.

Breeding. Singing bird perched on top of a nest Tinkiro, Feb (Walsh *et al.* 1990). Carrying food near Bafilo, May. Song: Kara area, Feb and Jun–Nov; Aledjo, Oct; Notsé, Jun.

525.   TCHAGRA AUSTRALIS   R(B)

Brown-headed Bush-Shrike
Tchagra à tête brune

Common resident (*T. a. ussheri*) of Southern Guinea Savanna and forest edge, occurs at higher altitudes than *T. senegala* but also reaches the coast (Robinson 1972). Collected Ahoué-houé (De Roo *et al.* 1969) and Ounabé (De Roo 1970). Often seen in the Badou area.
Breeding. Display flight with wing-clapping during descent Klabé Apégamé, Feb 1987. Song Badou, Jul.

526.   LANIARIUS FERRUGINEUS   R(B)

Tropical Boubou
Gonolek à ventre blanc

Not uncommon resident (*L. f. major*) of Guinea Savanna. Locally common in both Southern Guinea Savanna, e.g. the Bouzalo area, and in Northern Guinea Savanna, e.g. Landa-Pozanda. Recorded throughout from Naboulgou in the north to the coast in the south (Browne 1980).

527.   LANIARIUS BARBARUS   R(B)

Gonolek
Gonolek de Barbarie

Common resident (*L. b. barbarus*), whose distinctive duetting calls can be heard throughout the northern savannas. Uncommon or absent in Southern Guinea Savanna but occurs commonly at the coast.

528.   LANIARIUS LEUCORHYNCHUS   R(B)

Sooty Boubou
Gonolek noir

Rare resident of forest and forest edge, known only from observation at Fazao, Apr 1984 (Minster Agriculture Limited 1984).

529.   TELOPHORUS SULFUREOPECTUS   R(B), Afm

Sulphur-breasted Bush-Shrike
Pie-grièche soufrée

Not uncommon and widespread (*T. s. sulfureopectus*), but status unclear. Occurs from the coast (Browne 1980), where may be resident, to at least as far north as Naboulgou, where only noted Apr–Aug. This suggestion of migration supported by lack of any records Nov to Jan. Collected Abala (? = Abalokopé or Balla), Jul, Bismarckburg, Apr, Misahöhe, Oct, and Podji, May (Reichenow 1902a). Other localities include Bagan, Mar, Bismarckburg, Jul (Douaud 1956b), Landa-Pozanda, Feb–Oct, Péwa, Apr and Jul, and Tchifoma, Jul (Douaud 1956b).

530.   TELOPHORUS MULTICOLOR   R(B)

Many-coloured Bush-Shrike
Pie-grièche variable (or Pie-grièche verte à ventre rouge)

Uncommon resident (*T. m. multicolor*) of forest and forest edge. Specimens from Ounabé
(De Roo 1970) and Misahöhe (De Roo *et al.* 1972), where several seen, Feb–Apr 1990.
Only other records are from Dzogbégan, 12 May 1988 and Balla, 29 Apr 1990.
  3 males, one of which was a black-breasted form, collected Agomé Tongwe, Ghana,
close to border with Togo (Reichenow 1902a).

531.   TELOPHORUS CRUENTUS   R(B)

Fiery-breasted Bush-Shrike
Pie-grièche verte ensanglantée

Scarce resident (*T. c. cruentus*) of forest and thickets at forest edge, 3 records only (all
at Misahöhe): one collected, Aug (De Roo *et al.* 1971); 3 seen on 3 Apr 1987; and one
in Jul 1990 (JBT).

532.   TELOPHORUS LAGDENI   R(B)

Lagden's Bush-Shrike
Pie-grièche verte de Lagden

Very rare, presumed resident (*T. l. lagdeni*), only one record: one sighted 10 km east of
the Ghana border on the Pagala to Ghana road, 11 Aug 1990 (JBT), where there were
considerable stands of forest vegetation. Listed as a candidate species for treatment as
threatened in Appendix G of Collar & Stuart (1985).

533.   TELOPHORUS BLANCHOTTI   R(B)

Grey-headed Bush-Shrike
Pie-grièche de Blanchot

Common resident (*T. b. blanchoti*) of thick Guinea Savanna woodland, at least as far
north as Dapaon and occasional in Southern Guinea Savanna, e.g. Moretan, and at
the coast (Browne 1980).
  Breeding. Characteristic calls Kara area, Feb–Jul.

534.   NICATOR CHLORIS   R(B)

Nicator
Pie-grièche nicator

Common resident, restricted to forest and gallery forest in the southern part of the country.
Recorded from Bismarckburg (Reichenow 1891a), Agou (JBT), Ahoué-houé, Ebéva,
Kolokopé, Misahöhe and Tététou (De Roo *et al.* 1969, 1971, 1972), Djodji (Cheke *et al.*
1986), Kpalimé (TC), Pagala and Yégué (Douaud 1956b), Bethel and Idifiou.

PRIONOPIDAE

535.   PRIONOPS PLUMATUS   RB

Long-Crested Helmet-Shrike
Bagadais casqué

Common resident (*P. p. plumata*) of savanna, from the Burkina Faso border south to at least Notsé and Kpalimé. Usually in noisy, conspicuous groups of up to a dozen birds.

Breeding. Dependent young Mo, May. 3 birds at nest placed 10 m up in a tree, 15 km south of Notsé, 25 Nov 1988 (H&S).

536.   PRIONOPS CANICEPS   R(B)

Red-billed Shrike
Bagadais à bec rouge

Locally common resident (*P. c. caniceps*) throughout the forest zone, often in noisy flocks of up to 10 birds. Occasional in gallery forest, e.g. Mono R. at 7°06'N, Aug 1986, and Amou-Oblo, 24 Feb 1987.

DICRURIDAE

537.   DICRURUS LUDWIGII   RB

Square-tailed Drongo
Drongo de Ludwig

Not uncommon resident (*D. l. sharpei*) of densely-wooded Southern Guinea Savanna and forest. Collected Ahoué-houé, Jul (De Roo *et al.* 1969), and Apéyémé, Dec (De Roo *et al.* 1972). Other localities include Aledjo (Cheke *et al.* 1986), Atakpamé, Déguingué, Fazao, Klouto, Misahöhe, Nyivé and Wobé.

Breeding. A pair feeding a recently fledged juvenile, which was perched about 20 cm from its nest, Misahöhe, 31 Mar 1988 (Walsh *et al.* 1990).

538.   DICRURUS ATRIPENNIS   R(B)

Shining Drongo
Drongo de forêt

Uncommon forest resident. Presence confirmed by two males collected Bismarckburg, Feb and Mar (Reichenow 1891a). In Ghana and Nigeria doubts have arisen about identifications of this species because of the difficulty of separation from *D. adsimilis atactus*, which may be a hybrid of *D. adsimilis divaricatus* and *D. adsimilis coracinus* (Elgood 1982, Grimes 1987). However, there are no confirmed records of this form in Togo. Birds possessing long tails, considered to be *D. atripennis*, seen Kpété Béna, Mar 1990, Misahöhe, Jan and Feb 1988 (Walsh *et al.* 1990), and Tomegbé, Mar 1990. The Kpété Béna bird also uttered a call unlike that of *D. adsimilis*.

539.   DICRURUS ADSIMILIS   RB

Glossy-backed Drongo
Drongo brillant

Abundant widespread resident (*D. a. divaricatus = adsimilis*) of savanna from Cinkansé south to at least Tsévié; race confirmed by specimens (De Roo *et al.* 1969, 1971, 1972). Lack of records from forest zone suggests *D. a. atactus* absent or very rare.

Breeding. Carrying food to a nest, 7 m up in an *Afzelia africana* tree, Landa-Pozanda, 13 Jul 1989. Carrying nesting material and defending territory against a Black Kite *Milvus migrans* and a male Scarlet-chested Sunbird *N. senegalensis* near Atakpamé, 31 Jan 1988 (Walsh *et al.* 1990).

CORVIDAE

540.   PTILOSTOMUS AFER   RB

Black Magpie
Piac-piac

Common resident throughout the northern savanna zones. Also common along the coast and occurs in Lomé and Anécho (Millet-Horsin 1921a), but rare in Southern Guinea Savanna, where seen Ahepe, Ayengré, Davie and Sokodé. Usually in groups of 10–30, associating with cattle.
   Breeding. Dependent young being fed by adults in a *Borassus* palm Kpaya, Jun. Dependent young Kara, Jun and Oct. Recently-fledged juveniles Kara, Jun, and Niamtougou, Jul. Copulation Kara, Jun.

541.   CORVUS ALBUS   RB, Afm?

Pied Crow
Corbeau pie

Common resident throughout, including the coast and forest clearings, e.g. Badou. Flocks of 16 and 22 at Atakpamé, Jan–Feb, and 20 at Kpalimé, Mar, suggest that some may migrate northwards as has been found in Ghana (Grimes 1987).
   Breeding. 3 young, about 2 weeks old, in nest in *Ceiba pentandra* tree at Kara, 30 Jun 1989. Sitting on nest: Kandé, Apr; Kara, Apr. The Kara nest was destroyed in a storm and re-built, May. A pair at a nest on a pylon at Nangbeto, Jun. Building Lomé, May. Carrying stick near Sio R. at Lomé, Apr.

ORIOLIDAE

542.   ORIOLUS ORIOLUS   PM

Golden Oriole
Loriot d'Europe

Rare Palaearctic migrant (*O. o. oriolus*), only 3 records (all singles): Atakpamé, 3 Apr 1953 (Douaud 1957), Lomé, 10 Oct 1953 (Douaud 1957), and Kpayando, 17 Apr 1988.

543.   ORIOLUS AURATUS   R(B)

African Golden Oriole
Loriot doré

Common widespread resident (*O. a. auratus*) of savanna zones from Cinkansé south to Atakpamé and Tététou.
   Breeding. Almost certainly bred Kara, May–Jul 1989. Adults regularly seen at same site in large *Afzelia africana* tree, but nest was not found until after any young had flown. A female carrying food Pagouda, Jul. A male carrying food, and scolding at the same site the next day, Naboulgou, Aug.

544.   ORIOLUS BRACHYRHYNCHUS   R(B)

Black-headed Oriole
Loriot à tête noire

Not uncommon resident (*O. b. brachyrhynchus*) of the forest zone and occasional in gallery forest in the savanna, e.g. beside the Sio R. near Tsévié (Cheke *et al.* 1986).

Collected Misahöhe (Reichenow 1897), Ahoué-houé and Dzobégan (De Roo *et al.* 1969, 1972). Regularly sighted Misahöhe; other sightings at Déguingué, Idifiou and Wobé.

545.   ORIOLUS NIGRIPENNIS   R(B)

Black-winged Oriole
Loriot à ailes noires

Not uncommon resident of forest zone with similar status to *O. brachyrhynchus*, but penetrates further into forest outliers in the savanna, e.g. seen Ayagba and Tinkiro. Collected, Misahöhe (Reichenow 1897), and recently sighted there (Cheke *et al.* 1986) and at Agbenohoué, Déguingué, Tasso and Wobé.

STURNIDAE

Sturninae

546.   POEOPTERA LUGUBRIS   R(B)

Narrow-tailed Starling
Etourneau à queue etroite

Rare resident of forest zone, only one record: a flock of 5 perched in a dead tree, 2 km west of Tomegbé, 25 Jul 1989.

547.   ONYCHOGNATHUS FULGIDUS   R(B)

Chestnut-wing Starling
Etourneau roupenne

Rare forest resident (*O. f. hartlaubii*), known only from Misahöhe. Groups of 2–5 birds, Jan–Feb 1988 (Walsh *et al.* 1990), and subsequent sightings, Apr and Jul 1990 (JBT).

548.   LAMPROTORNIS CUPREOCAUDA   R(B)

Copper-tailed Glossy Starling
Merle métallique à dos bleu

Rare forest resident, only one record: one, amongst a group of *L. splendidus*, in riverside trees at Kpété Menou, 25 Mar 1990. Listed as near-threatened in Appendix C of Collar & Stuart (1985).

549.   LAMPROTORNIS PURPUREUS   RB

Purple Glossy Starling
Merle métallique pourpré

Common and widespread resident (*L. p. purpureus*) throughout the Northern Guinea Savanna zone and as far north as Cinkansé. Also occurs at the coast in the Lomé area (Browne 1980, JBT). Collected Borgou, Kirikri, Mango, Nanergou and Sokodé (De Roo *et al.* 1969, 1972, Reichenow 1902a). Occasionally seen in large pre-roost flocks: 100 at Kara, Oct; 25 at Ketao, Jul.
    Breeding. Dependent young Ketao, Aug. Carrying food Kpaya and Landa-Pozanda, Jun.

550.   LAMPROTORNIS CHALCURUS   R?(B)

Bronze-tailed Glossy Starling
Merle métallique à queue violette

Status unclear. Only recorded in northern savanna (*L. c. chalcurus*), where probably resident, but may occur further south as known to reach the Accra and Keta Plains near the coast in Ghana (Grimes 1987). Collected Mango, Jul (De Roo *et al.* 1971), and singles seen Naboulgou, 13 Aug 1989, and Namoundjoga, 8 Apr 1990.

551.   LAMPROTORNIS CHALYBAEUS   R?(B), AfM?/(NB)

Blue-eared Glossy Starling
Merle métallique commun

Status unclear. Resident or dry season visitor (*L. c. chalybaeus*) to the far north. Collected Namoundjoga, Jul and Aug (De Roo *et al.* 1971). Sight records from Tantigou (3 on 27 Apr 1987; 2 on 8 Apr 1988; 3 on 8 Apr 1990; 1 on 26 Jan 1990; 1 on 28 Feb 1989) and Namoundjoga (2 on 8 Apr 1990).

552.   LAMPROTORNIS CHLOROPTERUS   R(B)

Lesser Blue-eared Glossy Starling
Merle métallique de Swainson

Not uncommon widespread resident (*L. c. chloropterus*) throughout the savannas and also in forest clearings in the highlands, e.g. Badou, Djodji and Klabé Azafie. Northernmost record: 3 at Tantigou, 8 Apr 1990. Occasionally seen in large flocks: 250 at Djamdé, 23 Oct 1987; 80 at Fosse aux Lions, 27 Aug 1989; 70 at Landa-Pozanda, 17 Aug 1986. Many specimens collected Bismarckburg, between 7 Dec and 2 Feb (Reichenow 1891a); others from Podji, Nov (Reichenow 1897) and Togoville, Sep (De Roo *et al.* 1971).

553.   LAMPROTORNIS SPLENDIDUS   RB

Splendid Glossy Starling
Merle métallique à oeil blanc

Common resident (*L. s. chrysonotis*) of forest and forest edge. Since the first records in Togo (Dekeyser & Derivot 1966, Cheke *et al.* 1986), the species has been found to be very common in the forested parts of the highlands and their periphery. It has been noted at Amou-Oblo, Anonoe, Ayomé, Badou, Bénali, Bethel, Déguingué, Djodji, Dzogbégan, Ewa, Idifiou, Imoussa, Kouniohou, Kpété Béna, Kpimé-Tomégbé, Misahöhe, Tinkiro, Todomé, Tomégbé and Zogbé Kobé. Occasionally seen in large flocks, e.g. 100 at Zogbé Kobé, Jul; 50 at Todomé, Jul. Although Bannerman (1948) had no skins from Ghana to examine, the species was collected there by C. G. M. Nagtglas and is not uncommon in Ghana now (Grimes 1987). Perhaps there has been a marked increase in the population in recent years.

Dekeyser & Derivot (1966) ascribed the Togolese birds to the western form (*chrysonotis*) but the eastern *splendidus*, which occurs in Benin (Berlioz 1956, Brunel 1958), may also be present in Togo. Although inadvertently omitted from Thiollay's list for Côte d'Ivoire (Thiollay 1985b), the Splendid Starling is numerous along the coast there (Brunel & Thiollay 1969, Demey & Fishpool 1991), where it has also been referred to *chrysonotis* (Brunel & Thiollay 1969).

Breeding. A pair entering a tree-hole with food Bénali, 12 May 1988. Entering nest-hole with stick and repeatedly returning to hole, Ayomé, 5 Feb 1988. Entering nest-hole Badou, 25 Mar 1990, and Gonobé R. (07°34'N, 00°50'E), 25 Apr 1989.

554.   LAMPROTORNIS CAUDATUS   R(B), AfM/(NB)

Long-tailed Glossy Starling
Merle métallique à longue queue

Presumed resident in far north, where common Dapaon area, but only occurs in Northern Guinea Savanna, Jan–Aug. Occurs not uncommonly in the Kara area but rarely as far south as Bassar (PMC) and Pagala (TC). Sometimes in flocks, e.g. 10 at Titira, Jul. Collected Kandé, Mango and Korbongou, Aug (De Roo *et al.* 1969, 1971).

555.   LAMPROTORNIS PULCHER   AfM/(B)

Chestnut-bellied Starling
Etourneau à ventre roux

Status uncertain, probably wet season visitor, Apr–Sep, to far north only, where may breed. Only 4 records: singles near Dapaon, 26 Jul 1979 (Cheke & Walsh 1980), and Cinkansé, 4 Jul 1987; pairs, 6 km south of Cinkansé, 27 Apr 1987 and 24 May 1988.

556.   CINNYRICINCLUS LEUCOGASTER   AfM/(B)

Amethyst Starling
Merle améthyste

Common visitor (*C. l. leucogaster*) to coast, forest clearings and Guinea Savanna woodland to at least as far north as Barkoissi, Nov–Aug. Details of movements unclear, but suggestive of coastal arrival Nov, followed by northward progression beginning Feb. Recorded at the coast, Nov–Mar (Browne 1980), and one record of a juvenile male at Misahöhe, 22 Nov 1894 (Reichenow 1897). Earliest Guinea Savanna record – 2 males at Tinkiro, 9 Feb; latest – 8 at Naboulgou, 13 Aug. Arrives Kara area late Mar. Sometimes occurs in flocks, e.g. 11 at Mo, Jun, 30 at Kpété Béna, Mar.
   Collected Bismarckburg, Mar, Misahöhe, Apr and Nov (Reichenow 1891a, 1897), and Aledjo, Jul (De Roo *et al.* 1971).
   Breeding. Male carrying green leaf, presumably for lining nest, Djamdé, Jun (Cheke & Walsh 1980).

Buphaginae

557.   BUPHAGUS AFRICANUS   R(B)

Yellow-billed Oxpecker
Pique-boeuf à bec jaune

Uncommon resident (*B. a. africanus*), now restricted to the Keran Park and its immediate vicinity. Within the park, 1–4 birds seen together in association with Buffalo *Syncerus caffer* (Cheke 1980), Roan Antelope *Hippotragus equinus* and Warthog *Phacochoerus aethiopicus*, but never with the abundant Kob *Kobus kob*. Two recent records outside the park: 2 on cows at Domaine Gravillou, 8 Apr 1988 and one with 3 Buffalo, Mandouri, 24 Jan 1989. Millet-Horsin (1923) mentioned that oxpeckers occasionally reached the coast, with cattle herded from the north by Hausa.
   Absence or extreme rarity of oxpeckers outside reserves, in both Togo and Ghana (Grimes 1987), probably attributable to the widespread introduction of acaricide treatments for cattle.

PASSERIDAE

558.   PASSER GRISEUS   RB

Grey-headed Sparrow
Moineau gris

Abundant resident (*P. g. griseus*) of towns and large villages throughout; occasional in open bush country especially in the dry season, when forms flocks, e.g. Keran Park, 10 km south of Mango, Dec–Mar. Noted at Atakpamé, Badou, Bafilo, Dapaon, Domaine Gravillou, Fazao, Kara, Lomé, Mango, Naboulgou, Notsé, Sokodé, Tantigou, Titira and Tsévié. Collected at Aledjo, Borgou, Lomé, Mango, Namoundjoga, Nanergou, Paio and Togoville (De Roo *et al.* 1969, 1971, 1972). Collected Mango by G. Thierry, date unknown (Reichenow 1899, 1902a); specimens described as *Passer diffusus thierryi* Reichenow. Millet-Horsin (1923) said Grey-headed Sparrows were regularly eaten by the local populace.

Breeding. 2 young in nest, which fledged late Aug 1989, Kara. Pairs carrying food to nests in garage roof at Kara, Sep 1986 and Oct 1987 (Walsh *et al.* 1990). Entering nests, also in roofs of garages, Atakpamé and Kara, Jun 1989. Adult at nest Lomé, Sep 1989.

559.   PETRONIA DENTATA   AfM/(B), R?(B)

Bush Petronia
Petit moineau soulcie

Locally abundant dry season visitor to the drier northern savannas, Oct–Apr, especially in Keran Park. Common further south at least to the Kara region, and occasional as far south as Atakpamé and Ayengré. Collected Mango, 18 Aug (De Roo *et al.* 1969), and 6 sighted Cinkansé, 13 Aug 1988, which suggests that some may be resident in the north.

Breeding. One carrying nesting material into a hole in a tree at Kandé, Dec (Cheke & Walsh 1980).

[SPOROPIPES FRONTALIS

Scaly-fronted Weaver
Tisserin à front écailleux

No confirmed records but likely to be present in northern savannas, as breeds as far south as 9°10'N in Benin (Claffey 1995).]

560.   PLOCEPASSER SUPERCILIOSUS   RB

Chesnut-crowned Sparrow-Weaver
Moineau-tisserin

Uncommon resident of well-wooded savanna. Locally common in Keran Park from Naboulgou northwards; only other known localities are Kara (Cheke & Walsh 1980) and Nangbeto (JBT).

Breeding. One carrying straw Naboulgou, Apr 1987. Unoccupied nests with adults in vicinity Naboulgou, Feb 1987. Old nests, with associated polistine wasp combs, Naboulgou, Aug.

PLOCEIDAE

[BUBALORNIS ALBIROSTRIS
Buffalo-Weaver
Alecto à bec blanc

No records as yet but Buffalo-Weavers occur in Burkina Faso only 5km north of Cinkansé. The species has extended its range southwards by c. 20 km in the vicinity of Tenkodogo during 1974–1990, so it may soon reach Togo.]

561.   PLOCEUS PELZELNI   RB

Little Weaver
Tisserin nain

Locally uncommon resident (*P. p. monachus*) of wetlands near the coast. Occurs, in low numbers, beside the Sio R. near Lomé, and at Tokpli.
    Breeding. Breeds lower Sio R. near Lomé: building, Jul; a pair at a nest, Apr; young being fed in 13 nests, Aug. Some nests still active mid Sep. The record of *P. luteolus* nesting at Glidgi, 11 Jun 1919 (Millet-Horsin 1923), probably refers to *P. pelzelni*.

562.   PLOCEUS LUTEOLUS   RB

Slender-billed Weaver
Tisserin minulle

Not uncommon resident (*P. l. luteolus*) of riverine vegetation throughout the Northern Guinea Savanna and Sudan Savanna habitats. Records around the Anécho lagoon (Millet-Horsin 1923) probably refer to *P. pelzelni*.
    Breeding. Two adults emerging from a nest at Landa-Pozanda, Jun, and male building nest in *Acacia* tree there, Aug. Active nest Domaine Gravillou, Aug. Fresh nest Naboulgou, Apr. Old nests noted Mare aux Lions, Feb, and Borgou, Apr. Nesting Glidgi, 11 Jun 1919 (Millet-Horsin 1923) probably refers to *P. pelzelni*.

563.   PLOCEUS NIGRICOLLIS   RB

Spectacled Weaver
Tisserin à lunettes

Common resident (*P. n. brachypterus*) of well-wooded savanna and forest clearings from Fosse aux Lions (H&S) southwards to the coast, where found at Porto Séguro (De Roo *et al.* 1969) and Lomé, both in the town (De Roo *et al.* 1971, JBT) and beside the Sio R.
    Breeding. A pair with a nest in a *Raphia* palm Sara-Kawa, Aug (Walsh *et al.* 1990). One with nest Landa-Pozanda, Aug. Female at nest Mango, Oct.

564.   PLOCEUS AURANTIUS   RB

Orange Weaver
Tisserin orangé

Uncommon resident (*P. a. aurantius*) of vegetation fringing L. Togo, probably declining as urbanisation spreads. Millet-Horsin (1923) reported the species as occurring in great quantity around the lagoon, where the birds built colonies on vegetation overhanging the water. Quentin *et al.* (1986) obtained nematode parasites from a *P. aurantius* which had been collected at Lomé, May 1982.
    Breeding. Nest, contents unknown, Zébé, 15 Jun 1919 (Millet-Horsin 1923).

565.   PLOCEUS HEUGLINI   RB

Heuglin's Masked Weaver
Tisserin masqué

Not uncommon resident of Northern Guinea Savanna woodland. Recorded from
Ebéva north to Namoundjoga, but most common in the Kara-Naboulgou area.
Also noted at the coast (Browne 1980).

De Roo *et al.* (1972) collected *P. heuglini* from Ebéva in Nov. Specimens from
Mango, Dec, were identified as *Textor* (= *Ploceus*) *heuglini neglectus* (De Roo
et al. 1972) but are *P. melanocephala* (M. Louette, pers. comm.). Also, a bird
collected Namoundjoga, Jul, and identified as *Pachyphantes* (=*Ploceus*)
superciliosus by De Roo *et al.* (1971) was *P. heuglini* (M. Louette, pers. comm.).

Breeding. Breeds during the rainy season, usually in association with
polistine wasps. Several active colonies with associated wasps, between Défalé
and Kpessidé, Aug. Nests being built in Oil Palm and young *Butyrospermum*
tree at Ketao, Jul. Colonies there active in early Sep. Male building in *Acacia
gourmanensis* tree, with wasp combs already in place, Panseni, Jul (Walsh *et al.* 1990).
Unattended nests: Défalé, Feb; Fosse aux Lions (colony of 50 nests), Apr; Landa-
Pozanda, Feb.

566.   PLOCEUS VELATUS   RB

Vitelline Masked Weaver
Tisserin à tête rousse

Not uncommon resident (*P. v. vitellinus*) of Guinea Savanna, recorded as far south
as Okpahoué, but most abundant in Northern Guinea Savanna. Usually seen in
pairs or small groups.

Breeding. A pair attending a fresh nest Naboulgou, Aug, when initial stage of
nest-building also seen. Male building and female entering a second nest Domaine
Gravillou, 5 Aug 1989, and nest built there, 5–17 Jun 1990. 4 new nests Gando,
8 Mar 1988 and one Mango, 27 Aug 1989. A male building Mango, 10 Oct 1988.
Unoccupied nests with attendant polistine wasp combs Naboulgou, Feb and Apr.
Unoccupied nest Domaine Gravillou, Apr.

567.   PLOCEUS CUCULLATUS   RB

Village Weaver
Tisserin gendarme

Abundant resident (*P. c. cucullatus*) throughout. Usually associated with towns
and villages; stated to be part of the local diet by Millet-Horsin (1923).

Breeding. Millet-Horsin (1923) located a colony which extended for 600 m
along the edge of the lagoon at Agoué, with a line density of 10 nests per m.
He also illustrated a nest found at Anécho, 25 Jun 1919. Probably breeds
throughout the year, but records only Jan–Oct. Display and nest-building in colony
in *Borassus* palms at Kara, Jul. Nest-building: Atakpamé, Mar; Badou-Dzindzi,
Mar; Kara, Mar and Aug; Lomé, Jun; Sokodé, Mar; Tchifoma, Jul (Douaud
1956b). Active colonies: Agbandé, Jul; Amoussokopé (mixed colony with
P. nigerrimus), Oct; Anié, Jul; Atakpamé, Jul; Ayagba, Jul; Badou, Jul; Défalé,
Apr; Kara (beside Kara R. in *Borassus* palms), May–Jun; Kissibo, Jul; Landa-
Mono (beside Mono R.), Sep; Lomé, Jan, Apr and Jun; Mango, Jul; Oga, Mar;
Zogbégan, Jul.

568.   PLOCEUS NIGERRIMUS   RB

Chestnut and Black Weaver
Tisserin noir de Vieillot

Locally common resident (*P. n. castaneofuscus*) of Southern Guinea Savanna. Recorded from Agou (JBT), Ahoué-houé (De Roo *et al.* 1969), beside the Sio R. some 7 km east of Adeta, Adina (De Roo *et al.* 1970), Amakpavé, Amoussokopé (Cheke *et al.* 1986), Atakpamé (De Roo *et al.* 1970), Edifou (De Roo *et al.* 1970), Logoba (Reichenow 1897), Tokpli and Tsévié (Cheke *et al.* 1986).

Breeding. Nests in Coconut Palms at Logba (? = Logoba), Feb (Reichenow 1897). E. Baumann (in Reichenow 1897) stated that the nest sites differed from place to place. In the high grass savanna, they were attached between the final quarters of two blades of grass. In the villages, they hung on coconut palms together with nests of other weavers. In the lower grass savanna, the nests were hung from the fronds of lone-standing *Elaeis* or Phoenix palms. In mixed colonies invariably nest beneath *P. cucullatus*.

Mixed colony with *P. cucullatus* Amoussokopé, Oct (Cheke *et al.* 1986) and Tsévié, Sep; colony Agou, Feb (JBT).

569.   PLOCEUS MELANOCEPHALUS   RB

Black-headed Weaver
Tisserin à tête noire

Uncommon resident (*P. m. capitalis*), found both at the coast and at river edges in Northern Guinea Savanna. In the south, common beside the Sio R., Lomé, and also 20 noted Tokpli, Feb. In the north, only recorded from the Oti R. at Mango and at Domaine Gravillou. A specimen from Mango ascribed to *P. heuglini* by De Roo *et al.* (1972) was *P. melanocephalus* (M. Louette, pers. comm.).

Breeding. C/3 Mango, Aug. Nest building Mango, Oct. Active nests Domaine Gravillou and Lomé, Aug, where males in full breeding dress also seen, Sep. Birds in non-breeding plumage, Feb.

570.   PLOCEUS TRICOLOR   RB

Yellow-mantled Weaver
Tisserin tricolore

Common widespread resident (*P. t. tricolor*) of forests and forest edges. Also occurs in gallery forest in Southern Guinea Savanna, e.g. Tohoun (Dekeyser 1951).

Breeding. Breeds in small colonies of about a dozen nests in forest trees. Building: Koniouhou, Mar (Cheke *et al.* 1986); Misahöhe, Apr. Entering nests: Misahöhe, Mar–Apr; Idifiou, Feb (Walsh *et al.* 1990). Juvenile birds: Misahöhe, Jan–Apr.

571.   PLOCEUS SUPERCILIOSUS   R(B)

Compact Weaver
Tisserin gros-bec

Uncommon resident of edges of wetlands in Southern Guinea Savanna. Collected Bismarckburg and Sebbe (Reichenow 1902a). De Roo (1970) reported specimens from Adina, Ebéva, Edifou, Evou, Kamina, Lomnava and Témedja. The specimen from Namoundjoga (see De Roo *et al.* 1971) was a misidentified *P. heuglini* (M. Louette, pers. comm.). Sight records from beside the Sio R. near Lomé, Fazao and Kpayando.

Breeding. Male beside nests, 20 km north of Lomé, 18 Aug 1989, and at Wahala, 20 Aug 1989.

572.   MALIMBUS SCUTATUS   R(B)

Red-vented Malimbe
Malimbe à queue rouge

Uncommon resident of forest (*M. s. scutatus*), only 2 records: sighted Misahöhe, Feb 1990 (JBT) and Apr 1990.

573.   MALIMBUS NITENS   RB

Blue-billed Malimbe
Malimbe à bec bleu

Uncommon resident of forest zone. Collected Bismarckburg, Apr (Reichenow 1891a), Ahoué-houé, Jul (De Roo *et al.* 1969) and Ebéva, Oct (De Roo *et al.* 1972). Also collected on the Ghana side of the Togo border at Agomé Tongwe, Jul (E. Baumann, MNB). Sight records Misahöhe, Apr 1990, and Pagala, Aug 1990 (JBT).
  Breeding. Nest and C/2 collected by R. Büttner at Bismarckburg, 8 Apr (Reichenow 1891a). Adults bringing food to nests in colony at Pagala, 11 Aug 1990 (JBT).

574.   MALIMBUS MALIMBICUS   R(B)

Crested Malimbe
Malimbe huppé

Uncommon resident (*M. m. nigrifrons*) of forest zone. A male and a female collected Misahöhe on different dates in Dec 1894 (Reichenow 1897), also collected Dzogbégan, Dec (De Roo *et al.* 1972). Also collected (a juvenile male) on the Ghana side of the Togo border at Agomé Tongwe, 22 May 1894 (Reichenow 1897). Sight records from Badou, once in company of *M. rubricollis*, Mar 1990, Djodji, Mar 1990, Kpalimé, Nov 1989 and Apr 1990 (JBT), and Misahöhe, Apr 1990.

575.   MALIMBUS RUBRICOLLIS   RB

Red-headed Malimbe
Malimbe à tête rouge

Common resident (*M. r. bartletti*) of forest zone and occasional in gallery forest in Southern Guinea Savanna, e.g. beside the Sio R. at Kati, and near the Benin border (JBT). Collected Batja (= Badja), Jun 1894 (Reichenow 1897) and Misahöhe, Aug and Dec (De Roo *et al.* 1971, 1972).
  Breeding. Building Badou, 25 Mar 1990. Many active nests Djodji and elsewhere in the Badou region, Mar. One mobbing an African Wood Owl (*Strix woodfordii*) at Kati, 10 Feb 1986.

576.   ANAPLECTES RUBRICEPS   RB

Red-winged Malimbe
Tisserin à ailes rouges

Not uncommon, widespread but sparsely distributed resident (*A. r. leuconotus*) of Northern Guinea Savanna.
  Breeding. Fresh nests near Mango, Dec 1978, and Kpayando, Mar 1990. Nests of unknown age noted Aledjo, Apr, Djamdé, Aug, Landa-Pozanda, Jul, Naboulgou, Feb and Apr, Oti R. at 10°39'N, 00°21'E, Aug, and Sawaga, Apr.

577. QUELEA ERYTHROPS   AfM/(B), R?(B)

Red-headed Dioch
Travailleur à tête rouge

Common intra-African migrant found in all types of savanna; some resident
populations occur. Recorded from the coastal strip (Sio R. near Lomé, Lomé
(Browne 1980), Togokomé (De Roo *et al.* 1969) and Tokpli), at numerous localities
in Southern Guinea Savanna (De Roo 1970, De Roo *et al.* 1971, 1972), the Kara,
Mango and Dapaon areas in the Northern Guinea Savanna, where usually in
flocks of 20–30, and Sudan Savanna (Borgou, De Roo *et al.* 1972; Namoundjoga,
De Roo *et al.* 1971).

[QUELEA QUELEA

Black-faced Dioch
Travailleur à bec rouge

Millet-Horsin (1923) identified bands of *Quelea sanguinirostris* (= *Q. quelea*), which
he also described as "le quelea à bec rouge, le travailleur, le mange-mil", in the Anécho
area. However, it is likely that these were *Q. erythrops*, a species which he did not list.
There are no records of *Q. quelea* in Togo in the extensive archive for this pest compiled
by the Centre for Overseas Pest Research (P. J. Jones, pers. comm.). If it does occur, it
would be expected in the far north, as in Ghana (Grimes (1987)].

578. EUPLECTES AFER   R(B)

Yellow-crowned Bishop
Vorabé

Locally common resident (*E. a. afer*) of wetlands in the coastal plain and in northern
savannas. Collected in both habitats, Aug (De Roo *et al.* 1969), and at Mango, date
unknown (Reichenow 1902a). Plentiful near Lomé and especially in the Mango area,
where 500 counted, and Domaine Gravillou, Jul 1989. Surprisingly rare elsewhere.
   Breeding. Males in breeding dress, May–Aug.

579. EUPLECTES HORDEACEUS   RB

Fire-crowned Bishop
Monseigneur

Common widespread resident (*E. h. hordeaceus*) of thick grassland near water
throughout. Most common in Northern Guinea Savanna, less so elsewhere but occurs in
Southern Guinea Savanna, at the coast (Millet-Horsin 1923, De Roo *et al.* 1969, Browne
1980) and as far north as Borgou and Namoundjoga (De Roo *et al.* 1971, 1972).
   Breeding. Copulation Sala R., near Bafilo, 26 Aug 1984. Nest, contents unknown,
Agoué, 29 Jul 1919 (Millet-Horsin 1923). Female building Mango, 26 Aug 1989. Males
moulting into breeding dress Sio R., near Lomé, 1 May 1990.
   Taxonomic note. The race *E. h. hordeaceus* is included now in the monotypic
E. hordeaceus (Craig 1993a).

580. EUPLECTES FRANCISCANUS   RB

Red Bishop
Ignicolore

Abundant resident throughout savanna zones and at the coast. Prefers grassland, edges
of marshes and farmland.

Breeding. Nest being constructed Zébé, 25 Jun 1919, and nest, contents unknown, Anécho, 10 Jul 1919 (Millet-Horsin 1923).

Taxonomic note. *E. franciscanus* is now considered a monotypic species, separate from *E. orix* (Hall & Moreau 1970, Craig 1993a).

581.   EUPLECTES MACROURUS   R(B)

Yellow-mantled Whydah
Veuve à dos d'or

Common widespread resident (*E. m. macrourus*) throughout the savanna zones and at the coast, preferring rank grassland near water. In his description of *E. m. pallidus*, now considered synonymous with *macrourus* (Craig 1993b), Neunzig (1928) listed specimens from Bassar and Mango.

Breeding. Males entering breeding dress Kpaya, early Jun.

582.   EUPLECTES ARDENS   R(B)

Red-collared Widow-bird
Veuve noire

Rare, presumed resident (*E. a. ardens*). Craig (1993b) argued that there are no known criteria to separate *concolor* from *ardens* and suggested that *concolor* should no longer be used. Three males collected Misahöhe, 18–19 Nov 1893, and another Kuma Adamé, 14 Oct 1894 (Reichenow 1897), but the latter site may have been in Ghana. Males at Djodji, 26 Jul 1989, and Pagala, Aug 1990 (JBT), are the only recent records.

Breeding. One of the specimens from Misahöhe, Nov, is in full breeding dress and all have long tail streamers.

583.   ANOMALOSPIZA IMBERBIS   R(B)

Parasitic Weaver
Tisserin-coucou

Rare, presumed resident. Collected Namoundjoga, Jul (De Roo *et al.* 1971), and pairs sighted Kara, 10 Jul 1987, and Tététou, 26 Jan 1988.

584.   AMBLYOSPIZA ALBIFRONS   RB, Afm?

Grosbeak Weaver
Gros bec à front blanc

Uncommon presumed resident (*A. a. capitalba*) of marshes and reed-beds in the coastal plain and the southwest. May be subject to local movements. A male collected Kpalimé, 18 Oct 1894, by E. Baumann (Reichenow 1897, 1902a), 2 collected Apéyémé, Dec (De Roo *et al.* 1972) and seen Kpaza R., date unknown.

Breeding. Bred in a reed-bed beside the main road, 20 km north of Lomé, in 1989. Activity at small colony first noted Jul (JBT). A nest, 1 m above the water in reeds, being built by a female with attendant male, 17 Aug 1989; the male uttered trilling calls and stretched out its wings. A second nest, incomplete, being entered by a female, 20 Aug. A third nest, contents unknown, with attendant adult, 7 Sep 1989, was seen being destroyed by a monitor lizard *Varanus* sp., 14 Sep. Absent from the site in 1990. Nest in tall grass at side of Kpaza R. (08°30'N, 00°53'E), date unknown but during wet season.

ESTRILDIDAE

585. NIGRITA BICOLOR   R(B)
Chestnut-breasted Negro-Finch
Sénébrun à ventre roux

Uncommon forest resident (*N. bicolor bicolor*). Collected Ahoué-houé (De Roo *et al.*
1969) and Misahöhe (De Roo *et al.* 1972), where seen, Jan 1988 (Walsh *et al.* 1990) and
Nov 1989 (JBT). Also observed Badou, and Djodji, both in Mar 1990, and Balla, Apr 1990.

586. NIGRITA LUTEIFRONS   R(B)
Pale-fronted Negro-Finch
Sénégali à nègre à front jaune

Rare resident (*N. l. luteifrons*) of forest, only one record: one seen at Misahöhe, 28 Apr
1990.

587. NIGRITA CANICAPILLA   R(B)
Grey-crowned Negro-Finch
Sénégali nègre

Common widespread resident (*N. c. emiliae*) of forest, gallery forest, forest edge and
clearings. Recorded from the coast (Browne 1980) north to Aledjo (Cheke *et al.* 1986).
  Breeding. Moss being collected from a dead tree and being added to a large, domed
nest near Pagala, Aug 1990.

588. NESOCHARIS CAPISTRATA   RB
Grey-headed Olive-back
Bengali vert à joues blanches

Uncommon resident of well-wooded Guinea Savanna. Apart from singles, near Binako,
Feb 1994 (PMC), and Badou, date unknown (TC), only known from the Kara area,
where seen 5 km south of Kara (Cheke 1982b) at Djamdé, Kpaya, Kpayando and
Landa-Pozanda. Noted feeding on figs near Landa-Pozanda, Mar 1990.
  Breeding. Nest-building Landa-Pozanda, Jul 1987 (Walsh *et al.* 1990). Occupied
nest (a football-sized tangle of grasses 6 m up on a side-branch of a tall tree in riverine
woodland with lush grass undergrowth) Landa-Pozanda, 3 Aug 1989; nest had been
destroyed, perhaps by monkeys, when re-visited on 10 Aug.

589. PYTILIA PHOENICOPTERA   RB
Red-winged Pytilia
Diamant aurore

Not uncommon resident (*P. p. phoenicoptera*) of savannas from the far north to at
least as far south as Ayagba (Cheke *et al.* 1986). Usually singly or in pairs, but 4 at
Mare aux Lions, Feb 1987.
  Breeding. Dependent young, only 1–2 days out of the nest, Kpayando, 6 Mar 1988
(Walsh *et al.* 1990).

590. PYTILIA MELBA   R(B), AfM?/NB
Melba Finch
Beaumarquet

Rare, presumed resident of northern savannas or dry season visitor (*P. m. citerior*) from the north, only one certain record: one beside the Oti R. at Mango, 27 Dec 1984 (H. Lege). A female collected at Bismarckburg, 27 Mar (Reichenow 1891a), is questionable: the locality is far south of its normal range and the specimen was not found in the MNB. Not recorded in Ghana (Grimes 1987).

591.   PYTILIA HYPOGRAMMICA   R(B)

Yellow-winged Pytilia
Pytilie à ailes jaunes

Uncommon resident of well-wooded Southern Guinea Savanna. Collected Binaparba (De Roo *et al.* 1969), Ebéva (De Roo *et al.* 1972) and Edifou (De Roo 1970). Sight records: 5 birds together at Kpayando, Mar 1987 and Mar 1988; pairs at Ketao, Sep 1989, and Fazao, Jan 1989.

592.   MANDINGOA NITIDULA   R(B)

Green-backed Twin-spot
Bengali vert tacheté

Rare, presumed resident (*M. n. schelgeli*) within forest, only one record: a female collected by E. Baumann at Misahöhe, 15 Feb 1895 (Reichenow 1897).

593.   PYRENESTES OSTRINUS   R(B)

Black-bellied Seed-cracker
Gros-bec ponceau à ventre noir

Uncommon resident (*P. o. ostrinus* and *P. o. frommi*) of thickets in savanna and forest clearings.
   Although a male, collected by E. Baumann at Misahöhe, 5 Jul 1894 (Reichenow 1897), was used by Neumann (1910) for his description of *P. o. ostrinus*, the specimen was later assigned to *P. o. maximus* (Anon on the label and Bannerman 1949). Mackworth-Praed & Grant (1973) subsumed *maximus* within *frommi*, and raised this to specific status as the Large-billed Seed-cracker *P. frommi*, and included Togo in its geographical distribution.
   Specimens collected at Tchonou are *P. o. ostrinus* (De Roo 1970). Sight records from Anonoe, Mar 1990, and Titira, Dec 1987.

594.   SPERMOPHAGA HAEMATINA   R(B)

Blue-billed Weaver
Gros-bec sanguin

Uncommon forest resident (*S. h. togoensis*). Collected Bismarckburg (Reichenow 1891a), Misahöhe (Reichenow 1897) and Togoville (De Roo *et al.* 1971). The Bismarckburg and Misahöhe specimens were used by Neumann (1910) to describe *togoensis*. Sight records: Badou, Mar; Balla, Apr; Djodji, Mar (Cheke *et al.* 1986); Misahöhe, Feb–Mar.

595.   LAGONOSTICTA RUFOPICTA   R(B)

Bar-breasted Fire-Finch
Amarante pointé

Common widespread resident (*L. r. rufopicta*) of savanna habitats from the coast (Reichenow 1902a, Browne 1980) north to Dapaon, where 12 together, Apr 1988, and Nanergou (De Roo *et al.* 1969).

Breeding. A young bird (with large white gape flanges) in group of 9 birds Landa-Pozanda, Aug 1986 (Walsh *et al.* 1990). 3 fledglings with large gape flanges, accompanied by 2 adults, Kara, 19 Nov 1988.

596.   LAGONOSTICTA SENEGALA   R(B)

Senegal Fire-Finch
Amarante commun

Common resident (*L. s. senegala*) throughout Northern Guinea Savanna, often in towns and villages, occasionally in flocks of 20–30 birds, e.g. Tantigou, Apr and Jul. Less abundant further south but recorded at Blitta and Nangbeto (JBT) in Southern Guinea Savanna, and at Lomé (Browne 1980), and collected Porto Séguro (De Roo *et al.* 1969), Sebbe (Reichenow 1902a) and Togoville (De Roo *et al.* 1971) along the coastal strip. Grimes (1987) discounted Browne's records as misidentifications for *rufopicta*, mistakenly stating that he did not record the latter. However, Browne did indeed list *rufopicta*, and the coastal specimens suggest that his identification was correct.

597.   LAGONOSTICTA RARA   R(B)

Black-bellied Fire-Finch
Sénégali à ventre noir

Common resident (*L. r. forbesi*), widespread in Northern Guinea Savanna in cultivated ground and zones with good tree cover, including riparian woodland, and extending as far north as Titira. Payne (1982) quotes a record from Borgou, but this has not been traced. Not uncommon in Southern Guinea Savanna including Notsé (De Roo *et al.* 1969) and the Fazao and Mo areas. Usually seen in pairs.
Breeding. Two pairs with 3 fledglings Kara, date unknown. A pair accompanied by 2 recently fledged Indigobirds (*Vidua ?camerunensis*) Kara, 9 Dec 1988.

598.   LAGONOSTICTA RUBRICATA   R(B)

Blue-billed Fire-Finch
Amarante flambé

Uncommon resident (*L. r. polionota*) of both Guinea Savanna zones, recorded from the coast (Browne 1980) north to Titira; occurs singly or in pairs. Collected Adina (De Roo 1970), Atakpamé (De Roo 1970) and Bismarckburg (Reichenow 1891a).

599.   LAGONOSTICTA LARVATA   R(B)

Black-faced Fire-Finch
Amarante masqué

Locally not uncommon resident (*L. l. togoensis*) of Guinea Savanna woodland recorded from Notsé (De Roo *et al.* 1969) north to Kara. The type specimen of *togoensis*, described by Neumann (1907), was collected at Kété Kratschi, now in Ghana.
Breeding. Male carrying grass in bill (suggesting courtship display) Kara, Jul (Cheke & Walsh 1980).

600.   URAEGINTHUS BENGALUS   RB

Red-cheeked Cordon-bleu
Cordon bleu

Abundant resident (*U. b. bengalus*) of all savanna habitats from Tabligbo northwards but most common in Northern Guinea Savanna and Sudan Savanna. Occasionally in flocks of 20 or more birds.

Breeding. C/4, (nest 2 m up in *Acacia* tree with associated polistine wasp nests) Landa Pozanda, 10 Aug 1989. Similar nest nearby was being built, 24 Jun 1989, but, although complete by 22 Jul, remained empty. A wasp collected from this nest association was *Ropalidia cincta*, the species also identified in association with *U. bengalus bengalus* and other species in Ghana (McCrae & Walsh 1974). The wasp specimen has been deposited in the BMNHL. Nest building Kara, Jul, and Ketao, Sep.

601.   ESTRILDA CAERULESCENS   R(B)

Lavender Fire-Finch
Sénégali gris-bleu

Uncommon resident of Northern Guinea Savanna, often in small groups of 4–6 birds. Recorded Aledjo (De Roo *et al.* 1969), Djamdé, Defale, Kara, Naboulgou and Péwa.

602.   ESTRILDA MELPODA   R(B)

Orange-cheeked Waxbill
Joues-oranges

Abundant resident of open grassland areas, rank grass beside wetlands and rivers, and disturbed habitats throughout the savanna and at the coast. Also penetrates into forest clearings, e.g. Badou and Klouto.

Breeding. 2 parties with fledglings Kara, 15 Oct 1988.

603.   ESTRILDA TROGLODYTES   RB

Black-rumped Waxbill
Bec de corail cendré

Common resident of Guinea Savanna and Sudan Savanna. Most records from Kara northwards but also seen at the coast (Browne 1980). Usually in small groups of 4–15 birds but flock of over 60 Domaine Gravillou, 27 Jan 1990, and 50 there, Mar 1988.

Breeding. Dependent young Kara, Oct (Walsh *et al.* 1990). Family party (3 young with pronounced gapes) Mango, Oct.

604.   AMANDAVA SUBFLAVA   R?/(B), AfM?/(B)

Zebra Waxbill or Goldbreast
Ventre orange

Locally not uncommon presumed resident (*A. s. subflava*), but only recorded Jan–Jul in north so may be intra-African migrant. Usually seen in flocks of 20–100 in Northern Guinea Savanna, e.g. Domaine Gravillou, Kandjo, and the Kara area, but also occurs in the south in the Lomé area (Browne 1980) and Tokpli, Nov 1989 (JBT) and 21 Feb 1990.

605.   ORTYGOSPIZA ATRICOLLIS   R(B)

Quail-Finch
Astrild-caille

Locally common resident (*O. a. ?atricollis*) preferring large open grasslands, usually near water. Occurs from Ayengré north to Tantigou, and at the coast (*O. a. ?ansorgei*) (Browne 1980). Often in parties of 10–50 birds, but 100 together at Tantigou, Apr.

606. **LONCHURA MALABARICA**   AfM/(B), R?(B)

Warbling Silver-bill
Bec d'argent

Uncommon (*L. m. cantans*) mostly found in the far north, but one record as far south as Naboulgou (6 together in Apr 1990). Although presumed to be mainly a dry season visitor some may be resident. Collected Nanergou (De Roo *et al.* 1969), Aug, but all sight records at Domaine Gravillou, Kanbouanga (Cheke & Walsh 1980), Naboulgou, Nataré and Tantigou, Oct–Apr. Max. of 10 at Domaine Gravillou, Mar.

607. **LONCHURA CUCULLATA**   RB

Bronze Mannikin
Spermète nonnettte

Abundant resident (*L. c. cucullata*) of grassland, farms and town gardens, throughout. Often in small groups of 4–10 but sometimes occurs in flocks of 50–100.
   Breeding. Extended. C/3 (nest in *Gmelina* tree) Kara, Oct (Walsh *et al.* 1990); C/5 Kara, Aug. Nest with 2 newly hatched young Kara, Jul. Noisy young (nest in *Eucalyptus* tree with polistine wasp nest within 40 cm) Kara, Oct (Walsh *et al.* 1990). Young in nest Atakpamé Aug. Dependent young Kara, Aug. Nest Zébé, 28 Jun 1919 (Millet-Horsin 1923). Juveniles Kara, Mar. Active nest in *Acacia* tree, Sara-Kawa, Jun (Walsh *et al.* 1990), and 20 km north of Lomé, Aug. Building: Kara, May–Jun, Aug (in abandoned nest of *Apus affinis*) and Sep; Ketao, Jul and Aug (in abandoned *Ploceus* nest); Péwa, Jun; Landa-Pozanda, Apr and Jun. Display: Kara, Jun.

608. **LONCHURA BICOLOR**   R(B)

Black and White Mannikin
Spermète à bec blue

Not uncommon resident (*L. b. bicolor*) of the coastal strip and forest clearings in the south. Recorded Agoué and Anécho (Millet-Horsin 1923) and collected Adina, Ahoué-houé, Atakpamé, Badou, Ebéva, Edifou, Misahöhe, Tététou and Tomégbe, (De Roo 1970, De Roo *et al.* 1969, 1971 1972). Sighted Kpalimé and L. Togo (JBT), Lomé (Cheke & Walsh 1984), Djodji, Kamétonou, Tokpli and Klabé Apégamé. Sometimes in flocks of up to 10 birds.

609. **LONCHURA FRINGILLOIDES**   R(B)

Magpie Mannikin
Spermète pie

Uncommon resident of coastal areas (Browne 1980), forest clearings and Southern Guinea Savanna. Collected Ahoué-houé (De Roo *et al.* 1969) and Aledjo (De Roo *et al.* 1972).
   Breeding. 6 juveniles in party of 10, which included a displaying male, Badou, Jan (Walsh *et al.* 1990). Nest-building Badou, Feb.

610. **AMADINA FASCIATA**   AfM?/(B)

Cut-throat Weaver
Cou-coupé

Rare, presumed dry season visitor only (*A. f. fasciata*) to the far north. Only one record: a pair at Kpani, 9 Feb 1988 (Walsh *et al.* 1990).

611.   PHOLIDORNIS RUSHIAE   R(B)

Tit-Hylia
Astrild-mésange

Rare resident (*P. r. ?ussheri*) of forests, only one sight record: 3 at Balla, Apr 1990.

VIDUIDAE

Taxonomic note: The species and nomenclature used follow Payne (1982) and his subsequent revisions (Payne 1985, 1994, 1996, Payne & Payne 1994). These may differ from those eventually published in the *Birds of Africa* as the studies on this group are not yet complete.

612.   VIDUA CHALYBEATA   R(B)

Village Indigobird
Combassou du Sénégal

Payne's presumption that the ranges of this indigobird overlapped that of its host *Lagonosticta senegala* in Togo (Payne 1982) has now been confirmed. Males with distinctive black primaries have been seen at Mango and Naboulgou, Nov, Landa-Pozanda, 11 Sep 1988, and at Kara, 29 Aug 1988. One at Kara, Oct, mimicked the song of *L. senegala*. One was collected in Ghana near the Morago river (Payne 1982), at a site very close to the Ghana/Togo border.

[VIDUA RARICOLA

Goldbreast Indigobird
Veuve de Jambandu

Payne & Payne (1994) report an association between *V. raricola* and the Goldbreast *Amandava subflava* in Cameroon and Sierre Leone. As the Goldbreast occurs in Togo so probably does this indigobird.]

613.   VIDUA WILSONI   R(B)

Bar-breasted Firefinch Indigobird
Combassou noir

One collected 11 km south of Kandé, Aug, and listed as *Hypochera funerea wilsoni* by De Roo *et al.* (1969), is considered to be this species by Payne (1982). One very dark bird seen Sara-Kawa, Sep, had a blackish-purple gloss and brown flight feathers and was probably *wilsoni* and not *chalybeata*. A similar bird at Kara, Sep, and 2 near Mango, Nov. Likely to occur throughout the Togo range of its host *Lagonosticta rufopicta*.

614.   VIDUA CAMERUNENSIS   R(B)

Cameroon Indigobird
Combassou de Cameroun

A juvenile with a female Black-bellied Firefinch *Lagonosticta rara* at Landa Pozanda, 4 Nov 1989, and 2 fledglings with a pair of Black-bellied Firefinch at Kara, 9 Dec 1988. No previous records for Togo but occurs in Ghana and Nigeria (Payne 1982, where named *V. raricola*). It is now realised that the type of *V. raricola* mimicked the songs of *Amandava subflava* rather than *L. rara*. Viduines mimicking the latter are now assigned to *V. camerunensis* and those mimicking *A. subflava* to *V. raricola* (see

Payne & Payne 1994 for further details). One collected at Mole, Ghana (specimen UMMZ 220766) was listed originally as *V. raricola* (Payne 1982) but is now considered to be *V. camerunensis* (Plate 1 of Payne & Payne 1994).

615.   VIDUA LARVATICOLA   R(B)

      Black-faced Firefinch Indigobird
      Combassou de Bako

Specimens from Mango, date unknown, were listed as *Hypochera ultramarina* by Reichenow (1902a) and those from Paio, Aug, as *H. nigeriae* by De Roo *et al.* (1969). These are now considered to be *V. larvaticola* (Payne 1982). De Roo *et al.* (1971, 1972) also recorded "*H. nigeriae*" at Borgou, Dec, and Niamtougou, Jul. A very glossy blue male with brown flight feathers seen at Kara, Jul 1979, was probably *larvaticola*.

    V. larvaticola parasitises the Black-faced Firefinch *Lagonosticta larvata* and so would be expected to overlap with the latter's range in Togo.

      [VIDUA NIGERIAE

      Quail-finch Indigobird
      Combassou de astrild-caille

Payne & Payne (1994) report an association between *V. nigeriae* and the Quail-finch *Ortygospiza atricollis* in Cameroon and Nigeria. As the Quail-finch occurs in Togo so probably does this indigobird.]

616.   VIDUA MACROURA   R(B)

      Pin-tailed Whydah
      Veuve dominicaine

Abundant resident of savanna zones. Occurs at the coast and in Southern Guinea Savanna, e.g. Anié and Fazao, but most common in northern Guinea and Sudan Savanna.
    Breeding. Parasitises *Lonchura cucullata*, *Estrilda melpoda* and *E. troglodytes* in southern Ghana (Macdonald 1980), and probably does so in Togo. 3 recently fledged birds Kara, 19 Nov 1988. Display flights Kara, Oct. Males in breeding dress, May–Oct.

617.   VIDUA TOGOENSIS   R(B)

      Togo Paradise Whydah
      Veuve à collier d'or togolaise

Uncommon resident of Guinea Savanna woodland. Following Payne (1985), *V. togoensis* is known to occur on the basis of specimens from Mango and Paio, which had been listed as *Steganura orientalis togoensis* Grote by De Roo *et al.* (1969). The Togo Paradise Whydah was named as *Steganura paradisea togoensis* by Grote (1923) using E. Baumann and J. von Zech's specimens from Kete (?= Keta) and Kété Kratschi in Ghana, and G. Thierry's from Mango. The latter specimen and one collected by R. Büttner at Bismarckburg were listed as *S. paradisea* by Reichenow (1892, 1902a).
    Breeding. Parasitises *Pytilia hypogrammica* (Payne 1985).

618.   VIDUA INTERJECTA   R(B)

      Uelle Paradise Whydah
      (named Exclamatory Paradise Whydah by Payne 1994)
      Veuve à collier d'or d'Uelle

Status uncertain but probably uncommon resident whose Togo range overlaps that of its host *Pytilia phoenicoptera*. No specimen from Togo was available for Payne (1985) but he emphasised that in male *interjecta* the maroon on the breast extends further posteriorly than in males of *togoensis*, giving a two-tone appearance to the underparts of *interjecta*, compared with the more uniformly amber underparts of *togoensis*. Using this criterion, a male *interjecta* was seen at Naboulgou, 19 May 1980, and another at Landa-Pozanda, 11 Sep 1988. Other males, either *interjecta* or *togoensis*, sighted Defale, Apr, Mango, Nov, Naboulgou, Oct, and Palakoko, Nov.

FRINGILLIDAE

619.   SERINUS LEUCOPYGIUS   R(B)

Grey Canary
Chanteur d'Afrique

Rare resident (*S. l. riggenbachi*) of Northern Guinea Savanna and Sudan Savanna, 4 records only: 3 near Barkoissi, 10 Apr 1988 (Walsh *et al.* 1990); one Cinkansé, 13 Aug 1988; one Kpani, 3 Mar 1990; one Mango, date unknown (TC).
Breeding. Song Cinkansé, Aug.

620.   SERINUS MOZAMBICUS   R(B)

Yellow-fronted canary
Serin du Mozambique

Common resident (*S. m. caniceps*) throughout the savanna zones, recorded from Notsé (De Roo *et al.* 1969) north to Namoundjoga (De Roo *et al.* 1971).

621.   SERINUS GULARIS   R(B)

Streaky-headed Seed-eater
Serin gris à tête blanche

Not uncommon resident (*S. g. canicapilla*) of well-wooded Guinea savanna and forest clearings. Collected Misahöhe, 27 Mar 1895 (Reichenow 1897), Tchonou (De Roo *et al.* 1969), Ebéva (De Roo *et al.* 1972) and Kolékopé (Louette 1975). Occasionally occurs in flocks when feeding on millet, e.g. 94 at Mo, Aug 1984 (Cheke *et al.* 1986). Birds also seen Badou, Djamdé, Landa Pozanda and Péwa.
Breeding. Song flight Péwa, 25 Jun 1989.

EMBERIZIDAE

622.   EMBERIZA TAHAPISI   AfM/(B), R(B)

Rock Bunting
Bruant cannelle

Common dry season visitor (*E. t. goslingi*) to the Northern Guinea Savanna and Sudan Savanna zones, especially on stony ground, Oct–Apr, when migrants arrive from the north, probably to breed. Some resident populations also, e.g. Péwa, the Kara area and Defale. Usually only 1–6 birds seen but a party of 10 and a flock of 40 Defale, 3 Apr 1988.

623.   EMBERIZA AFFINIS   R(B)

Brown-rumped Bunting
Bruant à ventre jaune

Uncommon resident of Northern Guinea Savanna (*E. a. nigeriae*). Collected Mango, Aug, and Paio, Aug (De Roo *et al.* 1969). Only 3 other records: singles Naboulgou, 20 Feb 1988, and 16 km northwest of Mango, Nov 1988 (H&S); a pair Naboulgou, 7 Apr 1990.

624.   EMBERIZA CABANISI   R(B)

Cabanis's Yellow Bunting
Bruant de Cabanis

Not uncommon resident (*E. c. cabanisi*) of Guinea Savanna, preferring areas with scattered trees, often in rocky terrain such as the Bafilo ridge, where common. Recorded from Bismarckburg and Misahöhe (Reichenow 1891a, 1897) north to Paio (De Roo *et al.* 1969).

Breeding. Carrying food Defale, Aug (Walsh *et al.* 1990). Song Aledjo Kadara, Jul.

APPENDIX 1

Some observations of the environment and social life of people of the Bismarckburg area at the end of the 19th. century.

What follows is based on a translation of the original account (Büttner 1893) by the late Dudley J. Cheke (father of R. A. Cheke).

"On the 2nd. of June 1888 Surgeon-Major Dr. L. Wolf raised the German flag on Mt. Adado. This was in the area of Adélé which until then had never been trodden on by a whiteman. He began to build the station which was later to receive the name of Bismarckburg.

On that day with what feelings of hope and joy must Wolf and his companions, First Lieutenant Kling and the technician Bugslag, have looked at the broad landscape with its mountain ranges and peaks; that rolling sea of grass and the dark green strips of woodland, which stretched like nets, and surrounded the pure gravel beds of the mountain streams in such a delightful way. Looking to the southeast they could see the way which they had already taken, as far back as the mountain peak of Gibia. The horizon was closed by the mountain region of Aposso whose difficult character, with its steep cliffs and extremely stony paths and wild mountain streams, had presented very considerable difficulties to the expedition in its attempt to move forward. This landscape itself was virgin territory for the explorers, because the attempt of the French Catholic missionaries to establish a station in the hinterland had got no further than Atakpamé. Even today, a grave stands witness to them and to so many others who failed in their attempts to penetrate. To the south of Atakpamé a level or slightly rolling land of grass steppe or savanna, with scattered shrubs which are typical of a greater part of tropical Africa, stretches as far as the coast where the expedition had started, in Klein-Popo. In the dry season, grass fires spread over the savanna and the streams dry up so that the thirsty caravans have to dig in the river beds for water; or pay dearly for dirty clayey liquid, known as water, which the natives gather in their pots. In the rainy season the coastal district, which takes some six days march to cross, still represents a considerable problem to explorers when the rivers overflow their banks, so that for hours at a time one has to wade in water and gets bogged down on the slippery paths. The three founders of the station were men of true enthusiasm; they did not so much look back to the road they had taken as forwards to the rich field of activity which lay before them. As far as the eye could see everything was new and unknown and was impatiently waiting for research.

There were manifold tasks which lay before the research station at Bismarckburg. It had to be the base for further expeditions into the hinterland, especially in the northern direction where they had to pass more than 6 degrees of latitude to join the wide bend of the Niger in order to hit Barth's route (1853). The establishment at Adélé had also got a commercial purpose: namely to attract, in a southerly direction towards the German coast, the Hausa, who until then had travelled via Salaga and on into the English territory. In addition attention had to be paid to the practical questions: what could be grown there, what products, and also to health in the hinterland. It included anthropological and ethnographical research. It was also necessary to study the meteorology, geology, flora and fauna.

These men set about the giant task with great zeal until they were cut off by death. Only Ludwig Wolf rests in the actual field of his activity. He died on the 26th of June 1889 in Ndali in the Barbar land, while Bugslag and Kling are buried in their homeland, worn out by the effects of their repeated stays in African territory. Bugslag was buried in the beginning of December 1891 in his home town of Apenrade. Kling died on the 15th of September 1892 in Berlin.

The gaps had to be filled by others. On the 15th of May 1890 the mechanic Stohr arrived in Bismarckburg and on the 20th of June in the same year, I undertook the direction of the research station. Fate allowed both of us to return to our homeland, whereas the man named to be my successor, Dr. Kuster, was not even to arrive at the goal of his wishes. He died on the way to the station, after a very short stay in Africa, on the 24th April 1892 in Akroso on the Volta. Now, Bismarckburg is under the direction of L. Conradt who arrived in August 1892 and to whom the technician Hille, who has been in Adélé since January 1892, has been assigned.

I have only to add to this list of individuals the names of von Francois and Dr. Henrici who each visited the station once on their journeys in Togo. Then I have completed the entire list of Europeans who looked out on Mt. Adado, into that wide landscape which is now no longer so unknown.

The dead as well as the living should be given their due for what they did for the research station. Just as the railway lines stream out in all directions in Europe, the map of Togo is marked with the routes taken by the Bismarckburg researchers in all directions of the compass. These were: in the southeast, towards Aposso; in the south across Tribu and Buem to Misahöhe; between them the Kebu route; in the west via Dutukpene to Kratshi; in the west northwest to Salaga; in the northwest to Adjuti; in the north to Fasugu; in the northeast to Tshautyo; in the east to Anyanga. French researchers in the west and the north of Togoland were able to complete their famous journeys in the areas which the researchers in Bismarckburg would like to have explored. This was not due to any fault of the station but because of a shortage of funds and personnel in the research field and in the instructions they were given.

The Hausa caravans are still taking the route via Tshautyo, Fasugu, Yerrepa, Naparri to Salaga which they have passed over for at least several decades. Salaga is the base for trade into the English territory. Indeed why should they travel via Bismarckburg which isn't even on their route and go out of their way to come through German territory when they too are short of funds and cannot be offered paths free of danger or be given any other kind of support?

From the day of its foundation the station has devoted itself earnestly to cultivation, although we are still far from having become self-supporting. Anyway the products of the native plants are of so little value; also, the labour which has to be brought in from distant Liberia or the coast is extremely dear. Like the natives we planted our fields with manioc, yams, maize, peanuts, beans and bananas. Adélé is a mountainous territory, not favourable to variable cultivation. Hence its inhabitants are only very marginally inclined to work in the fields. Their main crop is manioc, followed by yams. The neighbouring areas cultivate mainly yams, followed by grains and in the east, for instance in Anyanga, millet and on the western side, rice. In the station's garden we grew a great number of European vegetables, some of them of very high quality, in addition to the native crops: in the rainy season we used the mountain garden, in the dry season the stream garden. In great quantity, and frequently within the year, we harvested potatoes, beans, peas, salad, cabbage, cucumber, melons, pumpkins, carrots, onions, radishes, black radishes, parsley, celery and also tomatoes, egg-plants, papaya, pineapples, bananas, marakuyas. No doubt it would be possible to grow a great number of other fruits. Nor were we without flowers: dahlias, balsams, carnations, and mignonette grew from European seed. Cotton and tobacco, also grown from imported seed, and since both plants are also found in the native cultures there is no doubt that they would have grown perfectly well. We do not know what their quality is. Finally I laid out a large nursery of kola nut trees and urged my successors to look after it with the greatest care. When I left the station in December 1891, the seedlings were already a metre high and they would be ready to be planted out in the spring at the beginning of the rainy season. I don't doubt that the kola nuts will do well in Adélé and, also, will become an important item of commerce with the Hausas. But I am very much concerned about young seedlings which are to be given to the natives: in view of the lack of interest and idleness of the people of Adélé, it is hardly to be expected that these little trees will grow into fruit-bearing trees under their hands.

I have frequently referred to the lack of interest of the people of Adélé to cultivate the land. Unfortunately there is a clear reason for it. They rush with true zeal into the bush to harvest rubber. At the time of the foundation of the research station the way to use the milk sap of Landolphi was not yet known. It was Dr. Wolf who first brought the knowledge of this method to them. In the first years the outcome was very considerable, but unfortunately not to our advantage nor to that of the land itself. No merchants from the German coast came but there was a strong contingent of black English merchants, who took the rubber in endless loads to the English coast. In exchange there streamed in wares from the coast; cotton goods, arms, powder, and a thousand and one little things which the natives love, with the result that they abandoned the fields and bought the necessities of life at high prices from neighbouring territories. The goods which we could offer in exchange, which cost a great deal to bring up from the coast, became less and less desirable. If the necessities of life ever did reach the station they had to be paid for at very greatly increased prices. The small number of pigs, goats, sheep and poultry in the land were far from sufficient for the needs of the people. We ourselves had to get pigs from Anyanga and cattle even from Fasugu and Tshautyo, so it can easily be seen how difficult it was to feed the staff at the station which numbered between forty and fifty people. If there isn't some change in the circumstances, it will be impossible to maintain the station, at least to the extent of its present work. However, I am hoping for just such a change as a result of the harvesting of the Landolphis. These have been treated in such a robber – like way that in a wide district around the villages the rubber lianes have been destroyed. The rubber collectors go to great distances to the most remote places so that now it takes them two weeks to obtain what they used to get in the same number of days. When the lianes are completely plundered the people will have to return to working on the land.

Balls of rubber are the only product which Adélé sends to the coast. Even when we had other products, their export would have been made impossible by the very distance alone: a laden caravan can hardly make the distance between Adélé and the coast in under twenty days.

Apart from collecting rubber, a great deal of the time of the natives was taken up in fetish palavers. Adélé is indeed the fetish-land par excellence. In the grove of Pereu sits Najo, in the grove of Dipongo, Avriko, the two senior gods. The high priest of Najo is Nunu Elisi, all the other fetish people are under her jurisdiction. Nothing happens in Adélé without prolonged fetish palavers; whether it is a matter of the people as a whole or just private interests, you have to go to Pereu to make offerings there and discover the will of Najo. The power of that woman over their souls is very great indeed. Her position was however shattered for a time when at the head of the Ketshenki people she attacked the station with the national totem and was driven back with severe loss and the fetish stool fell into our hands. Then, abasing herself in the station yard before all the people she made peace with the oboroni, the whites, and returned to her holy place.

Although the station has only been established for a fairly short time it is already closely knit with the interests of the land and the people, who despite all their unquestioned weaknesses we feel a lively sympathy for. In particular true friendship in danger, need and sickness tied us with Kontu, the chief of the neighbouring village Jegge (= Yégué), and his family. May this good entente, valuable to the land and the station, be forever maintained and advanced by Bismarckburg.

Now I hasten to the scientific tasks of the station. These I think have been pursued with love, persistence and success in a systematic way which is better than in any of the other protected territories.

Meteorological observations have been maintained unbroken for years at the station. Three times daily, barometer, thermometer and humidity measurements have been made and the winds and the clouds observed. The tables of the self-registering instruments are changed weekly. The weather conditions are noted and the precipitations measured. If these observations are to have any value they must be made with extreme care and, therefore, are one of the tasks which cannot be entrusted to even the most civilised of the blacks. Of those who have carried out these observations the longest, let me thank Bugslag and Stohr above all.

The research into the flora and fauna of the land was first done by Kling and later fell to my lot. The flora of Adélé is not as rich as I had thought and hoped. (The Royal Botanical Museum of Berlin received, from Dr Wolf, von Francois and from Kling, 343 herbarium plants and 14 items of spirit material from Togoland; from Dr Büttner from Togoland 673 herbarium plants, 68 items of spirit material and dry objects). The principal form of vegetation of the savanna is uniform. Colourful tuberous growths appear with the beginning of the rainy season, later mainly Compositae, Convolvulacae, Scrophulariacae, Cucubitacae, Malvacae, Euphorbiacae, Papilionacae, Melastomacae all covering the wide expanses of grass. There is nowhere any primeval forest but, on the other hand, the banks of the watercourses are covered with a thick, though narrow, girdle of bushes. In this bushland there are some of the giants of the primeval forest. Bushlike vegetation covers the undergrowth. To the eye of the botanist the main items in the flora in this area beside the rivers and streams are ferns, *Selaginella*, strange Aracae, enormous Zingiberacae, Orchidacae and Comellinae, fragrant Rubiacae, prickly Acanthacae, snaky Apocynacae and Asclepiadacae, bright Verbenacae,

Bignoniacae, bush-like Violacae, Sterculiacae, Olacacae and Ochnacae, Connaracae and Combretacae. The flora of bogs and broad stretches of water is completely absent in Adélé, to some advantage to the inhabitants.

The animals prefer the shady and cool stretches of the bush to the sunny and hot savanna and therefore the collector is always enticed thither attempting, alas in vain, to exhaust the richness of types. An individual European, otherwise very much taken up with other things, could never master this richness in years of work. Happy is he when he can find a clever helper. How often I envied Djo, from the Wei tribe, when I saw his lithe almost naked body in metre high grass in the deepest and thickest of bushes; untroubled by thorns and lianas, furious ants and other horrors such as scorpions, centipedes, and poisonous snakes, he all the time making no sound. A European will never learn this silent gliding after the smallest of booty. A European's poorly developed sense of direction soon has him lost after a few paces in the grass or the bush, and hundreds of times the booty escapes in the brambles or in the mud. Djo never went after invertebrate animals and I never had a worse outcome than when I tried to teach him how to collect insects. Other members of the Wei tribe also contributed to my collections, not actually out of scientific interest but rather for 'dash', West African for backsheesh. These sons of a freer nature are gifted with a good sense of observation and to them I owe a considerable number of smaller mammals, snakes and other reptiles, fishes and amphibians. The natives of the land too, among whom some were good patient huntsmen, have provided some items. The Weis, Djali and Mumru, deserve the highest praise: they quickly learnt the techniques of using collecting flasks, quivers, sieves, nets and all kinds of capturing methods and in the course of time brought in various insects, other arthropods, worms and shells. So much so that Dr Karsch told me that the little area of Adélé in the hinterland of Togo is probably better known faunistically than any other part of tropical Africa, despite the few years of research undertaken there.

I now have the most happy memories of my collecting activity. The wonderful Jegge (= Yégué) stream with its beautiful vegetation, the unending life on its shores: these things hold my memory magically.

I had no less joy in the work every evening: selecting, preparing, pinning and wrapping up all the various finds. This was the work that had to be done at the end of every day at the station. Two young helpers in all this were my boys: the 12 or 13 year old Palawe who came from the Grussi area who also served to catch mice and snakes and prepare birds, and the even smaller Quassi a boy from the coast.

Last but not least I think of my co-worker Stohr. He often brought me rare birds and butterflies. He was always anxious to increase our collections whether he was in the workplace, in the fields, in the bush or in the neighbouring villages. I can never be grateful enough to him for the way that he packed and soldered all the items, despite the damp and the insects eating him up.

The research in this land is by no means complete. May the research station have a long life and flourish and may enthusiastic researchers bring the work to its completion."

APPENDIX 2

Recoveries of birds ringed outside Togo and recovered within Togo, and two recoveries of birds ringed in Togo

EURING data cover period ending July 1990. Some additional data up to February 1995 have been included. Age at ringing according to EURING codes (1 = Pullus; 2 = full-grown, age unknown; 3 = born in year of ringing; 4 = born at least 1 year before year of ringing; 6 = born at least two years before year of ringing). Dist. = Grand Circle distance (km); Dir = Compass direction (0-360 degrees) to Togo. Dur. = duration of interval between ringing and recovery (days). Dates within brackets indicate date of letter containing information; ? indicates unknown.

	RINGING DATA					RECOVERY DATA						
SPECIES	COUNTRY	RING NUMBER	AGE	DATE	COORDINATES OF LOCALITY	DATE	LOCALITY	COORDINATES	DIST. (km)	DIR.	DUR. (days)	SOURCE OF INFORMATION
Ardea cinerea	'Prusse orientale'	?	?	?	?	11.i.35	?	?	?	?	?	Rydzensky (1956), Douaud (1957)
	Hungary	?	?	?	?	?	?	?	?	?	?	Brown et al. (1982)
	Switzerland	?	?	?	?	?	?	?	?	?	?	Brown et al. (1982)
	Germany	?	?	?	?	?	?	?	?	?	?	Brown et al. (1982), Cramp & Simmons (1977)
Pandion haliaetus	Finland	M25314	1	09.vii.88	62°21'N, 24°09'E	14.x.88	?	10°30'N, 00°40'E	6085	208	97	J. Haapala (in litt.)
	Finland	M31170	1	29.vi.92	60°27'N, 26°34'E	13.ii.95	Atakpamé	07°34'N, 01°14'E	6266	210	959	J. Haapala (in litt.)
	Sweden	9201108	1	29.vi.65	54°54'N, 15°35'E	01.i.67	near Lomé	06°10'N, 01°21'E	5996	198	551	B-O. Stolt (in litt.)
	Sweden	9227459	1	06.vii.85	57°00'N, 11°49'E	14.xi.85	Ago Déké, 10 km E of Lomé	06°10'N, 01°21'E	5775	192	131	EURING
Buteo buteo	Sweden	9005870	1	30.vi.62	63°44'N, 16°10'E	28.ii.68	Atakpamé	07°34'N, 01°14'E	6365	198	2069	B-O. Stolt (in litt.), Grimes (1987)
Milvus migrans	France	?	?	07.vi.47	nr. Villeneuve	06.ii.57	Wome nr. Palime	06°52'N, 00°45'E	?	?	3532	Douaud (1957), Anon (1957)
	France	DA76620	1	04.vi.72	47°42'N, 07°30'E	04.ii.73	?	06°48'N, 00°42'W	4613	190	245	EURING
	Germany	322070	1	31.x.36	51°25'N, 11°56'E	20.ii.55	Wome nr. Palime	06°52'N, 00°45'E	5059	192	6840	EURING, Jokele (1974)
	Germany	3003344	1	31.v.63	51°52'N, 11°19'E	03.iii.65	Agou-Akplolo	06°57'N, 00°34'E	5090	191	613	EURING, Jokele (1974)
	Germany	3027678	1	17.vi.73	49°55'N, 08°24'E	10.iii.74	near Tsevie	08°23'N, 01°06'E	4666	188	266	EURING
	Switzerland	812460	1	09.vii.59	46°20'N, 06°05'E	late 1970	?	06°20'N, 01°10'E	?	?	?	R. J. Dowsett (in litt.)
	Switzerland	?	?	?	?	02.xi.??	?	?	?	?	?	Heim de Balsac & Mayaud (1962)
Pernis apivorus	Belgium	K11555	1	27.vii.75	50°12'N, 05°06'E	11.xi.78	Abobo, W of Lake Togo	06°12'N, 01°24'E	4903	184	1203	EURING
	Finland	D159149	1	31.vii.92	63°26'N, 22°59'E	03.viii.93	near Kpalimé	06°55'N, 00°44'E	6553	260	368	J. Haapala (in litt.)
Falco tinnunculus (male)	Tunisia	EA93711	4	06.iv.47	37°05'N, 11°02'E	15.iv.68	45 km NW of Kande	10°23'N, 00°35'E	?	?	3755	R. J. Dowsett (in litt.)
?Coturnix coturnix		?	?	?	?	?	near Kpessi	08°04'N, 01°16'E	?	?	?	Douaud (1957)
Charadrius dubius	UK	NJ00258	1	12.vi.83	53°23'N, 00°58'E	28.i.84	near Lomé	06°08'N, 01°14'E	5255	178	230	EURING, Mead & Hudson (1985)
Charadrius hiaticula	Finland	P240382	4	26.vii.69	61°36'N, 21°36'E	01.i.72	Wogba, SW of Vogan	06°18'N, 01°30'E	6378	196	889	EURING
	Finland	PT47100	1	16.vii.93	64°29'N, 24°14'E	06.ii.95	near Lomé	06°10'N, 01°20'E	6754	206	570	J. Haapala (in litt.)

Species	Country	Ring no.	Age	Ringing date	Ringing coords	Recovery date	Recovery locality	Recovery coords					Source
Charadrius hiaticula	UK	NV15382	3	30.ix.86	58°49'N, 02°55'W	30.i.90	Akparne	06°10'N, 01°12'E	5863	176	1218	EURING	Mead & Clark (1991)
Pluvialis squatarola	Denmark	688145	2	20.x.58	55°38'N, 12°34'E	05.x.59	near Aného	06°17'N, 01°40'E	5572	190	350	EURING	
Numenius phaeopus	Denmark	583805	2	12.vii.56	55°38'N, 12°34'E	14.ix.56	near Sokodé	08°59'N, 01°11'E	5283	191	33	EURING	
Tringa glareola	Sweden	4148133	3	03.vii.78	56°05'N, 15°51'E	08.ii.79	near Aného	06°15'N, 01°35'E	5689	189	198	EURING, B-O. Stolt (in litt.), Urban et al. (1986)	
Actitis hypoleucos	Togo	BB38207	3	25.xii.70	06°12'N, 01°24'E	24.v.73	Finland	66°42'N, 24°30'E	?	?	881	R. J. Dowsett (in litt.)	
Calidris alba	UK	NR25684	3	14.ix.88	57°14'N, 07°26'W	01.xii.88	Lomé	06°10'N, 01°91'E	5731	172	78	EURING	Mead & Clark (1989)
Gallinago gallinago	Togo	DS63167	2	01.i.71	06°14'N, 01°13'E	22.ii.72	Platani Cammarata, Sicily	37°38'N, 13°40'E	?	?	418	Sharland (1979)	
Stercorarius parasiticus	UK	EH47200	1	28.vi.79	06°08'N, 02°05'W	(16.vi.80)	Lomé	06°08'N, 01°13'E	6008	177	353	EURING	Spencer & Hudson (1981)
Chlidonias niger	Morocco	SA621804	3	16.ix.80	32°48'N, 08°48'W	19.x.81	Lomé area	06°06'N, 01°12'E	3143	161	246	EURING	Urban et al. (1986)
	Netherlands	H137454	3	07.vii.81	52°30'N, 05°25'E	24.iii.83	Akparne	06°10'N, 01°12'E	5163	184	594	EURING	
	Netherlands	H170648	6	17.vii.83	52°30'N, 05°25'E	18.i.88	Lomé area	06°10'N, 01°38'E	5154	184	1646	EURING	
	Netherlands	H172691	6	17.vii.84	52°30'N, 05°25'E	02.xi.84	Lomé area	06°08'N, 01°13'E	5168	184	108	EURING	
Sterna caspia	Finland	?	?	?	?	??.x.??	?	?	?	?	?	R. J. Dowsett (in litt.)	
Sterna dougallii	Eire	CK08791	1	30.vi.62	52°17'N, 06°23'W	08.vi.63	Lomé area	06°10'N, 01°21'E	5175	172	343	EURING	
	Eire	CK47130	1	21.vii.67	52°18'N, 06°24'W	19.xii.67	Lomé area	06°12'N, 01°24'E	5174	172	151	EURING	
	Eire	CK48833	1	30.vi.67	52°18'N, 06°24'W	02.ii.68	Lomé area	06°12'N, 01°24'E	5174	172	217	EURING	
	Eire	CK73246	1	24.vi.68	52°18'N, 06°30'W	20.xii.68	Lomé area	06°12'N, 01°24'E	5174	172	179	EURING	
	Eire	CK73038	1	22.vi.69	52°18'N, 06°30'W	07.xi.69	Lomé area	06°12'N, 01°24'E	5176	172	138	EURING	
	Eire	CC53822	1	25.vi.71	52°18'N, 06°24'W	(08.x.73)	Lomé area	06°12'N, 01°18'E	5173	172	836	EURING	
	Eire	CR97355	1	23.vi.73	52°18'N, 06°24'W	07.xii.73	Lomé area	06°12'N, 01°24'E	5174	172	167	EURING	
	Eire	CR97547	1	25.vi.74	52°18'N, 06°24'W	(21.iii.75)	Lomé area	06°12'N, 01°24'E	5174	172	269	EURING	
	Eire	XS39865	1	19.vii.86	53°36'N, 06°00'W	02.ii.88	Lomé area	06°10'N, 01°21'E	5315	173	563	EURING	
	UK	CK42399	1	03.vii.65	53°14'N, 04°31'W	28.xii.65	Lomé area	06°10'N, 01°21'E	5259	174	178	EURING	
	UK	CK89627	1	11.vii.65	54°06'N, 06°12'W	11.i.68	Lomé area	06°12'N, 01°24'E	5369	173	914	EURING	
	UK	CK57735	1	06.vii.68	53°12'N, 04°30'W	14.ii.71	Lomé area	06°06'N, 01°18'E	5262	174	954	EURING	
Sterna hirundo	Denmark	8707625	1	18.vi.72	54°38'N, 11°31'E	15.x.72	Lomé	06°08'N, 01°14'E	5471	190	119	EURING	
	Denmark	8707627	1	24.vi.72	54°38'N, 11°31'E	16.xi.72	Lomé	06°08'N, 01°14'E	5471	190	145	EURING	
	Finland	A106666	1	07.vii.62	62°53'N, 21°23'E	07.x.75	Lomé area	06°10'N, 01°21'E	6523	195	4840	EURING	
	Finland	A359797	1	04.vii.70	61°36'N, 26°06'E	19.x.70	Lomé area	06°12'N, 01°24'E	6505	199	107	EURING	Robinson (1972)
	Finland	AT7563	1	13.vii.74	61°55'N, 26°40'E	26.vi.75	Lomé area	06°10'N, 01°21'E	6559	209	348	EURING	
	Finland	AT11739	1	10.vii.70	60°36'N, 27°12'E	28.x.73	Lomé area	06°12'N, 01°24'E	6441	210	1205	EURING	
	Finland	AT30997	1	22.vi.74	60°27'N, 21°42'E	06.x.80	Lomé area	06°10'N, 01°21'E	6292	204	2296	EURING	
	Finland	AT55932	1	10.vii.80	63°16'N, 29°54'E	29.vii.81	Lomé area	06°10'N, 01°21'E	6774	213	384	EURING	
	Finland	AT96452	1	12.vii.88	63°16'N, 29°54'E	23.xii.88	Lomé area	06°10'N, 01°21'E	6773	213	164	J. Haapala (in litt.)	
	France	GA30863	1	15.v.67	48°18'N, 07°42'E	08.ii.68	Lomé area	06°06'N, 01°12'E	4731	188	269	EURING	
	Germany	614924	2	01.vii.47	53°47'N, 07°51'E	30.xi.52	Lomé area	06°08'N, 01°20'E	5329	186	1978	EURING	
	Germany	713181	1	18.vii.48	53°47'N, 07°58'E	07.vii.49	at sea	04°52'N, 01°08'E	5473	187	386	EURING	

| | RINGING DATA | | | | | | RECOVERY DATA | | | | | |
SPECIES	COUNTRY	RING NUMBER	AGE	DATE	COORDINATES OF LOCALITY	DATE	LOCALITY	COORDINATES	DIST. (km)	DIR.	DUR. (days)	SOURCE OF INFORMATION
Sterna hirundo	Germany	7135563	1	16.vii.48	54°39'N, 08°21'E	26.vi.49	at sea	44°55'N, 01°05'E	5567	187	346	EURING
	Germany	614924	3	01.vii.47	53°48'N, 07°54'E	30.xi.52	Lomé area	06°06'N, 07°18'E	5336	186	1978	EURING
	Germany	He7288363	?	15.v.57	53°57'N, 08°25'E	27.iv.58	Lomé	06°10'N, 01°21'E	?	?	347	Schloss (1962)
	Germany	He7299303	1	23.vi.57	54°00'N, 08°24'E	03.xi.61	Kodjoviakope (Lomé)	06°10'N, 01°21'E	5351	187	1594	Neubauer (1973)
	Germany	He7302734	1	16.vii.57	53°48'N, 07°54'E	23.xii.60	Lomé	06°10'N, 01°21'E	5324	186	1255	Schloss (1962)
	Germany	He7320746	1	09.vi.59	54°00'N, 08°24'E	08.v.60	Lomé	06°10'N, 01°21'E	5351	187	333	Schloss (1962)
	Germany	He7320798	1	09.vi.59	54°00'N, 08°24'E	09.i.61	Lomé	06°10'N, 01°21'E	5351	187	610	Neubauer (1973)
	Germany	7483079	1	03.vii.72	54°24'N, 08°36'E	15.x.72	Lomé area	06°12'N, 01°24'E	5397	187	104	EURING
	Netherlands	K442513	1	17.vii.71	52°24'N, 04°48'E	15.x.72	Lomé area	06°30'N, 01°30'E	5111	183	455	EURING
	Netherlands	K591909	1	21.vi.76	53°29'N, 06°12'E	02.i.82	Lomé area	06°08'N, 01°16'E	5282	185	2022	EURING
	Netherlands	K765915	1	21.vi.83	52°32'N, 05°26'E	10.xii.83	Lomé area	06°08'N, 01°13'E	5172	184	172	EURING
	Netherlands	K611230	1	06.vi.87	52°54'N, 05°30'E	19.iii.88	Lomé area	06°10'N, 01°21'E	5208	184	286	EURING
	Netherlands	K611419	1	20.vi.87	52°54'N, 05°30'E	05.iii.88	Lomé area	06°10'N, 01°21'E	5208	184	258	EURING
	Netherlands	K850187	1	06.vii.88	51°48'N, 04°09'E	04.xii.88	Lomé area	06°10'N, 01°21'E	5078	183	151	EURING
	Norway	797252	1	03.vii.66	60°30'N, 05°31'E	02.i.68	Lomé area	06°09'N, 01°20'E	?	?	548	Holgersen (1969)
	Norway	7129206	1	04.vii.72	59°43'N, 05°20'E	10.x.72	Lomé area	06°08'N, 01°14'E	?	?	98	Holgersen (1974)
	Sweden	4032529	1	29.vi.63	59°35'N, 18°54'E	27.vi.65	Lomé	06°10'N, 01°21'E	6130	201	729	Released 28.vi.65 but recaptured 01.vii.65, died 02.vii.65
	Sweden	4032529	1	29.vi.63	59°35'N, 18°54'E	01.vii.65	Lomé	06°10'N, 01°21'E	6130	201	732	Specimen in Stockholm Museum. B-O. Stolt (in litt.)
	Sweden	4032812	1	08.vii.63	59°16'N, 15°41'E	25.xii.63	Lomé	06°10'N, 01°21'E	6036	198	150	B-O. Stolt (in litt.)
	UK	708602	1	18.vii.59	55°37'N, 01°37'W	09.ii.61	Lomé area	06°10'N, 01°21'E	5502	177	571	EURING
	UK	722570	1	20.vii.60	55°20'N, 01°32'W	10.iii.61	Lomé area	06°10'N, 01°21'E	5471	177	205	EURING
	UK	729786	1	24.vii.61	55°20'N, 01°32'W	30.i.62	Lomé area	06°10'N, 01°21'E	5471	177	190	EURING
	UK	CK39626	1	22.vii.63	55°18'N, 01°30'W	02.xii.67	Lomé	06°08'N, 01°14'E	5463	177	1594	Robinson (1972)
	UK	CE24988	1	29.v.77	51°47'N, 00°00'E	(29.i.80)	Lomé area	06°10'N, 01°21'E	5072	179	975	EURING
	UK	XS77865	1	17.vii.84	56°30'N, 05°43'W	29.vi.86	Lomé	06°08'N, 01°14'E	5632	174	713	Mead & Clark (1988)
	UK	XS30831	1	26.vi.87	56°03'N, 02°38'W	(26.vii.90)	Lomé	06°08'N, 01°14'E	5559	176	1126	EURING
	UK	XS60634	4	22.vii.88	54°37'N, 01°11'W	25.ix.88		06°29'N, 01°14'E	5353	178	34	EURING
	UK	XS97493	1	12.vi.88	51°47'N, 00°00'E	24.xii.88	Lomé	06°10'N, 01°14'E	5075	179	195	EURING
	UK	XR13249	1	16.vi.88	57°40'N, 04°20'W	(17.vii.89)	Lomé area	06°10'N, 01°21'E	5746	175	397	EURING
	UK	XR60775	1	14.vii.89	56°30'N, 05°43'W	09.i.90	Lomé area	06°10'N, 01°15'E	5629	174	179	EURING
Sterna hirundo/paradisaea	Finland	A2371	1	02.vii.35	60°12'N, 24°54'E	03.iii.36	Lomé area	06°12'N, 01°24'E	6340	208	244	J. Haapala (in litt.)
Sterna paradisaea	Denmark	740292	1	20.vii.61	62°00'N, 07°20'W	04.xi.61	Lomé area	06°10'N, 01°21'E	6796	174	107	EURING

Species	Country	n	Ring no.	Ringing date	Ringing site	Recovery date	Recovery site	Recovery coords				Source	Reference
Sterna paradisea	Finland	1	AT58798	13.vii.80	65°22'N, 24°50'E	06.x.80	Lomé area	06°10'N, 01°21'E	6851	196	85	EURING	Schloss (1968)
Sterna sandvicensis	Germany	1	He7349407	07.vi.59	54°18'N, 08°48'E	14.i.61	Lomé	06°10'N, 01°21'E	5388	187	586	EURING	
	Denmark	1	7010079	26.vi.68	56°43'N, 10°15'E	20.x.68	Lomé area	06°10'N, 01°21'E	5674	188	116	EURING	
	Denmark	1	7006438	13.vi.70	56°43'N, 10°15'E	05.ii.71	Lomé	06°08'N, 01°14'E	5679	188	237	EURING	
	Eire	1	DS17581	30.vi.67	52°18'N, 06°24'W	13.xii.67	Lomé area	06°12'N, 01°24'E	5174	172	166	EURING	
	France	1	FT8263	15.vi.66	44°42'N, 01°12'W	(23.i.69)	Lomé area	06°12'N, 01°30'E	4287	176	952	EURING	
	France	1	GX10829	12.vi.68	47°30'N, 03°00'W	20.x.68	Lomé area	06°06'N, 01°12'E	4619	175	130	EURING	
	France	1	FU28123	25.vi.70	44°42'N, 01°12'W	09.xii.70	Lomé area	06°06'N, 01°12'E	4296	177	167	EURING	
	Germany	1	6262548	24.vi.71	54°06'N, 08°42'E	20.xi.72	Lomé area	06°12'N, 01°30'E	5364	187	514	EURING	
	Netherlands	1	2028662	01.vii.67	53°18'N, 05°18'E	24.iv.73		06°30'N, 01°00'E	5216	184	2124	EURING	
	Netherlands	1	2028801	07.vi.68	53°18'N, 05°18'E	15.x.68	Lomé area	06°30'N, 01°24'E	5247	184	130	EURING	
	Sweden	1	5080339	05.vi.71	55°58'N, 14°26'E	(28.ii.72)	Lake Togo	06°20'N, 01°30'E	5637	192	268	EURING	B-O. Stolt (in litt.)
	UK	1	P18735	20.vi.61	55°37'N, 01°37'W	01.i.61	Lomé area	06°10'N, 01°21'E	5502	177	134	EURING	
	UK	1	2074656	30.vi.62	57°20'N, 02°00'W	26.xii.62	Lomé area	06°10'N, 01°21'E	5695	177	179	EURING	
	UK	1	DS0471	28.vii.62	55°37'N, 01°37'W	01.xii.62	Lomé area	06°10'N, 01°21'E	5502	177	126	EURING	
	UK	1	DS34542	02.vii.66	55°37'N, 01°37'W	09.xi.66	Lomé area	06°10'N, 01°21'E	5502	177	130	EURING	
	UK	1	DS43825	04.vii.66	56°27'N, 02°49'W	11.xii.66	Lomé area	06°17'N, 01°40'E	5590	176	160	EURING	
	UK	1	DS61576	08.vii.67	55°18'N, 01°30'W	29.xi.67	Lomé area	06°12'N, 01°24'E	5463	177	174	EURING	
	UK	1	DS36070	08.vii.67	54°06'N, 06°12'W	18.xii.67	Lomé area	06°12'N, 01°24'E	5369	177	163	EURING	
	UK	1	XX85131	19.vi.70	57°18'N, 02°00'W	27.xi.70	Lomé area	06°12'N, 01°24'E	5687	177	161	EURING	
	UK	1	DR18138	23.vi.75	55°36'N, 01°36'W	30.xii.75	Lomé area	06°12'N, 01°24'E	5497	177	190	EURING	
	UK	1	DN56936	01.vii.86	54°32'N, 05°39'W	29.xi.86	Lomé	06°08'N, 01°14'E	5416	173	151	EURING	
Cuculus canorus	Netherlands	3	1029416	26.vii.66	53°18'N, 05°00'E	13.x.66	near Akoumapé	06°24'N, 01°24'E	5223	184	48	EURING	Cramp (1985)
Hirundo rustica	France	1	1781248	21.vi.73	46°18'N, 02°48'E	14.i.74	Lomé area	06°12'N, 01°24'E	4459	182	207	EURING	
	France	4	2115584	14.ix.76	47°54'N, 01°54'E	08.iii.77	near Kpalimé	06°54'N, 00°42'E	4558	181	175	EURING	
	France	2	2575398	24.xi.83	45°48'N, 00°30'W	30.xii.83	near Kpalimé	06°54'N, 00°36'E	4325	179	189	EURING	
	Switzerland	?	?	09.vii.56	Olten	24.x.56	Adokpe	?	?	?	137	Douaud (1957)	Anon (1956)
Motacilla flava	Italy	?	L144538	23.iv.72	43°15'N, 13°45'E	?.x.73	Lomé	06°08'N, 01°14'E	?	?	142	R. J. Dowsett (in litt.)	
	Sweden	3	2379838	03.ix.71	55°27'N, 12°59'E	23.i.72	near Kpalimé	06°55'N, 00°44'E	5505	192	224	EURING	B-O. Stolt (in litt.)
Saxicola rubetra (male)	Tunisia	4	HX9405	24.ix.56	33°54'N, 10°06'E	04.xii.56	You, 5 km S of Blitta	08°18'N, 01°00'E	2994	198	858	EURING	Douaud (1957)
Acrocephalus scirpaceus	Germany	2	He9974050	10.vi.61	53°38'N, 13°42'E	15.xii.63	Dzedzrame, nr Klouto	06°58'N, 00°39'E	5322	193	158	EURING	Reiser (1973)
	Switzerland	?	?	28.viii.40	Sempach	02.ii.41	Kpalimé	06°54'N, 00°37'E	?	?	935	Douaud (1957)	
Sylvia borin	Sweden	4	2476583	25.vi.75	59°15'N, 13°30'E	15.i.78	Akpsor	06°50'N, 00°40'E	5931	191	161	EURING	EURING, B-O. Stolt (in litt.), Dowsett et al. (1988)
Phylloscopus trochilus	Norway	2	9553016	19.vii.80	Revtangen	27.xii.80	Tokoin - Ouest	06°09'N, 01°13'E	?	?	?	EURING	Holgersen (1981)
	Sweden	2	1520658	26.viii.70	56°12'N, 16°24'E	31.iii.71	near Apeyeme	06°58'N, 00°39'E	5653	200	217	EURING	B-O. Stolt (in litt.), Dowsett et al. (1988)
Muscicapa striata	Germany	3	9Z09084	15.vii.81	53°25'N, 10°08'E	03.v.82	north Togo	10°52'N, 00°29'E	4808	190	292	EURING	Dowsett et al. (1988, Fig. 14)

APPENDIX 3

Analysis of avian families recorded in Togo.

RB = Residential breeder. R(B) = Resident, breeding not proven.
PM = Palaearctic migrant. AfM = All intra-African migrants whether breeding or not.
NB each species is only categorised once, even if, for instance, it has populations which are both resident and migratory.

Family	No. of Genera	No. of Species	HABITAT				STATUS				
			Aquatic	Marine	Forest	Savanna	RB	R(B)	PM	AfM	Other
NON-PASSERINES											
Procellaridae	1	1		1							1
Hydrobatidae	1	1		1							1
Podicipedidae	1	1	1					1			
Sulidae	1	2		2							2
Phalacrocoracidae	1	1	1				1				
Anhingidae	1	1	1					1			
Pelecanidae	1	2	2								2
Ardeidae	9	17	16			1	2	8	4	2	1
Scopidae	1	1	1				1				
Ciconiidae	5	8	8				2		2	4	
Threskiornithidae	3	3	3					1	1	1	
Anatidae	8	10	10				1	2	3	1	3
Accipitridae	30	46	2		9	35	8	20	10	4	4
Sagittaridae	1	1				1			1		
Falconidae	1	9				9		6	3		
Phasianidae	5	10			3	7	3	5	1	1	
Turnicidae	2	3				3		2		1	
Rallidae	7	10	9			1	2	6		2	
Gruidae	1	1				1				1	
Heliornithidae	1	1	1					1			
Otididae	2	3				3		1		2	
Jacanidae	1	1	1				1				
Rostratulidae	1	1	1							1	
Haematopodidae	1	1	1					1			
Recurvirostridae	2	2	2							2	
Burhinidae	1	2				2	1		1		
Glareolidae	3	7	5			2	1			4	2
Charadriidae	3	14	12			2	3	3	4	1	3
Scolopacidae	11	24	23		1				24		
Stercoracidae	1	3		3					3		
Laridae	1	4		4					3		1
Sternidae	4	16	1	15					10	2	4
Rynchopidae	1	1	1								1
Pteroclidae	1	2				2				2	
Columbidae	5	16			5	11	7	6	1	1	1
Psittacidae	4	5			2	3		5			
Musophagidae	4	4			2	2	2	2			
Cuculidae	8	18			9	9	2	8	2	6	
Tytonidae	1	1				1		1			
Strigidae	5	7	1		1	5	1	6			
Caprimulgidae	2	7			1	6		2		5	
Apodidae	6	11			3	8	2	4	3	2	

Family	No. of Genera	No. of Species	HABITAT				STATUS				
			Aquatic	Marine	Forest	Savanna	RB	R(B)	PM	AfM	Other
Trogonidae	1	1			1			1			
Alcedinidae	6	10	4		2	4	1	5		4	
Meropidae	1	9			2	7	2	2	1	4	
Coracidae	2	5			1	4	1	1		3	
Phoeniculidae	1	2				2		2			
Upupidae	1	1				1			1		
Bucerotidae	3	11			8	3	2	8		1	
Capitonidae	6	13			10	3	2	11			
Indicatoridae	2	6			3	3		6			
Picidae	4	10			5	5	1	8	1		
Totals for non-Passerines	176	347	107	27	67	146	49	135	80	57	26
PASSERINES											
Eurylaimidae	1	2			2		1	1			
Pittidae	1	1			1			1			
Alaudidae	4	7				7		3		3	1
Hirundinidae	4	18	4		2	12	4	4	3	7	
Motacillidae	3	8				8	2	1	5		
Campephagidae	2	4			2	2		3		1	
Pycnonotidae	10	19			17	2	1	18			
Turdidae	13	19			6	13	2	11	6		
Sylviidae	15	41	4		10	27	7	22	11	1	
Muscicapidae	4	12	1		5	6	1	9	2		
Platysteiridae	3	6			4	2	1	5			
Monarchidae	2	4			2	2	2	2			
Timaliidae	3	6			4	2	1	5			
Paridae	1	1				1		1			
Remizidae	1	1				1		1			
Salpornithidae	1	1				1		1			
Zosteropidae	1	1				1		1			
Nectariniidae	2	18			9	9	6	9		3	
Laniidae	2	3				3	2		1		
Malaconotidae	6	15			6	9	3	11		1	
Prionopidae	1	2			1	1	1	1			
Dicruridae	1	3			2	1	2	1			
Corvidae	2	2				2	2				
Oriolidae	1	4			2	2		3	1		
Sturnidae	5	12			4	8	2	8		2	
Passeridae	3	3				3	2			1	
Ploceidae	7	24			5	19	16	7		1	
Estrildidae	14	27			7	20	5	20		2	
Viduidae	1	7				7		7			
Fringillidae	1	3				3		3			
Emberizidae	1	3				3		2		1	
Totals for Passerines	116	277	9	0	91	177	63	161	29	23	1
GRAND TOTALS	292	624	116	27	158	323	112	296	109	80	27

GAZETTEER

Abalokopé (? = Abala) 07°31'N, 01°24'E
Abobo 06°14'N, 01°23'E
Abomey (Benin) 07°11'N, 01°59'E
Aboudyo Kopé 06°39'N, 00°43'E
(= Aboudiokopé)
Ada (Ghana) 05°46'N, 00°39'E
Adado (not found,
near Bismarckburg)
Adamé 06°20'N, 01°47'E
Adédakopé 07°20'N, 01°20'E
Adélé (not found,
near Bismarckburg
Adeta 07°08'N, 00°44'E
Adina 07°31'N, 01°01'E
Adjacin (Benin) 06°29'N, 02°35'E
Adjuti (not found,
NW of Bismarckburg)
Adossa 07°34'N, 00°41'E
Agadji 07°27'N, 00°54'E
Agbadroufou 06°12'N, 01°29'E
(= Agbodrafo
= Porto Seguro)
Agbandé 08°13'N, 01°08'E
Agbatitoe 07°04'N, 01°08'E
Agbélouvé 06°40'N, 01°10'E
Agbenohoué 07°23'N, 00°41'E
Agbodrafo 06°12'N, 01°29'E
(= Porto Séguro)
Agbo Kopé 07°26'N, 00°41'E
Agbossomou Kopé 08°06'N, 00°37'E
(= Aboussoum Kopé)
Ago Déké 06°11'N, 01°22'E
Agomé-Glouzou 06°33'N, 01°40'E
Agomé-Palimé
(= Kpalimé) 06°54'N, 00°38'E
Agomé Seva 06°28'N, 01°44'E
Agomé Tongwe 06°56'N, 00°27'E
(= Agbome, Ghana)
Agou 06°53'N, 00°44'E
Agoué 06°12'N, 01°13'E
Ahepe 06°36'N, 01°24'E
Ahoué-houé 07°33'N, 00°36'E
Akaba 07°57'N, 01°03'E
Akloa 07°31'N, 00°37'E
Akoumapé 06°23'N, 01°27'E
Akparne 06°10'N, 01°12'E
Akposso 07°40'N, 00°45'E
Akroso (Ghana) 05°46'N, 00°46'W
Alamassou 07°41'N, 01°15'E
Aledjo 09°15'N, 01°12'E
Aledjo Kadara 09°15'N, 01°12'E
Aléhéridé 09°13'N, 01°12'E
Alokoégbé 06°26'N, 01°05'E
Amakpavé 06°47'N, 01°11'E
Amou-Oblo 07°23'N, 00°52'E

Amoussokopé
(= Amoussokoko) 06°41'N, 00°51'E
Amoutchou 07°23'N, 01°11'E
Anécho (= Klein Popo) 06°14'N, 01°36'E
Anié 07°45'N, 01°12'E
Anonoe 07°33'N, 00°35'E
Anyanga (not found,
E of Bismarckburg)
Apasso (Ghana) 07°32'N, 00°07'E
Apéyémé 07°12'N, 00°42'E
Aplahoué (Benin) 06°56'N, 01°41'E
Atakpamé 07°32'N, 01°08'E
Atchinedji 07°34'N, 01°21'E
Avegode 06°48'N, 01°36'E
Avétonou 06°48'N, 00°48'E
Ayagba 07°46'N, 00°48'E
Ayengré 08°40'N, 01°01'E
Ayomé 07°30'N, 00°57'E
Azafi 07°34'N, 01°03'E
Azongo (= Zongo) 06°21'N, 01°43'E
Badja 06°23'N, 00°59'E
Badou 07°35'N, 00°36'E
Badou-Dzindzi 07°35'N, 00°32'E
Bafilo 09°21'N, 01°14'E
Bagan 09°00'N, 00°40'E
Baguida 06°10'N, 01°20'E
Balla 06°59'N, 00°34'E
Baoulé 10°16'N, 00°35'E
Barkoissi 10°33'N, 00°17'E
Bassar (= Bassari) 09°15'N, 00°47'E
Béko (Benin) 06°36'N, 02°27'E
Bénali 07°35'N, 00°44'E
Bethel 07°32'N, 00°32'E
Binako 09°11'N, 00°54'E
Binaparba 09°14'N, 00°46'E
Bismarckburg 08°11'N, 00°41'E
Blitta 08°19'N, 00°59'E
Bodjécali (Benin) 11°51'N, 03°22'E
Borgou 10°46'N, 00°35'E
Boulo waterfall 08°46'N, 00°40'E
Bouzalo 09°06'N, 01°01'E
Brouffou 07°44'N, 00°41'E
Bueta (not found)
Chra (= Kra = Wahala) 07°11'N, 01°10'E
Chutes d'Ajarala 06°49'N, 01°36'E
Cinkansé 11°06'N, 00°01'E
(= Cinkassé = Senkansé)
Dadja 07°26'N, 01°10'E
Danyi monastery 07°14'N, 00°41'E
Danyi Plateau 07°09'N, 00°40'E
Dapaon (= Dapango) 10°51'N, 00°12'E
Davie 06°23'N, 01°12'E
Defale 09°53'N, 01°05'E
Déguingué 08°05'N, 00°38'E
Djamdé 09°32'N, 01°03'E

Djodji	07°40'N, 00°35'E	Kodegbé	07°31'N, 01°03'E
Djogma	09°23'N, 01°10'E	Kpandu (Ghana)	07°00'N, 00°18'E
Djougou (Benin)	09°42'N, 01°40'E	Kolokopé	07°48'N, 01°18'E
Domaine Gravillou	10°25'N, 00°29'E	Korbongou	10°53'N, 00°15'E
Dutukpene (Ghana)	08°06'N, 00°24'E	Koué	08°16'N, 00°43'E
Dzedrame	06°58'N, 00°39'E	Kouma	06°21'N, 01°36'E
Dzogbégan	07°14'N, 00°41'E	Koumongou	10°11'N, 00°27'E
Ebéva	07°32'N, 01°05'E	Kouniohou	07°40'N, 00°47'E
Edifou	07°29'N, 00°57'E	Kourniéré (? = Gurnia)	10°22'N, 00°38'E
Evou	07°33'N, 01°02'E	Koundjouaré	10°56'N, 00°39'E
Evou Apegamé	07°32'N, 00°02'E	Koussountou	06°56'N, 00°37'E
Ewa	07°37'N, 00°59'E	Koutoukpa	07°31'N, 00°59'E
Ezimé	07°29'N, 00°56'E	Koviakope	06°55'N, 00°49'E
Faille d'Aledjo	09°15'N, 01°12'E	Kovié (? = Kové)	06°39'N, 01°07'E
Fasugu (not found,		Kpalimé (= Palimé)	06°54'N, 00°37'E
N of Bismarckburg)		Kpani	10°16'N, 00°22'E
Fazao	08°42'N, 00°47'E	Kpaya	09°33'N, 01°08'E
Fosse aux Lions	10°46'N, 00°12'E	Kpayando	09°22'N, 01°09'E
Galangashie	10°31'N, 00°21'E	Kpélé	06°58'N, 01°08'E
Gambaga (Ghana)	10°31'N, 00°22'W	Kpéssi	08°04'N, 01°16'E
Gando	10°20'N, 00°45'E	Kpessidé (= Pessidé)	10°02'N, 00°56'E
Gaougblé	07°56'N, 01°12'E	Kpété Béna	07°26'N, 00°36'E
Glei	07°19'N, 01°10'E	Kpété Menou	07°41'N, 00°27'E
Glidgi	06°15'N, 01°36'E	Kpéya (= Péwa)	09°17'N, 01°14'E
Gonobé R.	07°37'N, 00°42'E	Kpimé-Tomegbé	07°01'N, 00°39'E
Hago	09°48'N, 01°11'E	Kratschi	07°48'N, 00°04'W
Haho	06°39'N, 01°19'E	(= Kété Kratschi, Ghana)	
Haho Baloué	06°58'N, 01°01'E	Kuluguna cascade	10°43'N, 00°05'E
Ho (Ghana)	06°36'N, 00°28'E	Kuma Adame (not found)	
Idifiou	07°37'N, 00°58'E	Kumasi (Ghana)	06°45'N, 01°35'W
Ife (Nigeria)	07°28'N, 04°32'E	Lake Alago	06°45'N, 01°36'E
Imoussa	07°33'N, 00°56'E	Lake Togo	06°15'N, 01°26'E
Jegge (= Yégué)	08°11'N, 00°39'E	Landa-Mono	08°36'N, 01°16'E
Kabou	09°27'N, 00°49'E	Landa-Pozanda	09°31'N, 01°17'E
Kalabo	08°13'N, 00°43'E	Leglebi (Ghana)	06°57'N, 00°29'E
Kambolé	08°45'N, 01°36'E	Liptako (Burkina Faso)	13°42'N, 00°30'E
Kamasse R.	09°01'N, 00°42'E	Logoba	06°23'N, 01°30'E
Kamé	07°01'N, 01°24'E	Lomé	06°08'N, 01°14'E
Kamétonou	06°58'N, 00°31'E	Lomnava	07°33'N, 01°05'E
Kamina	07°31'N, 01°11'E	Lyato	06°34'N, 01°40'E
Kanbouanga	10°43'N, 00°45'E	Mandouri	10°51'N, 00°49'E
Kandjo	09°35'N, 00°15'E	Mango	10°21'N, 00°28'E
Kandé (= Kante)	09°58'N, 01°02'E	(= Sansanné-Mango)	
Kara (= Lama Kara)	09°33'N, 01°11'E	Mankie (? = Mantje)	10°19'N, 00°21'E
Katchanké	08°12'N, 00°41'E	Mare aux Lions	10°10'N, 00°47'E
(near Bismarckburg)		Misahöhe	06°57'N, 00°35'E
Kati	06°54'N, 00°51'E	Mo	09°05'N, 01°03'E
Ketao	09°39'N, 01°19'E	Moretan	08°06'N, 01°21'E
Kete (= Keta) (Ghana)	05°54'N, 01°00'W	Mount Agou	06°54'N, 00°46'E
Kété Kratschi (Ghana)	07°48'N, 00°04'W	(Pic Baumann)	
Kévé	06°26'N, 00°56'E	Mpoti	08°14'N, 00°46'E
Kewa	09°00'N, 00°53'E	Mpoti	06°49'N, 00°08'W
Kirikri (= Adjeide)	09°12'N, 01°25'E	(= Mopti) (Ghana)	
Kissibo	07°42'N, 00°35'E	Naboulgou	10°09'N, 00°49'E
Klabé Apégamé	07°39'N, 00°53'E	Namoundjoga	10°54'N, 00°24'E
Klabé Azafie	07°36'N, 00°44'E	Nanergou	10°55'N, 00°09'E
Klein Popo (= Anécho)	06°14'N, 01°36'E	Nangbeto	07°25'N, 01°26'E
Klouto	06°57'N, 00°34'E	Nano	10°42'N, 00°06'E

Naparri (Ghana)	10°54'N, 00°12'E	Sotouboua	08°34'N, 00°58'E
Nataré	10°49'N, 00°25'E	Tabligbo	06°35'N, 01°30'E
Ndali (not found)		Tantigou	10°51'N, 00°12'E
Niamtougou	09°46'N, 01°06'E	Tatale	09°25'N, 00°15'E
Notsé	06°57'N, 01°10'E	Tasso	07°36'N, 00°42'E
(= Nuatja = Nuadja)		Tchanaga	10°30'N, 00°30'E
Nyamassila	07°59'N, 01°12'E	Tchébébé	08°26'N, 00°59'E
Nyivé	06°46'N, 00°35'E	Tchifoma (not found)	
Odjolo	07°32'N, 01°02'E	Tchimmbéré	09°05'N, 00°52'E
Oga	07°38'N, 00°55'E	Tchonou	07°30'N, 01°15'E
Okpahoué	07°37'N, 01°01'E	Témedja	07°31'N, 01°05'E
Oti-Toutionga	10°21'N, 00°34'E	Tenkodogo	11°47'N, 00°22'E
Oualé stream	10°55'N, 00°50'E	(Burkina Faso)	
Ouidah (Benin)	06°22'N, 02°05'E	Tététou	07°01'N, 01°30'E
Oulita	07°31'N, 00°55'E	Tinkiro	08°05'N, 00°46'E
Ounabé	07°34'N, 00°59'E	Titira	10°00'N, 01°07'E
Ounkémé-Monoto (Benin)	06°52'N, 01°36'E	Todomé	07°33'N, 00°43'E
Pagala	08°11'N, 00°58'E	Togodo	07°26'N, 00°56'E
Pagouda	09°45'N, 01°19'E	Togokomé	06°13'N, 01°25'E
Paio	10°14'N, 00°41'E	Togoville (= Toa-Go)	06°14'N, 01°29'E
Pakli Kopé	06°23'N, 01°06'E	Tohoun	07°02'N, 01°37'E
Palakoko	07°50'N, 01°06'E	Tokpli	06°45'N, 00°57'E
Panseni	10°48'N, 00°48'E	Tokpo	06°47'N, 00°55'E
Parawé	06°56'N, 01°41'E	Tomégbé	07°31'N, 00°36'E
(= Aplahoué) (Benin)		Tovegan	06°34'N, 00°54'E
Pasa	09°13'N, 01°21'E	Triku (not found)	
Pele Ele (= Kpélé Elé)	07°16'N, 00°48'E	Tsévié	06°25'N, 01°13'E
Péwa	09°17'N, 01°14'E	Tshautyo (not found,	
(= Kpéwa = Kpéya)		NE of Bismarckburg)	
Pobé (Benin)	06°58'N, 02°41'E	Tuntundi (? = Tuandi)	10°47'N, 00°51'E
Podji (= Kpodji)	06°57'N, 00°38'E	Wahala (= Chra = Kra)	07°11'N, 01°10'E
Porto-Novo (Benin)	06°29'N, 02°37'E	Wobé	07°32'N, 00°36'E
Porto Séguro		Wogba	06°17'N, 01°31'E
(= Agbodrafo)	06°12'N, 01°29'E	Yégué	08°11'N, 00°39'E
Sagbiabou	10°16'N, 00°39'E	Yendi (Ghana)	09°26'N, 00°01'W
Salaga (Ghana)	08°33'N, 00°31'E	Yerrepa (not found,	
Sara-Kawa	09°38'N, 01°01'E	NE of Bismarckburg)	
Sawaga (? = Sawagu)	10°45'N, 00°24'E	Yikpa-Dikpé	07°07'N, 00°36'E
Say (Niger)	13°07'N, 02°21'E	You	08°17'N, 01°00'E
Sebbe (= Zébé = Sébé)	06°15'N, 01°37'E	Zébé (= Sébé = Sebbé)	06°15'N, 01°37'E
Sika-Kondji	06°38'N, 01°35'E	Zogbégan	06°21'N, 01°39'E
Sirka	09°33'N, 01°18'E	Zogbé Kobé	06°26'N, 01°05'E
Sokodé	08°59'N, 01°08'E		

REFERENCES

AHL, E. 1931. Zur Systematik der Afrikanischen Arten der Baumfroschgattung *Hyperolius*. *Mitt. zool. Mus. Berl.* 17: 1–132.

ALLPORT, G. 1991. The status and conservation of threatened birds in the Upper Guinea forest. *Bird Conservation International* 1: 53–74.

ALLSWORTH-JONES, P. 1990. Togolese archaeology: recent developments. *The Nigerian Field* 55: 159–164.

ANON. (probably A. Reichenow). 1893. Nachrichten. *Ornithologische Monatsberichte* 1: 54.

ANON. (probably A. Reichenow). 1894a. *Ornithologische Monatsberichte* 2: 128.

ANON. (probably A. Reichenow). 1894b. *Ornithologische Monatsberichte* 2: 159.

ANON. (probably A. Reichenow). 1895. Nachrichten. Ernst Baumann †. *Ornithologische Monatsberichte* 3: 168.

ANON. 1918a. *Revue Française d'Ornithologie* 5: 216.

ANON. 1918b. *Revue Française d'Ornithologie* 5: 264.

ANON. 1956. Reprises d'oiseaux bagués. *Nos Oiseaux* 1956: 340.

ANON. 1957. Un milan noir dans ses quartiers d'hiver. *Nos Oiseaux* 1957: 80.

ANSANG, E. R. 1979. The seasonal cycle of the phytoplankton in the coastal waters of Ghana. *Hydrobiologia* 62: 33–45.

AUBREVILLE, A. 1937. Les forêts du Dahomey et du Togo. *Bull. Com. Et. Hist et Sci. de l'A. O. F.* 20: 1–112.

AUBREVILLE, A. 1938. La forêt coloniale: les forêts de l'Afrique occidentale française. *Annls. Acad. Sci. colon.*, Paris 9: 1–244.

AUBREVILLE, A. 1949. *Climats, forêts et désertifications de l'Afrique Tropicale.* Société d'Editions Géographiques, Maritimes et Coloniale: Paris, 351 pp.

BANNERMAN, D. A. 1930. *Birds of Tropical West Africa.* vol.1. The Crown Agents for the Colonies, London.

BANNERMAN, D. A. 1931. *Birds of Tropical West Africa.* vol.2. The Crown Agents for the Colonies, London.

BANNERMAN, D. A. 1939. *Birds of Tropical West Africa.* vol.5. The Crown Agents for the Colonies, London.

BANNERMAN, D. A. 1948. *Birds of Tropical West Africa.* vol.6. The Crown Agents for the Colonies, London.

BANNERMAN, D. A. 1949. *Birds of Tropical West Africa.* vol.7. The Crown Agents for the Colonies, London.

BANNERMAN, D. A. 1953. *The Birds of West and Equatorial Africa.* 2 Vols. Oliver and Boyd, Edinburgh and London.

BARNES, R. F. W. 1990. Deforestation trends in tropical Africa. *Afr. J. Ecology* 28: 161–173.

BAUDENON, P. 1952. Notes sur les bovidés du Togo. *Mammalia* 16: 49–61 & 109–121.

BAUMANN, E. 1894a. (Untitled) *Ornithologische Monatsberichte* 2: 160

BAUMANN, E. 1894b. (Untitled) *Ornithologische Monatsberichte* 2: 194.

BERLIOZ, J. 1956. Etude d'une collection d'oiseaux du Dahomey. *Bull. Mus. Nat. Hist. Nat.* 28: 261–264.

BOOTH, A. H. 1958. The Niger, the Volta, and the Dahomey gap as geographic barriers. *Evolution* 12: 48–62.

BOUET, G. 1913. L'autruche en Afrique occidentale Française. *Revue Française d'Ornithologie* 3: 121–125.

BOUET, G. 1914. Liste des oiseaux recueillis ou observés au Dahomey de 1908 à 1911. *Revue Française d'Ornithologie* 3: 263–269, 304–308.

BOUET, G. 1955. *Oiseaux de l'Afrique Tropicale (première partie).* ORSTOM, Paris.

BOUET, G. 1961. *Oiseaux de l'Afrique Tropicale (deuxième partie).* ORSTOM, Paris.

BRABY, R., BRABY, S. J. & SIMMONS, R. E. 1992. 5000 Damara Terns in the northern Namib Desert: a reassessment of world population numbers. *Ostrich* 63: 133–135.

BROWN, L., URBAN, E.K. & NEWMAN, K. 1982. *The Birds of Africa.* Vol. 1. Academic Press, London.

BROWNE, P. W. P. 1980. Birds observed near Lome, Togo in 1976 and 1977. *Malimbus* 2: 51–55.

BRUNEL, J. 1958. Observations sur les oiseaux du bas-Dahomey. *L'Oiseau et R.F.O.* 28: 1–38.

BRUNEL, J. & THIOLLAY, J. M. 1969. Liste préliminaire des oiseaux de Côte d'Ivoire. *Alauda* 37: 230–254.

BUTTNER, R. 1893. Vorwort. pp. 1–8 in Karsch, F. Die Insecten der Berglandschaft Adeli im Hinterlande von Togo (Westafrika). *Berlin Entomolog. Zeitschrift* 38. Part I.

CANE, W. P. & CARTER, M. F. 1988. Significant range extension for *Nectarinia reichenbachii* in West Africa. *Bull Br. Orn. Cl.* 108: 52–54.

CHAINEY, J. E. & CHEKE, R. A. 1994. A collection of Tabanidae (Diptera) from Togo with two new synonyms in *Haematopota*. *J. Afr. Zool.* 108: 225–229.

CHAPIN, J. P. 1932. The Birds of the Belgian Congo. Part I. *Bull. Amer. Mus. Nat. Hist.* 65: 1–756.

CHAPIN, J. P. 1954. The Birds of the Belgian Congo. Part 4. *Bull. Amer. Mus. Nat. Hist.* 75B: 1–846.

CHAPMAN, A. 1995. Breeding and moult of four bird species in tropical West Africa. *Tropical Zoology* 8: 227–238.

CHARDONNET, B., DUNCAN, P., WALSH, J. F. & DOGBE-TOMI, A. 1990. pp. 73–78 in East, R. (ed.) *Antelopes: global survey and regional action plans. Part 3. West and Central Africa.* I.U.C.N., Gland, Switzerland.

CHEKE, R. A. 1980. A small breeding colony of the Rock Pratincole *Glareola nuchalis liberiae* in Togo. *Bull. Br. Orn. Cl.* 100: 175–178.

CHEKE, R. A. 1982a. Additional information on the Rock Pratincole *Glareola nuchalis* in Togo. *Bull. Br. Orn. Cl.* 102: 116–117.

CHEKE, R. A. 1982b. More bird records from the Republic of Togo. *Malimbus* 4: 55–63.

CHEKE, R. A. 1986. The supposed occurrence of the White-necked Picathartes *Picathartes gymnocephalus* in Togo. *Bull. Br. Orn. Cl.* 106: 152.

CHEKE, R. A. 1995. An historical breeding record in Mali and description of the young of the Grasshopper Buzzard *Butastur rufipennis*. *Malimbus* 17: 106–107.

CHEKE, R. A. & WALSH, J. F. 1980. Bird records from the Republic of Togo. *Malimbus* 2: 112–120.

CHEKE, R. A. & WALSH, J. F. 1984. Further bird records from the Republic of Togo. *Malimbus* 6: 15–22.

CHEKE, R. A. & WALSH, J. F. 1989. Westward range extension into Togo of the Adamawa Turtle Dove *Streptopelia hypopyrrha*. *Bull. Br. Orn. Cl.* 109: 47–48.

CHEKE, R. A., WALSH, J. F. & SOWAH, S. A. 1986. Records of birds seen in the Republic of Togo during 1984–1986. *Malimbus* 8: 51–72.

CHEVALIER, A. 1900. *Les zones et les provinces botaniques de l'Afrique occidentale française.* Comptes rendu Academie Science, Paris.

CLAFFEY, P. M. 1995. Notes on the avifauna of the Bétérou area, Borgou Province, Republic of Benin. *Malimbus* 17: 63–84.

CLANCEY, P. A. 1990a. Size-variation and post-breeding movement in the Didric Cuckoo *Chrysococcyx caprius* (Boddaert). *Bull. Br. Orn. Cl.* 110: 130–137.

CLANCEY, P. A. 1990b. Comment on the geographical variation of the Malachite Kingfisher *Corythornis cristatus* of the Afrotropics. *Bull. Br. Orn. Cl.* 110: 137–138.

CLANCEY, P. A. 1993. The status of *Nectarinia olivacea* (Smith), 1840; a unitary species or two polytypic allospecies? *Le Gerfaut* 82–83: 25–29.

COLLAR, N. J. & STUART, S. N. 1985. *Threatened Birds of Africa and Related Islands.* The ICBP/IUCN Red Data Book, Part 1. Third Edition. ICBP/IUCN, Cambridge, U.K.

COLSTON, P. R. & CURRY-LINDAHL, K. 1986. *The Birds of Mount Nimba, Liberia.* British Museum (Natural History), London.

COLSTON, P. R. & MOREL, G. J. 1985. A new subspecies of the Rufous Swamp Warbler *Acrocephalus rufescens* from Senegal. *Malimbus* 7: 61–62.

CORNEVIN, R. 1987. *Le Togo: des origines à nos jours.* Académie des Sciences d'Outre-Mer, Paris.

CORSE, C. 1990. Wader studies in Orkney. *BTO News* No. 170: 8–9.

CRAIG, A. J. F. K. 1993a. Geographical variation and taxonomy of the genus *Euplectes* (Aves, Ploceidae) Part I: the short-tailed bishop birds. *J. Afr. Zool* 107: 83–96.

CRAIG, A. J. F. K. 1993b. Geographical variation and taxonomy of the genus *Euplectes* (Aves, Ploceidae) Part II: the long-tailed widow birds. *J. Afr. Zool.* 107: 139–151.

CRAMP, S. (ed.) 1985. *The Birds of the Western Palearctic.* Vol.4. Oxford University Press, Oxford.

CRAMP, S. (ed.) 1988. *The Birds of the Western Palearctic.* Vol.5. Oxford University Press, Oxford.

CRAMP, S. (ed.) 1992. *The Birds of the Western Palearctic.* Vol.6. Oxford University Press, Oxford.

CRAMP, S. & SIMMONS, K. E. L. (eds.) 1977. *The Birds of the Western Palearctic.* Vol.1. Oxford University Press, Oxford.

DAVIS, S. D., DROOP, S. J. M., GREGERSON, P., HENSON, L., LEON, C. J., VILLA-LOBOS, J. L., SYNGE, H. & ZANTOKSKA, J. 1986. *Plants in danger: what do we know?* IUCN, Gland and Cambridge.

DEKEYSER, P. L. 1951. Mission A. Villiers au Togo et au Dahomey (1950). III. – Oiseaux. *Études Dahomeennes* 5: 47–84.

DEMEY, R. 1986. Two new species for Ivory Coast. *Malimbus* 8: 44.

DEMEY, R. & FISHPOOL, L. D. C. 1991. Additions and annotations to the avifauna of Côte d'Ivoire. *Malimbus* 12: 61–86.

DE ROO, A. 1970. Contribution à l'Ornithologie de la République du Togo. 2. Oiseaux récoltés par M. C. Veronese. *Rev. Zool. Bot. Afr.* 81: 163–172.

DE ROO, A., DE VREE, F. & VAN DER STRAETEN, E. 1972. Contribution à l'Ornithologie de la République du Togo. *Rev. Zool. Bot. Afr.* 86: 374–384.

DE ROO, A., DE VREE, F. & VERHEYEN, W. 1969. Contribution à l'Ornithologie de la République du Togo. *Rev. Zool. Bot. Afr.* 79: 309–322.

DE ROO, A., HULSELMANS, J. & VERHEYEN, W. 1971. Contribution à l'Ornithologie de la République du Togo. *Rev. Zool. Bot. Afr.* 83: 84–94.

DE VREE, F., DE ROO, A. & VERHEYEN, W. N. 1969. Contribution à l'étude des chiroptères de la République du Togo. *Rev. Zool. Bot. Afr.* 80: 200–207.

DE VREE, F., HULSELMANS, J. & VERHEYEN, W. N. 1970. Contribution à l'étude des chiroptères de la République du Togo. 2. Liste préliminaire des chiroptères récoltés par la deuxième mission zoologique belge au Togo. *Rev. Zool. Bot. Afr.* 82: 41–46.

DE VREE, F. & VAN DER STRAETEN, E. 1971. Contribution à l'étude des chiroptères de la République du Togo. 3. Liste préliminaire des chiroptères récoltés par la troisième mission zoologique belge au Togo. *Rev. Zool. Bot. Afr.* 83: 159–164.

DIAMOND, A. W. & HAMILTON, A. C. 1980. The distribution of forest passerine birds and Quaternary climatic change in tropical Africa. *J. Zool. Lond.* 191: 379–402.

DICKERMAN, R. W. 1989. Notes on the Malachite Kingfisher *Corythornis* (*Alcedo*) *cristata. Bull. Br. Orn. Cl.* 109: 158–159.

DICKERMAN, R. W. 1994. Notes on birds from Africa with descriptions of three new subspecies. *Bull. Br. Orn. Cl.* 114: 274–278.

DOUAUD, J. 1955. Les oiseaux du Dahomey et du Niger. Notes de voyage. *L'Oiseau et R.F.O.* 25: 295–307.

DOUAUD, J. 1956a. L'hirondelle de fenêtre *Delichon urbica* au Togo. *Alauda* 24: 146–147.

DOUAUD, J. 1956b. Les oiseaux des monts du Togo (Afrique occidentale). *Alauda* 24: 221–227.

DOUAUD, J. 1957. Les migrations au Togo (Afrique occidentale). *Alauda* 25: 241–266.

DOWSETT, R. J. 1993. Afrotropical avifaunas: annotated country checklists. pp. 1–322 *in* Dowsett, R. J. & Dowsett-Lemaire, F. 1993 (eds.) *A contribution to the distribution and taxonomy of Afrotropical and Malagasy birds.* Tauraco Research Report No. 5.

DOWSETT, R. J., BACKHURST, G. C. & OATLEY, T. B. 1988. Afrotropical ringing recoveries of Palaearctic migrants 1. Passerines (Turdidae to Oriolidae). *Tauraco* 1: 29–63.

DOWSETT, R. J. & FORBES-WATSON, A. 1993. *Checklist of birds of the Afrotropical and Malagasy regions. Vol. 1. Species limits and distribution.* Tauraco Press, Liège, Belgium.

ECCLES, S. D. 1985. Reichenbach's Sunbird *Nectarinia reichenbachii* new to Ivory Coast. *Malimbus* 7: 140.

ELGOOD, J. H. 1982. *The Birds of Nigeria.* British Ornithologists' Union, Check-list No.4.

ELGOOD, J. H., HEIGHAM, J. B., MOORE, A. M., NASON, A. M., SHARLAND, R. E., & SKINNER, N. J. 1994. *The Birds of Nigeria. An annotated check-list.* B.O.U. Check-list no. 4. (second edition), Tring, Herts.

ERARD, C. & VIELLIARD, J. 1977. *Sarothrura rufa* (Vieillot) au Togo. *L'Oiseau et R.F.O.* 47: 309–310.

F.A.O. 1988. *An Interim Report on the State of Forest Resources in the Developing Countries.* F.A.O., Rome.

F.A.O./UNEP. 1981. Tropical Forest Resources Assessment Project. *Forest Resources of Tropical Africa. Part II. Country Briefs.* F.A.O., Rome.

FISCHER, G. 1923. *Jagd und wildschutz in den Deutschen Kolonien (Togoland) herausgegeben vom Reichs-Kolonialmant.* Jena.

FISHPOOL, L. D. C. & DEMEY, R. 1991. The occurrence of both species of "Lesser Golden Plover" and of Nearctic Scolopacids in Côte d'Ivoire. *Malimbus* 13: 3–10.

FISHPOOL, L. D. C. & POPOV, G. B. 1984. The grasshopper faunas of the savannas of Mali, Niger, Benin and Togo. *Bull. I.F.A.N. ser.A* (1981) 43: 275–410.

FRASER, F. C. 1951. Mission A. Villiers au Togo et au Dahomey (1950). V. Odonata and Neuroptera. *Bull. I.F.A.N.* 13: 1076–1092.

FRIEDMANN, H. 1955. *The Honey-Guides. Bull. U.S. Nat. Mus.* No. 208. Smithsonian Institution, Washington, D. C.

FRY, C. H., FRY, K. & HARRIS, A. 1992. *Kingfishers, Bee-eaters and Rollers.* Christopher Helm, London.

FRY, C. H., KEITH, S. & URBAN, E. K. 1988. *The Birds of Africa.* Vol. 3. Academic Press, London.

GANN, L. H. & DUIGNAN, P. 1977. *The Rulers of German Africa 1884–1914.* Stanford University Press, Stanford, California, 286 pp.

GAUD, J. 1989. Acariens sarcoptiformes plumicoles parasites des oiseaux piciformes d'Afrique. II. Acariens de la sous-famille Hyonyssinae (Analgoidea, Avenzoariidae). *J. Afr. Zool.* 103: 229–242.

GAUD, J. 1990a. Acariens sarcoptiformes plumicoles parasites des oiseaux piciformes d'Afrique. III. Parasites des Capitonidae et des Picidae – Acariens de la sous-famille Pteronyssinae – Genre *Anephippius. J. Afr. Zool.* 104: 229–239.

GAUD, J. 1990b. Acariens sarcoptiformes plumicoles parasites des oiseaux piciformes d'Afrique. IV. Parasites des Capitonidae et des Picidae – Acariens de la sous-famille Pteronyssinae – Genre *Conomerus. J. Afr. Zool.* 104: 313–333.

GAUD, J. 1993. Acariens sarcoptiformes plumicoles parasites des oiseaux piciformes d'Afrique. VI. Acariens de la famille Trouessartiidae (Analgoidea). *J. Afr. Zool.* 107: 121–134.

GEBHARDT, L. 1964. *Die Ornithologen Mitteleuropas. Ein Nachschlagewerk.* Brühlscher Verlag, Giessen.

GIRAUDOUX, P., DEGAUQUIER, R., JONES, P. J., WEIGEL, J. & ISENMANN, P. 1988. Avifaune du Niger: etat des connaissances en 1986. *Malimbus* 10: 1–140.

GOODMAN, S. M. & WATSON, G. E. 1983. Bird specimen records of some uncommon or previously unrecorded forms in Egypt. *Bull. Br .Orn. Cl.* 103: 101–106.

GRIMES, L. G. 1974. Dialects and geographical variation in the song of the Splendid Sunbird *Nectarinia coccinigaster. Ibis* 116: 314–329.

GRIMES, L. G. 1980. Observations of group behaviour and breeding biology of the Yellow-billed Shrike *Corvinella corvina. Ibis* 122: 166–192.

GRIMES, L. G. 1987. *The Birds of Ghana.* British Ornithologists' Union, Check-list No.9.

GROTE, H. 1923. *Steganura paradisea togoensis* nov. subsp. *Ornithologische Monatsberichte* 31:43.

HALL, B. P. & MOREAU, R. E. 1970. *An atlas of speciation in African passerine birds.* British Museum (Natural History), London.

HALL, J. B. & SWAINE, M. D. 1976. Classification and ecology of closed forest in Ghana. *Journal of Ecology* 64: 913–951.

HAYMAN, P., MARCHANT, J. & PRATER, T. 1986. *Shorebirds: an identification guide to the waders of the world.* Croom Helm, London.

HAYWARD, D. F. & OGUNTOYINBO, J. S. 1987. *The Climatology of West Africa.* Hutchinson, London.

HEDENSTROM, A., BENSCH, S., HASSELQUIST, D., LOCKWOOD, M. & OTTOSSON, U. 1993. Migration, stopover and moult of the Great Reed Warbler *Acrocephalus arundinaceus* in Ghana, West Africa. *Ibis* 135: 177–180.

HEDENSTROM, A., BENSCH, S., HASSELQUIST, D. & OTTOSSON, U. 1990. Observations of Palaearctic migrants rare to Ghana. *Bull. Br. Orn. Cl.* 110: 194–197.

HEIM DE BALSAC, H. & MAYAUD, N. 1962. *Les oiseaux du Nord-Ouest de l'Afrique*. Paul Lechevalier, Paris.

HELSENS, T. 1996. New information on birds in Ghana, April 1991 to October 1993. *Malimbus* 18: 1–9.

HOLGERSEN, H. 1969. Stavanger Museums Gjenfunn 1967–68. *Sterna* 8: 390–424.

HOLGERSEN, H. 1974. Stavanger Museums Gjenfunn 1971–1973. Del. 1. non-passeriformes. *Sterna* 13: 217–251.

HOLGERSEN, H. 1981. Bird-ringing report 1979–80, Stavanger Museum. *Sterna* 17: 85–123.

HOLYOAK, D. & SEDDON, M. B. 1990. Distributional notes on the birds of Benin. *Malimbus* 11: 128–134.

HOWARD, R. & MOORE, A. 1991. *A complete checklist of the Birds of the World*. 2nd. ed. Academic Press, London.

I.U.C.N. 1991. *Protected Areas of the World. A Review of National Systems*. Vol 3. *Afrotropical*. I.U.C.N. – The World Conservation Union, Gland, Switzerland.

I.U.C.N. 1994. Note by the Director General on taking of wild birds for the pet trade. Addendum 2 to General Assembly paper GA/19/94/3. I.U.C.N. – The World Conservation Union, 19th. Session of the General Assembly, Buenos Aires, Argentina, 17–26 January 1994. Gland, Switzerland.

JAGO, N. D. 1964. Aspects of the ecology and distribution of grasshoppers in Ghana as a contribution to the zoogeography of West Africa. *J. West Afr. Sci. Assoc.* 8: 190–204.

JENIK, J. & HALL, J. B. 1966. The ecological effects of the harmattan wind in the Djebobo Massif (Togo Mountains, Ghana). *Journal of Ecology* 54: 767–779.

JOKELE, I. 1974. Ringfunde des Schwarzen Milans (*Milvus migrans*). *Auspicium* 5: 229–243.

JOHN, D. M. & LAWSON, G. W. 1972. The establishment of a marine algal flora in Togo and Dahomey (Gulf of Guinea). *Botanica Marina* 15: 64–73.

KARSCH, F. 1893. Die Insecten der Berglandschaft Adeli im Hinterlande von Togo (Westafrika). *Berlin Entomolog. Zeitschrift* 38 (Part I): 1–266.

KEAY, R. W. J. 1953. *An outline of Nigerian vegetation*. 2nd. edition. Government Printer, Lagos.

KEAY, R. W. J. 1954. *Rhizophora* in West Africa. *Kew Bulletin* 8: 121–127.

KEAY, R. W. J. 1959. *Vegetation map of Africa south of the Tropic of Cancer. Explanatory notes*. With French translation by A. Aubréville Oxford University Press, Oxford.

KEITH, S., URBAN, E. K. & FRY, C. H. 1992. *The Birds of Africa*. Vol. 4. Academic Press, London.

KOSTER, S. H. & GRETTENBERGER, J. F. 1983. A preliminary survey of birds in Park W, Niger. *Malimbus* 5: 62–72.

LAMARCHE, B. 1980. Liste commentée des oiseaux du Mali. 1ère partie: non-passereaux. *Malimbus* 2: 121–158.

LEVEQUE, C., FAIRHURST, C. P., ABBAN, K., PAUGY, D. & CURTIS, M. S. 1988. Onchocerciasis Control Programme in West Africa: ten years monitoring of fish populations. *Chemosphere* 17: 421–440.

LIVINGSTONE, D. A. 1975. Late Quaternary climatic change in Africa. *Ann. Rev. Ecol. Syst.* 6: 249–280.

LOUETTE, M. 1975. Contribution à l'ornithologie de la République du Togo. 5. Oiseaux récoltés par la quatrième mission zoologique belge. *Rev. Zool. Bot. Afr.* 89: 618–620.

LOWE, W. P. 1937. Report on the Lowe-Waldron Expedition to the Ashanti Forest and Northern Territories of the Gold Coast. *Ibis* ser. 14: 345–368, 635–662, 830–864.

MACDONALD, M. A. 1979. Breeding data for birds in Ghana. *Malimbus* 1: 36–42.

MACDONALD, M. A. 1980. Observations on Wilson's Widowfinch and the Pintailed Whydah in southern Ghana, with notes on their hosts. *Ostrich* 51: 21–24.

MACDONALD, M. A. & TAYLOR, I. A. 1977. Notes on some uncommon forest birds in Ghana. *Bull. Br. Orn. Cl.* 97: 116–120.

MACKWORTH-PRAED, C. W. & GRANT, C. H. B. 1970. *African Handbook of Birds*. Series 3: *Birds of West Central and Western Africa*. vol.1. Longmans.

MACKWORTH-PRAED, C. W. & GRANT, C. H. B. 1973. *African Handbook of Birds*. Series 3: *Birds of West Central and Western Africa*. vol.2. Longmans.

MARTIN, C. 1991. *The Rainforests of West Africa. Ecology, Threats, Conservation*. Birkhaüser Verlag, Basel.

MCCRAE, A. W. R. & WALSH, J. F. 1974. Association between nesting birds and polistine wasps in North Ghana. *Ibis* 116: 215–217.

MEAD, C. J. & CLARK, J. A. 1988. Report on bird ringing in Britain and Ireland for 1987. *Ringing & Migration* 9: 169–204.

MEAD, C. J. & CLARK, J. A. 1989. Report on bird ringing for Britain and Ireland for 1988. *Ringing & Migration* 10: 158–196.

MEAD, C. J. & CLARK, J. A. 1991. Report on bird ringing for Britain and Ireland for 1990. *Ringing & Migration* 12: 139–175.

MEAD, C. J. & HUDSON, R. 1985. Report on bird-ringing for 1984. *Ringing & Migration* 6: 125–172.

MENSAH, M. A. 1969. Zooplankton occurrence over the shelf of Ghana. pp. 69–84 in *Proceedings of the Symposium on the Oceanography and Fisheries Resources of the Tropical Atlantic (1966)*. Abidjan, Côte d'Ivoire.

MILLET-HORSIN. 1921a. Souvenirs d'un naturaliste en Afrique occidentale Française. A. Au Togo. 4. La Pie Noire du Sénégal (*Cryptorrhina afra* L.). *L'Oiseau* 1921 (2) 17–19.

MILLET-HORSIN. 1921b. Souvenirs d'un naturaliste en Afrique occidentale Française. A. Au Togo. 5. Les Touracos verts (*Turacus buffoni*). *L'Oiseau* 1921 (2): 50–53.

MILLET-HORSIN. 1921c. Souvenirs d'un naturaliste en Afrique occidentale Française. A. Au Togo. 6. Le Coq de Pagode ou Coucal a éperons (*Centropus monachus* Rupp.). *L'Oiseau* 1921 (2): 75–79.

MILLET-HORSIN. 1921d. Société ornithologique de France. Communication du Dr Millet-Horsin. *Revue Française d'Ornithologie* 7 (13e année): 177–180.

MILLET-HORSIN. 1922. Rectification. *Revue Française d'Ornithologie* 8 (14e année): 323.

MILLET-HORSIN. 1923. Contribution a l'étude de la Faune ornithologique du Bas-Togo. *Bull. Comité d'Études Hist. et Sci. de l'Afr. Occid. Fr.* (Jan–Mai 1923): 1–27.

MINSTER AGRICULTURE LIMITED. 1984. Annexes 3.3 & 4.4 in *Amenagement des Reserves de Faune et Promotion du Tourisme*. Unpublished Report TG. 008/11.84 to Le Gouvernement de La Republique du Togo (Ministere du Plan de L'Industrie et de la Reforme Administrative & Ministere de L'Amenagement Rural et Haut Commissariat du Tourisme) and to La Commission des Communautes Europeenes. Oxford, U.K.

MOBERLEY, F. J. 1931. *Military Operations: Togoland and the Cameroons 1914–1916*. H.M.S.O., London.

MOREAU, R. E. 1966. *The bird faunas of Africa and its islands*. Academic Press, London.

MOREAU, R. E. 1969. Climatic changes and the distribution of forest vertebrates in West Africa. *J. Zool. Lond.* 158: 39–61.

MOREL, G. J. & CHAPPUIS, C. 1992. Past and future taxonomic research in West Africa. *Bull. Br. Orn. Cl.* 112A: 217–224.

MOREL, G. J. & MOREL, Y-M. 1990. *Les oiseaux de Sénégambie. Notices et cartes de distribution*. Editions de l' ORSTOM, Paris.

MULLIE, W. C. & KEITH, J. O. 1991. Notes on the breeding biology, food and weight of the Singing Bush-Lark *Mirafra javanica* in northern Senegal. *Malimbus* 13: 24–39.

NEUBAUER, W. 1973. Ringfunde der Flusseeschwalbe (*Sterna hirundo*). *Auspicium* 5: 11–33.

NEUMANN, O. 1904. Vögel von Schoa und Süd Athiopien. *J. Orn.* 52: 321–410.

NEUMANN, O. 1906. Diagnosen neuer afrikanischer Formen. *Ornithologische Monatsberichte* 14: 6–8.

NEUMANN, O. 1907. Neue afrikanische Webefinken. *Ornithologische Monatsberichte* 15: 166–168.

NEUMANN, O. 1910. Revision der Genera *Spermospiza* und *Pyrenestes*. *J. Orn.* 58: 522–530.

NEUNZIG, R. 1928. Beiträge zur Kenntis der Ploceiden VI. Neue Rassen. *Zool. Anz.* 78: 107–118.

NTIAMOA-BAIDU, Y. 1991. Seasonal changes in the importance of coastal wetlands in Ghana for wading birds. *Biol. Cons.* 57: 139–158.

OATLEY, T. B. 1983. Twenty-third ringing report for southern Africa. *Ostrich* 54: 141–149.

OUSTALET, E. 1898. Catalogue des oiseaux du Dahomey remis par M. Miegemarque au Muséum d'histoire naturelle, en 1895. *Bull. Mus. Hist. Nat.* 4: 361–364.

PAYNE, R. B. 1982. Species limits in the Indigobirds (Ploceidae, *Vidua*) of West Africa: mouth mimicry, song mimicry, and description of new species. *Miscellaneous Publications of the Museum of Zoology, University of Michigan* no. 162.

PAYNE, R. B. 1985. The species of parasitic finches in West Africa. *Malimbus* 7: 103–113.

PAYNE, R. B. 1994. Brood parasitism in Nigerian birds. pp. 53–56 in Elgood, J. H., Heigham, J. B., Moore, A. M., Nason, A. M., Sharland, R. E. & Skinner, N. J. *The Birds of Nigeria. An annotated check-list.* B.O.U. Check-list no. 4. (second edition), Tring, Herts.

PAYNE, R. B. 1996. Field identification of the indigobirds. *Bull. African Bird Cl.* 3: 14–24.

PAYNE, R. B. & PAYNE, L. L. 1994. Song mimicry and species associations of west African indigobirds *Vidua* with Quail-finch *Ortygospiza atricollis*, Goldbreast *Amandava subflava* and Brown Twinspot *Clytospiza monteiri*. *Ibis* 136: 291–304.

PIRAUX, M. 1987. *Togo today.* 2nd. edition. Les éditions j.a., Paris.

POISSON, R. 1951. Mission A. Villiers au Togo et au Dahomey (1950). IV. Hémiptères Cryptocérates *Bull. I.F.A.N.* 13: 1131–1140.

PONCHELET, H. 1993. Environnement. Togo. *Le Point* No. 1111: 36–37.

POPOV, G. B. 1985. Two new species of grasshopper from Africa (Orth., Acrididae). *Ent. mon. Mag.* 121: 199–205.

QUENTIN, J. C., SEUREAU, C. & KULO, S. D. 1986. Cycle biologique de *Tetrameres* (*Microtetrameres*) *inermis* (Linstow, 1879). Nématode Tetrameridae parasite du tisserin *Ploceus aurantius* au Togo. *Ann. Parasitol. Hum. Comp.* 61: 321–332.

REICHENOW, A. 1891a. Ueber eine Vogelsammlung aus Togoland. *J.Orn.* 39: 369–394.

REICHENOW, A. 1891b. *Turturoena büttikoferi*, Rchw. n. sp. *in* Berichte über die October-Sitzung der Allgemeine Deutsche Ornitholog. Gesellschaft zu Berlin (27 October 1891). *J.Orn.* 39: 437.

REICHENOW, A. 1892. Zur vogelfauna von Togoland. *J. Orn.* 40: 233–236.

REICHENOW, A. 1893. Die Vogelfauna der Umgegend von Bismarckburg. *Mitteilungen aus den Deutschen Schutzgebieten* 6: 181–206.

REICHENOW, A. 1894a. Nachrichten. *Ornithologische Monatsberichte* 2: 65.

REICHENOW, A. 1894b. Zur Ornis des Togolandes. *Ornithologische Monatsberichte* 2: 112.

REICHENOW, A. 1894c. Notizen. *Ornithologische Monatsberichte* 2: 146–147.

REICHENOW, A. 1894d. *Eremomela baumanni* n.sp. *Ornithologische Monatsberichte* 2: 157.

REICHENOW, A. 1895. Neue Arten aus Afrika. *Ornithologische Monatsberichte* 3: 96–97.

REICHENOW, A. 1897. Zur Vogelfauna von Togo. *J. Orn.* 45: 1–57.

REICHENOW, A. 1899. Zur Tierverbreitung in Afrika. *Ornithologische Monatsberichte* 7: 189–190.

REICHENOW, A. 1900–1904. *Die Vögel Afrikas.* vols 1–3 and atlas. Neudamm. J. Neumann.

REICHENOW, A. 1901. *in* Bericht Über die Märzsitzung. *J. Orn.* 49: 283–286.

REICHENOW, A. 1902a. Die Vögel des deutschen Schutzgebietes Togo. *J. Orn.* 50: 9–43.

REICHENOW, A. 1902b. *Thamnolaea coronata* Rchw. n. sp. *Ornithologische Monatsberichte* 10: 157–158.

REICHENOW, A. 1915. Uber *Pelecanus sharpei*. *J. Orn.* 63 :130.

REICHENOW, A. 1917. *in* Berichte über die Novembersitzung 1916. *J. Orn.* 65 :111–115.

REISER, K. H. 1973. Ringfunde des Teichrohrsängers (*Acrocephalus scirpaceus*). *Auspicium* 5: 47–58.

ROBBINS, C. B. 1978. The Dahomey Gap – a reevaluation of its significance as a faunal barrier to West African high forest mammals. *Bull. Carnegie Mus. Nat. Hist.* 6: 168–174.

ROBERTSON, W. B. 1969. Transatlantic migration of juvenile Sooty Terns. *Nature* 223: 632–634.

ROBINSON, N. 1972. Bird notes from Republique du Togo. *Bull. Niger. Orn. Soc.* 9: 85–89.

ROBINSON, N. 1973. The Republic of Togo. *The Nigerian Field* 38: 147–157.

ROBINSON, N. 1974. A roost of Pied Kingfishers – *Ceryle rudis*. *Bull. Niger. Orn. Soc.* 10: 56–61.

ROURE, G. 1967. *Rapport au Gouvernement du Togo sur sauver la faune du Togo.* Unpublished report no. AT2369, FAO, Rome.

RYDZENSKY, W. 1956. The nomadic movements and migrations of the European Common Heron. *Ardea* 1956: 71–187.

SAUROLA, P. 1994. African non-breeding areas of Fennoscandian ospreys *Pandion haliaetus*: a ring recovery analysis. *Ostrich* 65: 127–136.

SAYER, J. A., HARCOURT, C. S. & COLLINS, N. M. 1992. *The Conservation Atlas of Tropical Forests: Africa*. MacMillan, Basingstoke.

SCHIOTZ, A. 1967. The treefrogs (Rhacophoridae) of West Africa. *Spolia zool. Mus. haun.* 25: 1–346.

SCHLOSS, W. 1962. Ringfunde der Flusseeschwalbe (*Sterna hirundo*). *Auspicium* 1: 395–443.

SCHLOSS, W. 1968. Ringfunde der Küstenseeschwalbe (*Sterna macrura*). *Auspicium* 2: 384–402.

SCLATER, W. L. 1930. *Systema Avium Aethiopicarum*. Part II. British Ornithologists' Union, London.

SEEL, D. C. 1977. Migration of the northwestern European population of the Cuckoo *Cuculus canorus*, as shown by ringing. *Ibis* 119: 309–322.

SHARLAND, R. E. 1975. Albinism amongst Ethiopian birds. *Bull. Niger. Orn. Soc.* 11: 85.

SHARLAND, R. E. 1979. Ringing in Nigeria 1978. 21st. Annual report. *Malimbus* 1: 43–46.

SHULL, B., GRETTENBERGER, M. & NEWBY, J. 1986. Recent observations in W National Park (Niger). *Malimbus* 8: 23–24.

SIMMONS, R. 1993. A census of the desert-breeding Damara Tern *Sterna balaenarum* in Namibia. *Proc. VIII Pan-Afr. Orn. Congr.* 395–398.

SNOW, D. W. (Ed.) 1978. *An atlas of speciation in African Non-Passerine Birds*. British Museum (Natural History), London

SNOW, D. W. & LOUETTE, M. 1981. Atlas of speciation in African non-passerine birds – addenda and corrigenda 2. *Bull. Br. Orn. Cl.* 101: 336–339.

SPENCER, R. & HUDSON, R. 1981. Report on bird-ringing for 1980. *Ringing & Migration* 3: 213–256.

SPENCER, R. & HUDSON, R. 1982. Report on bird-ringing for 1981. *Ringing & Migration* 4: 65–128.

STERNFELD, Dr. 1909. *Die Fauna der deutschen Kolonien*. II. *Togo*. 1. *Die Schlangen Togos*. Berlin.

STRESEMANN, E. 1924. Über *Hieraaëtus ayresii* und *Spizaëtus africanus*. *Novitates Zoologicae* 31: 214–216.

TAYLOR, I. R. & MACDONALD, M. A. 1979. A population of *Anthus similis* on the Togo range in eastern Ghana. *Bull. Br. Orn. Cl.* 99: 29–30.

THIOLLAY, J. M. 1985a. The West African forest avifauna: a review. pp. 171–180 in Diamond, A. W. & Lovejoy, T. E. (Eds.) *Conservation of Tropical Forest Birds*. ICBP Technical Publication no. 4, Cambridge.

THIOLLAY, J. M. 1985b. The birds of Ivory Coast: status and distribution. *Malimbus* 7: 1–59.

THONNERIEUX, Y., WALSH, J. F. & BORTOLI, L. 1989. L'avifaune de la ville de Ouagadougou et ses environs (Burkina Faso). *Malimbus* 11: 7–40.

TREWARTHA, G. T. 1962. *The Earth's Problem Climates*. Methuen, London.

TURNER, B. D. & CHEKE, R. A. 1983. Psocoptera of the Togo-Benin gap, West Africa. *J. Nat. Hist.* 17: 379–404.

UNWIN, A. H. 1920. *West African Forests and Forestry*. London.

URBAN, E. K., FRY, C. H. & KEITH, S. (Eds.) 1986. *The Birds of Africa*. vol. II. Academic Press, London.

VANPRAET, C. L. 1980. *Systeme mondial de Surveillance de l'Environnement. Projet pilote sur la surveillance continue de la couverture forestière tropicale. Togo. Cartographie du couvert vegetal et etude de ses modifications*. FAO Rapport Technique 32/6.1102-75-005, FAO, Rome.

VILLIERS, A. 1951a. Mission A. Villiers au Togo et au Dahomey (1950). II. Ophidiens. *Études Dahomeennes* 5: 17–46.

VILLIERS, A. 1951b. La Faune (du Togo). pp. 403–408 in Guernier, E. (Ed.) *Encyclopédie de l' Empire Français. L' Encyclopédie Coloniale et Maritime*. vol. *Togo et Cameroun*. Paris.

VON SCHALOW, H. 1896. Berichte über die September-Sitzung. *J. Orn.* 44: 93.

WALSH, J. F. 1985. Extension of known range of the African Black Duck *Anas sparsa* in West Africa. *Bull. Br. Orn. Cl.* 105: 117.

WALSH, J. F. 1989. Wetlands of the moist-savanna region of West Africa, and their importance to migratory White Storks (*Ciconia ciconia*). pp 271–280, in Rheinwald, G., Ogden, J. & Schulz, H. (Eds.) Weissstorch – White Stork: Status and Conservation Proc. Int. Stork Conservation Symp., Walsrode 1985, Schriftenreihe des DDA 10, Bonn.

WALSH, J. F. 1991. On the occurrence of the Black Stork *Ciconia nigra* in West Africa. *Bull. Br. Orn. Cl.* 111: 209–215.

WALSH, J. F. & CHARDONNET, B. 1995. Togo. pp. 26–27 in East, R. (ed.) *Antelope Survey Update No.1.* I.U.C.N., Gland, Switzerland.

WALSH, J. F., CHEKE, R. A. & SOWAH, S. A. 1990. Additional species and breeding records of birds in the Republic of Togo. *Malimbus* 12: 2–18.

WALSH, J. F. & GRIMES, L. G. 1981. Observations on some Palaearctic land birds in Ghana. *Bull. Br. Orn. Cl.* 101: 327–334.

WALSH, J. F., SOWAH, S. A. & YAMAGATA, Y. 1987. Newly discovered colonies of the Northern Carmine Bee-eater *Merops nubicus* in Ghana and Togo. *Malimbus* 9: 129–130.

WERNER, F. 1898. Ueber Reptilien und Bratrachier aus Togoland, Kamerun und Tunis aus dem kgl. Museum für Naturkunde in Berlin. *Verhandlung Zool. Bot. gesellsch., Wien* 47: 395–408.

WHISTLER, H. 1949. *Popular Handbook of Indian Birds.* 4th. edition revised and enlarged by N. B. Kinnear. Gurney & Jackson, London.

WHITE, C. M. N. 1963. A revised check list of African flycatchers, tits, tree creepers, sunbirds, white-eyes, honey-eaters, buntings, finches, weavers and waxbills. The Government Printer, Lusaka.

WHITE, F. 1983. *The vegetation of Africa: a descriptive memoir to accompany the* UNESCO/AETFAT/UNSO *Vegetation Map of Africa.* UNESCO, Paris.

WORLD BANK. 1993. *Ecologically sensitive sites in Africa.* Vol. 1. Occidental and Central Africa. Compiled by the World Conservation Monitoring Centre for the World Bank, Washington, DC, U.S.A.

WORLD CONSERVATION MONITORING CENTRE. 1992. *Global biodiversity: status of the Earth's living resources.* Chapman & Hall, London.

INDEX OF SCIENTIFIC NAMES

(Page numbers in **bold** refer to the species accounts in the Systematic List)

INDEX OF ENGLISH NAMES

(Page numbers in **bold** refer to the species accounts in the Systematic List)